THE CHINA QUESTIONS

THE
CHINA
QUESTIONS

CRITICAL INSIGHTS INTO
A RISING POWER

Edited by

Jennifer Rudolph
Michael Szonyi

Harvard University Press

Cambridge, Massachusetts
London, England

2018

Third printing

Library of Congress Cataloging-in-Publication Data

Names: Rudolph, Jennifer M., editor. | Szonyi, Michael, editor. | Fairbank
  Center for East Asian Research.
Title: The China questions : critical insights into a rising power / edited
  by Jennifer Rudolph and Michael Szonyi.
Description: Cambridge, Massachusetts : Harvard University Press, 2018. | Includes
  index. | "In celebration of the 60th anniversary of the Fairbank Center for
  Chinese Studies at Harvard University"—Title page verso.
Identifiers: LCCN 2017023762 | ISBN 9780674979406 (cloth : alk. paper)
Subjects: LCSH: China—Forecasting. | China—Politics and government—2002– |
  China—Foreign relations—21st century. | China—Economic conditions—
  2000– | Environmental policy—China. | China—Social conditions—2000– |
  China—Civilization—2002–
Classification: LCC DS779.4 .C463 2018 | DDC 951.06—dc23
  LC record available at https://lccn.loc.gov/2017023762

In celebration of the 60th anniversary of the
Fairbank Center for Chinese Studies at Harvard University

CONTENTS

II. INTERNATIONAL RELATIONS

III. ECONOMY

THE CHINA QUESTIONS

INTRODUCTION

Michael Szonyi

IF YOU'VE picked up this book, you have probably already accepted
the premise that China matters, and therefore that understanding
China matters. In a certain obvious sense, China has always mattered
and always will. What happens to a fifth of the planet's population
is important. But today China matters not only to the Chinese people
themselves but also to Americans and to the entire world in some
new, unexpected, and interesting ways—and not only because of
China's large and growing role in the world economy. Of the many
pressing problems facing our world—from climate change to economic growth to maritime security to counterterrorism—none can
be solved or even addressed effectively without China's participation.
It is this reality, and not simple trade volumes, that makes the relationship between the United States and China the most important
bilateral relationship of the twenty-first century.

Another new and mostly unexpected way in which China matters
is that, for better or worse, Chinese policies increasingly have an impact beyond China's borders. Whether through its Belt and Road
Initiative or by its contribution to the depletion of global fisheries,
the actions of China's government and its people affect all of us. China
is also playing a new role in the global marketplace of ideas. In areas
as diverse as approaches to economic development and poverty reduction, to aging and mental health, to pollution reduction and re-
newable energy sources, it just makes good sense to pay attention to
some of its ideas. This is not to say that we should embrace every

aspect of the ways that the People's Republic of China (PRC) does things. Many Americans have profound objections to aspects of China's government and politics (and so, for that matter, do many Chinese). Nonetheless, it is still better to know more about the Chinese positions on these issues rather than less.

Because China matters, understanding China matters. In a certain obvious sense, understanding China has never been easier. The amount of information about China to which Americans have access is growing almost as explosively as the country's economy. Americans travel to China in record numbers. More and more are even studying the Chinese language (though nothing like the numbers of Chinese who study English). All leading global media have a presence in China, which means that when China is in the headlines, as it is almost daily, it is often world-class journalists who are telling the story. But even the very best and most neutral mainstream journalism is mostly driven, as it ought to be, by the news of the day. It tends to focus on what is most visible or striking; journalists cannot be expected to have deep knowledge of every story they cover. More and more of our information about China comes from Chinese people themselves, who are writing and publishing in English in greater volume and frequency. But just because they are insiders does not necessarily mean they understand the situation in China better. Americans today also have access to information about China through China's own state-owned media, which embarked several years ago on an aggressive global expansion. Their representation of China, unsurprisingly, has its own agenda, as positive about China as some US media is negative. Thus despite the increase in the amount of information available about China, it is still tough to make sense of it all. We might even say that just as the United States has a trade deficit with China, it also has an understanding deficit.

That is why we have put together this book. We invited thirty-six scholars to identify a big question that they think Americans should ask about the past, present, or future of China. And then we invited them to answer that question. Each of the authors is an expert who writes with the benefit of decades of exploring and analyzing these big questions. They have thought deeply about their question, and about how to summarize pressing issues while still recognizing complexity.

The chapters as a whole have a few key messages about China's past, present, and future. The key message about the past is that history matters; about the present, that complexity matters, and about the future, that China's challenges matter.

PAST

Is the China of today completely new, or does the past still play a role? One could easily make the argument that history does not matter in contemporary China, that the extraordinary transformations of the last forty years mean that China is all about the future, or that the retreat of the Chinese Communist Party (CCP) from ideological commitment means that what matters in China is the future, not the past. This conclusion would be premature.

For one thing, it is not that long ago that China tried and failed to eliminate its history in the Great Proletarian Cultural Revolution and other mass movements of the Maoist era. Xiaofei Tian writes in this volume of "the paradox of the [Cultural Revolution's] pledge to demolish the past and create a new society, even though the movement was itself deeply embedded in the past." Many of the chapters argue the importance of history on this or some other grounds. It is simply impossible to understand why the Chinese people feel so strongly about visits by Japanese leaders to the Yasakuni shrine, or about the Taiwan independence movement, without an understanding of the history behind these matters.

History also matters because it draws our attention to some intriguing continuities that have somehow endured despite centuries of radical change. Peter Bol suggests that the tension between intellectuals and politicians is a perennial feature of Chinese society that can help us make sense of political debates currently taking place in China. Roderick MacFarquhar shows that, for all their differences, Xi Jinping has in some ways taken a page from Mao Zedong's book. Yuhua Wang highlights the problem Chinese leaders have encountered—and continue to encounter—while they try to maintain power in the face of challenges from powerful elites.

Perhaps the most compelling, and surprising, way that history matters in China today is because the ruling CCP takes it so seriously. Claims about history have become crucial to how the CCP asserts the legitimacy of its rule, to the point that its General Office issued in 2013 a document forbidding public discussion of "historical nihilism." What this document calls historical nihilism really means any critical assessments of the Party's own history. The CCP no longer claims only to be heir to the ideas of a nineteenth-century German philosopher; it also justifies its existence on the basis of inheriting, transmitting, and promoting the five-thousand-year history of the Chinese people.

The authors who touch on history in this book would all agree that to understand China's past what is crucial is a critical perspective (precisely what the CCP would call historical nihilism), not a spoon-fed official version. For example, while the PRC government and media often suggest that Japan was unrepentantly hostile to China throughout the twentieth century, Ezra Vogel shows that this is not in fact accurate. Similarly, claims about the unitary origins of Chinese civilization or about the historic Silk Road are not neutral claims based on an objective archaeology—they are motivated by particular interests. A critical understanding of the history is essential to making informed judgments about those claims.

We do not want to suggest that being shaped by its history makes China unique or even exceptional. No country, regime, or society can be fully understood without an understanding of its history and culture. But the important role of history in contemporary political discourse—not to mention in the self-perception of many ordinary Chinese people—means that history perhaps matters especially in China.

PRESENT

If there is one word that can best characterize contemporary China, it might be complexity. Older readers may still remember photographs of Chinese cities from the early 1980s, where Soviet-style concrete buildings predominated, most everyone dressed in uniform colors and styles, and bicycles were everywhere. China today looks nothing like that—its big cities are centers of architectural innovation, fashion, and luxury automobiles. But the meaningful complexity goes well beyond appearances. Chinese politics are complex; Chinese society is complex; Chinese people are complex. Even a seemingly straightforward statement like "China has an authoritarian political system" is no longer straightforward. The Chinese Party-state has retreated in many ways from regular interference in the lives of ordinary people. But even after the end of the One-Child Policy, it still continues to limit the reproductive choices of ordinary people. It also continues to have an enormous propaganda apparatus, though as Jie Li points out the reception of that propaganda is now sometimes ironic. A naive strand in Western thinking has long held that China's political system would become more like ours as China's economy developed. It is now clear that China is creating a new kind of political system.

China's society is complex. Sharp new cleavages have emerged between urban and rural, young and old, and rich and poor. Economic growth has created a new middle class—hundreds of millions strong and growing—with new expectations and new demands. The embrace of economic reform by both government and society has created a new social contract that neither Marx nor Mao would recognize, and in which continued economic growth is critical to popular support for the current order. More broadly, the reform era has unleashed a wide range of new social forces, to which the CCP is having a hard time accommodating itself, and which it cannot easily control.

The complexity is not just evident at the social level; it extends down to the level of the individual person. Reform has dramatically changed what it means to be a person in contemporary China. As Arthur Kleinman puts it, a new "Chinese self" is emerging—more individuated, more globally connected. Chinese people are answering familiar questions—what does a good life mean?—in new ways. They are also asking new questions, some of which would never have occurred to their parents. What is an environmentally sustainable life? What should be the limits of the power of the state? Newly wealthy philanthropists are asking how best to give back to society. In a time of religious flux, changing family norms, and rapidly developing health care, many are asking: what is a good death?

Again, our argument is not that China is more or less complex than other societies. All societies are complex. Rather, the point is that appreciating that complexity is essential to a better understanding of China today.

FUTURE

Several authors explore the big challenges that China, and in particular the Chinese government, faces in the future. Can the CCP successfully root out corruption? Can it retain its legitimacy as its revolutionary origins become less and less relevant? Most important of all, can economic growth continue? Unlike some analysts who cherry-pick either the good or the bad, all our contributors seek to give a balanced view of these potential fault lines. Even more importantly, they ask about the resources that the Chinese have available to address these challenges, and in turn, the likelihood that they will be addressed in an orderly or chaotic way. These are issues that will affect all our futures.

Our contributors offer plenty of advice—to the Chinese government, to the US government, and, in a few essays, to the people of the world. However China responds to these challenges, whether it heeds the advice of our contributors or not, whether it is able to sustain high levels of economic growth and maintain political and social stability or not, we can all learn something from China's experiences to this point. This is not to say that there is such a thing as a "China model" that can be applied wholesale to other contexts, but simply that China's experiences, both its undeniable successes and instructive failures, provide a resource for other societies—for promoting economic development and reducing poverty, for managing care for the elderly and mental health, even for restructuring education or producing energy.

Past, present, and future are of course linked. Policy choices made in the past affect the situation in the present and will continue to do so in the future—decisions about education, health care, and infrastructure policy taken during the Maoist era shape the options open to China's leaders today. One can take this back even further and ask how ideas about political organization in the period before the PRC was founded, or about the role of religion in a modern society, continue to inform how Chinese officials think about the present and future. The reappearance of aspects of Maoist politics—noted by Roderick MacFarquhar—sometimes make it appear that China is going *back* to the future. And the extraordinary resonance that David Der-wei Wang points out between how Chinese intellectuals imagined the future a century ago, and what China is actually like today, make it seem that this imagined "future" has become reality.

Experts of all stripes can help us make sense of the history, the complexity, and the challenges. It's no secret why we invited these particular Chinese experts and not others. They are all scholars affiliated with the Fairbank Center for Chinese Studies at Harvard University (http://fairbank.fas.harvard.edu/). Over its sixty-year history, the Fairbank Center has always aspired to be the world's leading research institute for the study of China. While its main focus continues to be academic research, the center has also always had a public role. Our founder, John King Fairbank, trained not only generations of leading Chinese historians but also journalists like Theodore ("Teddy") White, Harrison Salisbury, and Richard Bernstein. In more recent years, the Fairbank Center has been home not only to scholars but also to policy makers, dissidents, and even corporate executives. And some members of the Fairbank Center community have always felt a responsibility to move beyond the ivory tower and help inform public opinion and shape public policy. With US-China relations moving into uncharted waters, we think this public role of educating and informing policy makers and the general public is more important than ever.

I | POLITICS

1 | IS THE CHINESE COMMUNIST REGIME LEGITIMATE?

Elizabeth J. Perry

NO QUESTION is more fundamental to a political regime's stability and survival than that of popular legitimacy. In the eyes of its people, does the regime in power have a "right to rule"? Even if citizens may dislike the particular policies or personnel of the ruling regime, do they nonetheless feel morally obliged to acquiesce to its authority? The connection to regime durability is obvious; only the most coercive of police states can endure for long without a general acceptance of regime legitimacy on the part of the populace.

Writing over a century ago, the historical sociologist Max Weber identified three basic sources of regime legitimacy: traditional, charismatic, and rational-legal. In the traditional type, people obey the state's dictates simply because it is customary to do so. Weber pointed to imperial China as an archetypical example. The revolution of 1911, which replaced China's two-thousand-year-old imperial system with a new republican form of government, shattered its traditional legitimacy. In the charismatic type of regime legitimacy, popular obedience derives from devotion to the supreme leader. Many scholars have characterized Mao's China as a classic case of charismatic rule. As the supreme leader of a Communist Revolution that restored Chinese sovereignty, Mao Zedong's personal aura shone brighter than that of any of his contemporaries or successors. His death in 1976 closed the chapter on charismatic legitimacy. In the rational-legal type of legitimacy, which sustains modern democracies, impersonal laws and bureaucratic administrative procedures are the basis for citizens' compliance. Few observers, however, would suggest that at any point in China's long history of authoritarianism has rational-legal legitimacy prevailed; today, as in the past, rule of man consistently trumps rule of law.

To be sure, there have been efforts in the post-Mao period to generate rational-legal legitimacy through various institutional reforms: convening regular party and government congresses, clarifying respective party and government responsibilities, constructing a collective leadership with separate portfolios for members of the Politburo Standing Committee, imposing mandatory retirement ages and term limits on party and government officials, and so on. But the movement toward institutionalization appears to have reversed course in recent years. Under Xi Jinping, power has been recentralized in the paramount leader, the Party's unquestioned supremacy over government has been reasserted, and norms surrounding age and term limits have been challenged in preparation for the 19th Party Congress.

If none of Weber's three classic types of legitimacy applies to contemporary China, how then do we explain the paradox that—more than forty years after Mao's death and nearly thirty years after the fall of communism across central Europe—a communist regime remains firmly in place in Beijing? Coercion is surely part of the explanation for the regime's survival, but it is not the whole story. Internal security forces operate less intrusively and ruthlessly in China than was true under some previous communist regimes (consider the East German Stasi, for example). In addition, numerous public opinion surveys conducted by a wide variety of pollsters agree that popular support for the Chinese communist regime remains surprisingly strong. In *Populist Authoritarianism,* political scientist Wenfang

Tang finds that "when political support was measured in different ways, including confidence in the key political institutions, national identity, satisfaction with government performance, support for one's own political system, or support for incumbent leaders, Chinese respondents consistently demonstrated one of the highest levels among the countries and regions where survey data were available . . . the overall level of political support in China is significantly higher than in many liberal democracies" (159).

Support is not the same thing as legitimacy, of course. Approval of one's political leaders and their programs does not necessarily mean that one accords the regime a moral right to rule. Struggling to explain the paradox of regime sustainability in contemporary China, several scholars, including Dingxin Zhao and Yuchao Zhu, have suggested that the PRC survives only by virtue of an instrumental "performance legitimacy" derived from the impressive economic growth of the post-Mao period and China's attendant ascent in international influence. Popular support that is generated simply by favorable governance outcomes does not, however, qualify as "legitimacy" in Weber's terms. Weber's famous typology was motivated by the deeper question of why some regimes, even in the face of *unfa-vorable* performance, continue to enjoy popular validation. The question is of clear relevance to contemporary China, where a slowing economy and deteriorating international environment threaten to erode the stunning accomplishments of recent decades. Will dwindling political support under conditions of adversity spell the downfall of the regime, as proponents of a "performance legitimacy" explanation predict, or does the Chinese communist regime command a level of popular legitimacy that may allow it to withstand the substantial domestic and global challenges looming on the horizon?

Due to restrictions on freedom of expression, it is impossible to know for certain whether an authoritarian regime is deemed legitimate in the eyes of its people. Yet it is clear that the question of regime legitimacy not only preoccupies those who study China; it concerns those who rule China as well. Wang Qishan, the chief architect and executor of President Xi Jinping's anti-corruption campaign, broached the subject himself during a meeting with foreign dignitaries in the fall of 2015. Wang did not cite tradition, charisma, or rational-legal authority, nor did he mention regime performance, in offering his defense of CCP legitimacy. Rather, Wang pointed to history. As he framed it, "The legitimacy of the Chinese Communist Party has its source in history, and rests on the will and choice of the people."

The idea of a powerful and popular "historical legitimacy" as an explanation for CCP authority is intriguing. But it is also inherently ambiguous. In a country that boasts some five thousand years of history, the ninety-five-year-old CCP can lay claim to but a miniscule portion of China's fabled past. For better and for worse, the last century has seen momentous change, much of which can be attributed to CCP initiative. The Communist Revolution (1921–1949) was itself an extraordinary feat, as a ragtag peasant army emerged victorious following battles against superior Japanese and Nationalist military might. In just the first few years after its revolutionary rise to power, the CCP managed moreover to expel "foreign imperialism" (if only to replace it for a time with "Soviet revisionism"), implement massive (albeit bloody) land reform, collectivize and nationalize agriculture and industry, and deliver basic medical care and education to its people. These historic achievements probably did generate widespread acceptance for the CCP and its paramount leader, Mao Zedong. However, the record for the rest of Mao's reign surely stirs less positive memories. The Anti-Rightist Campaign of 1957 silenced many of China's most gifted intellectuals. The Great Leap Forward of 1958–1961 delivered the worst famine in human history, causing tens of millions of deaths. The Cultural Revolution of 1966–1976 produced violent factional strife, stagnant incomes, and "ten lost years" in higher education and economic innovation. Indeed, the current leadership's mantra of "stability maintenance," which calls for massive state investment in surveillance and security, is rationalized as a necessary measure to prevent a recurrence of the turmoil that marred earlier periods of PRC history.

The Chinese Communist Party's effort to wrap itself in the mantle of historical legitimacy thus raises some thorny issues. Exactly which episodes in China's complex history should be credited with bestowing an unassailable "right to rule" on the CCP? And just how durable is such legitimacy, especially when objective inquiry may contradict the official narrative of events on which the regime's legitimacy is purportedly based?

The PRC hopes to finesse these questions by exerting tight party control over the interpretation of Chinese history and politics. As reported by multiple news outlets, in May 2016 President Xi Jinping presided over a national symposium on philosophy and social science at which he called for developing new analytical approaches that would be imbued with "Chinese characteristics" suited to the country's "socialist practices." Xi stressed that Communist Party leadership was essential in this urgent theory-building exercise. He proposed that efforts be made to "care for, foster, and make full use of " the many intellectuals working in the fields of philosophy and social science so as to ensure that they would be "advocates of advanced thinking, trailblazers of academic research, guides of social ethos, and staunch supporters of Party governance."

Xi Jinping is no doubt correct to believe that cultivating a loyal intelligentsia willing to provide a credible justification for continued Communist Party rule is crucial to its long-term survival. As Peter Bol's essay in this volume explains, Chinese rulers have for centuries depended on intellectuals to help construct political legitimacy, an assignment that often involved the rewriting of history. But today this is by no means an easy order. If Chinese history is to stand as the ultimate arbiter of regime legitimacy, what should we make of the inconvenient reality that the political institutions and ideology of the PRC were imported almost wholesale from the Soviet Union and bear very little resemblance to those of pre-revolutionary China? For a regime struggling to present itself as the custodian of five millennia of "glorious" Chinese history, this is a problem. Even if the claim to legitimacy rested solely on the CCP's achievement of having "restored" China's territorial integrity and national sovereignty with the founding of the PRC in 1949, the contention is problematic. Throughout much of its history, China was physically divided, its imagined coherence residing primarily in cultural, rather than political, unity. As historian Peter Perdue points out, ironically, the full extent of the geographical expanse that the contemporary PRC claims as its historical birthright was acquired through conquest only in the eighteenth century, when the imperial throne was occupied by the foreign Manchu dynasty.

The CCP may still enjoy a reservoir of legitimacy amassed during and after its revolutionary rise to power, but even the deepest reservoir will eventually evaporate unless regularly replenished. The unfulfilled promises of the Communist Revolution remain to be fully researched, let alone realized. The CCP has proclaimed a moratorium on examinations of its own historical mistakes, condemning such discussion as one of "seven speak-nots," public mention of which invites swift reprisals.

Efforts to anchor regime legitimacy in a distorted rewriting of the historical record are unlikely to withstand critical challenge in the long run. An earnest attempt to implement the ideals of social justice that first helped inspire the Communist Revolution might be a sturdier scaffold on which to construct a moral rationale for CCP rule. This calls for more than an anti-corruption campaign directed at official malfeasance; it demands dramatic measures to shrink substantially the huge income gap between rich and poor that has accompanied post-Mao economic reforms. Xi Jinping's call for "Precision Poverty Alleviation" in poor rural villages is certainly a step in the right direction, but it is only one step. A more ambitious approach could draw support from the ancient Chinese concept of the Mandate of Heaven, whereby a ruler's popular legitimacy was based on a comprehensive concern for social welfare.

If the Chinese communist regime continues to command some vestige of historical legitimacy, it is in danger of being depleted by current governance practices. There is, however, no surefire signal of an authoritarian regime's imminent loss of legitimacy; the only definitive proof lies in its demise. Yet with democratic regimes in such disarray around the globe these days, chances are slim that China will opt for that alternative anytime soon.

2 CAN FIGHTING CORRUPTION SAVE THE PARTY?

Joseph Fewsmith

CORRUPTION IS NOT new in China. Students protesting in Tiananmen Square in 1989 denounced "official profiteering." Three years later, a major upsurge in corruption appears to have followed Deng Xiaoping's 1992 trip to the special economic zone of Shenzhen, next to Hong Kong, when the ideological strictures imposed after the Tiananmen protests were broken. By 2001, the respected economist Hu Angang had estimated that corruption already accounted for 13–16 percent of China's gross domestic product, a figure that seems high but nevertheless reflects the sense that corruption was deepening. Yet a new wave of corruption appears to have hit China after the central government provided a 5 trillion *renminbi* (RMB, "people's currency") stimulus (about $750 billion) to the economy following the global financial crisis of 2008. Every year, the Central Discipline Inspection Commission (CDIC) issued stern statements about the need to crack down on corruption, but the odds of being caught and prosecuted remained low. However, Xi Jinping's campaign, begun immediately after his assuming the position of CCP general secretary in November 2012, has kicked efforts to stem corruption into a higher gear.

Why now? Given corruption's long history, what caused the breaking point? Was it, as some have suggested, simply that corruption had reached such a level that it threatened continued CCP rule? Or, closely related, that it threatened the legitimacy of the Party along with such other factors as social instability, demands for rule by law, forces of globalization, and so forth? Or was factional struggle the cause? All these played a role, but the specific roots of Xi's campaign against corruption surely lie in disgraced CCP official Bo Xilai's efforts to overturn the decision of the 2007 17th Party Congress (which designated Xi the next party boss) and take a leadership position for himself.

The story of Bo's efforts is remarkable and, no doubt, many details will remain unknown for a long time, perhaps forever. What is clear, however, is that the Party—meaning the Central Committee and, particularly, the leadership headed by the outgoing President Jiang Zemin—had decided that Xi Jinping would succeed Hu Jintao as general secretary in 2012. Bo Xilai would not even join the Politburo Standing Committee, the small group in which ultimate power is concentrated. Remarkably, Bo, who had been born and raised in the Party, the son of one of the "eight immortals" who had decided CCP policy during the tense days of the Tiananmen protests of June 1989, had decided to go against the CCP decision. If there is any rule that is central to the CCP, it is that decisions must be obeyed. Even Zhao Ziyang, the premier who was later accused of splitting the party, could not bring himself to openly oppose Deng's judgment that the demonstrators in Tiananmen Square were an "extremely small group" involved in a "planned conspiracy" to bring down socialism and the ruling party. But Bo Xilai had no problem building a program in Chongqing, the huge southwestern city where he headed the Communist Party, in which he essentially portrayed himself as more socialist than those who ruled in Beijing.

More than that, however, Bo apparently conspired with others to gain membership in the Politburo Standing Committee that had been denied to him. If there is any party rule stronger than the one that prohibits defying CCP decisions, it is the prohibition on forming factions to conspire against CCP leadership. We do not know details of this conspiracy, but no less a figure than Xi Jinping has declared that it existed. As Xi said:

> Among the Party's discipline and rules, none is greater than political discipline and political rules. In recent years, we have investigated high-level cadres' serious violation of discipline and law, especially the case(s) of Zhou Yongkang, Bo Xilai, Xu Caihou, Ling Jihua and Su Rong. Their violation of the Party's political discipline and political rules was very serious; it had to be viewed seriously. These people, the greater their power and the more important their position, the more they ignored the Party's political discipline and political rules, even to the extent of being completely unscrupulous and reckless! Some had inflated political ambitions, and violated the Party's organization to engage in political conspiracies, to immorally violate and split the Party!

These are powerful words in the Party's lexicon. To accuse Zhou Yongkang, a former member of the Politburo Standing Committee, and Xu Caihou, former vice chair of the Central Military Commission, of engaging in "political conspiracies" to "split the party" echoes words not heard since the Cultural Revolution fifty years prior. They speak to the depth of party divisions on the eve of its 18th Party Congress in 2012.

Bo Xilai had been detained for various crimes before Xi became general secretary, so he is not one of the 184 "tigers" (senior officials) that the campaign against corruption has targeted so far. But it is apparent that many followers of Zhou Yongkang, Ling Jihua, Xu Caihou, and others were targets. Clearly, Xi's first and most important priority was to purge his political enemies.

But the campaign was not limited to political struggle. Indeed, as the struggle against Bo Xilai and others suggests, the more important problem was that party discipline had broken down in ways that threatened its continued existence. Certainly, as Xi and his allies saw it, the Party faced serious challenges that could destroy it, much as similar challenges had brought down the Communist Party of the Soviet Union. As Xi Jinping put it shortly after his elevation as party chief, "Why did the Soviet Union disintegrate? Why did the Soviet Communist Party collapse? An important reason was that their ideals and convictions wavered. . . . Finally, all it took was one quiet word from Gorbachev to declare the dissolution of the Soviet Communist Party, and a great party was gone." Xi concluded, "In the end nobody was a real man, nobody came out to resist." Since then, he and those close to him have repeatedly invoked the specter of the Soviet collapse. As an important commentary in the official *People's Daily* newspaper later wrote, "Today, the Soviet Union, with its history of 74 years, has been gone for 22 years. For more than two decades, China has never stopped reflecting on how the communist party and nation were lost by the Soviet Communists."

What has brought China to this crisis of legitimacy? As Xi indicated, it was the loss of "ideals and convictions." Or perhaps, as Xi might have said if he were an academic, an alternative discourse had emerged, one that emphasized "rule of law" and "institutionalization," implying the end of the Party's revolutionary mission in favor of institutionalized government. This alternative agenda was rooted in the CCP's own rhetoric. Since promulgating a new constitution in 1982, in the wake of the disastrous Cultural Revolution, the CCP has emphasized the "rule of law." Indeed, Xi Jinping, giving a speech on the thirtieth anniversary of the promulgation of the constitution, declared, "To manage state affairs according to law, first we must run the country in accordance with the Constitution. The key to holding power in accordance with the law is to first rule in accordance with the Constitution. The Party leadership formulates the Constitution and the law, and the party itself must act within the scope of the Constitution and the law to truly achieve the Party leadership's establishment of the law, ensuring the enforcement of the law, and taking the lead in abiding by the law."

Unfortunately for them, some liberal intellectuals believed this speech signaled that Xi would pursue a liberal agenda, supporting rule of law and, more broadly, the emergence of civil society. In January 2013, the liberal newspaper *Southern Weekend* picked up on Xi's "China Dream" and rule-of-law rhetoric and published an editorial titled, "China's Dream is the Dream of Constitutional Government." The idea of "constitutional government" was rooted in a rights-protection movement that had been developing over the previous decade. Its basic goal was to use the law not only to protect the rights of citizens but also to strengthen the rule of law and gradually force the Party to operate solely within the confines of legality, thereby living up to its stated aims. While this vision offered hope of a path toward "peaceful evolution," it also undermined the Party's legitimacy. That perceived danger led Xi and other leaders to view the *Southern Weekend* editorial—which received national attention—as pushing China down the path of the former Soviet Union. On April 22, 2013, the Party's General Office issued Document No. 9, which outlined seven areas that should not be publicly discussed, starting with constitutional government but also including "universal values," "civil society," "freedom of the press," and "historical nihilism."

The CCP's concern with "historical nihilism," which really means the writing of good, solid, and honest history based on archival research—and which inevitably conflicts with the Party's approved historiography—was reflected in discussion of the "two thirty-year" periods that emerged in December 2013, around the time of the 120th anniversary of Mao Zedong's birth. It had become clear to Xi and others that an overemphasis on the first thirty years of the People's Republic of China—the harsh Maoist period—would undermine later reforms, just as an overemphasis on reform risked repudiating Chairman Mao, and hence the validity of the revolution itself. In recent years, many have asked how a revolution nearly seventy years ago, no matter how valid one thinks it was at the time, justifies the Party continuing in power today. In response, the CCP Central Party History Research Office issued an authoritative article arguing that "negating" Mao Zedong and Mao Zedong Thought (his political philosophy) would lead to "serious political consequences." Raising again the specter of the Soviet collapse, the article said, "One important reason for the disintegration of the Soviet Union and the collapse of the CPSU [Communist Party of the Soviet Union] is the complete negation of the history of the Soviet Union and the CPSU, the negation of Lenin and other leading figures, and the practice of historical nihilism, which confused people's minds."

Like the effort, discussed in Roderick MacFarquhar's essay, to bolster Xi Jinping's leadership role, the campaign against corruption is directly related to interpretations of CCP history and issues of legitimacy because the emergence of corruption speaks directly to the loss of "ideals and convictions" by CCP members. If CCP members have lost their ideological way, they indeed need to be restrained by civil society and the rule of law. But if party discipline and idealism instead can be restored by attacking corruption, then perhaps the notion that only the ruling party represents the true interests and ideals of the people is sustainable.

But is it? The emergence of widespread corruption in the CCP reflects broader changes in Chinese society, just as the rights–protection movement and other popular movements reflect the emergence of a more diverse, better educated, more open, and more participatory society. It is a society that might acknowledge the revolution's historical value but sees the future as being more "democratic," without defining precisely what that might mean. But certainly it means some sort of broader, more supervisory role for society so that corruption does not corrode both the political system and social mores.

The campaign against corruption has now been going on for four years. It has detained not only the 184 "tigers" (defined as those of vice ministerial rank or above), but also tens of thousands of "flies" (lower ranked officials). Strangely, however, there has been no theoretical effort to explain why this corruption exists. Official rhetoric blames the selfishness of flawed officials who are willing to take advantage of their positions to accumulate wealth. But an official discussion of how the Party's own structure provides incentives for corruption has been lacking. And without frank recognition of these underlying structural issues, it seems difficult to make the changes needed to diminish future corruption. The only structural change to date has been an enhancement of the Discipline Inspection Commissions at various levels within the CCP, though it seems unlikely that the Party truly wants to continue relying on this praetorian guard of sorts for its functioning. The Discipline Inspection Commissions and their predecessors have never played a sustained role in the Party's history, and when their role has temporarily been elevated in the past, they were often blamed for various excesses and trimmed back. So it is difficult at present to see just what structural changes can control corruption, restore legitimacy, and obviate the need for rule of law and societal supervision.

Although the initial thrust of the campaign against corruption was targeted at Xi's political enemies, the campaign should not be seen as simply a factional struggle, though that is part of it, but rather as part of a broad-ranging effort to stem the tide of societal changes that have been eroding the CCP's legitimacy. Ironically, the more successful Xi is in the short term, the greater the risk to political and social stability in the long term. Somehow Xi, and the ruling party more broadly, need to think about incorporating the societal forces emerging in China. Suppressing them is not enough.

3 | DOES MAO STILL MATTER?

Roderick MacFarquhar

CHAIRMAN MAO ZEDONG died over forty years ago. In the four decades since, China has been totally transformed into a country that Mao would not recognize. Unleashed by Deng Xiaoping's "reform and opening up" policy, the Chinese people have transformed a backward agricultural country into the world's second-largest economy and its industrial workshop. Hundreds of millions of Chinese have become well off, hundreds of thousands of Chinese tourists go everywhere buying up luxury goods, billionaires have appeared. The Sino-American opening signaled by Mao and Richard Nixon in 1972 has, since the Chairman's death, entangled the two countries in a multiplicity of relationships at all levels: official and popular, economic and educational, political and military.

China has indeed "stood up" and is a power recognized by all, particularly its neighbors. That power Mao would almost certainly have relished. But what of his Cultural Revolution dreams of equality and collectivism? China is now one of the most unequal countries in the world, and it is not just those billionaires who run private companies. How relevant today is Mao Zedong Thought? Are Mao's portrait on Tiananmen and mausoleum in the square of any political significance today? Does Mao still matter?

Nobody is more conscious of the importance of these questions than China's current ruler, Xi Jinping. President Xi constantly admonishes Chinese not to divide the history of the PRC into a Maoist period and a reform period. He fears that such a division would imply that there was a bad period and a good period, like the Stalinist and post-Stalinist periods (after Khrushchev's "secret speech" denouncing Stalin in 1956) in Soviet historiography. Xi values the basic elements of the Leninist state set up under Mao in 1949 because he clearly sees in them the only way to preserve Communist Party rule in the future.

What were those elements? First and foremost was Mao himself, the maximum leader, wearing the laurels of the revolutionary victory. He had assumed the leadership after other contenders had failed. With the help of colleagues, he had hammered the Communist Party and its armies into the tightly disciplined, highly motivated institutions that had won the civil war against the Nationalists and thereafter ruled China. Marxism-Leninism became the new state ideology, but Mao's ideas on war and peace, codified in Mao Zedong Thought, were the basis for ruling the country.

Mao oversaw the major movements in the early 1950s that spread communist rule down to the grass roots throughout China, and it was he who made the major policy decisions during the twenty-seven years that he lived after the revolution. Mao initiated the abandonment of "New Democracy" in favor of a rapid advance to socialism; after the triumph of rural collectivization, it was Mao who initiated the thaw that morphed into the relatively liberal "hundred flowers" era, and it was he who then reversed course into the Anti-Rightist Campaign. In his subsequent leftist phase, Mao conceived of the Great Leap Forward, the Socialist Education Movement, and, finally, the Great Proletarian Cultural Revolution. Despite these disasters, to the end of his days, nobody dared challenge Mao. For better or worse, his was the outsize personality that overawed all his colleagues, bestriding the country like a colossus to whom all Chinese citizens had been inculcated to give obedience. The signs suggest that Xi aspires to a similar Maoist role.

In sharp contrast to his immediate predecessors, Jiang Zemin and Hu Jintao, Xi has made no bow to collective leadership but has made it clear that he is the supreme ruler. There are two primary proofs. First, in addition to the offices always attached to the post of general secretary—the chairmanship of the CCP's central Military Affairs Committee (MAC) and the state presidency—there is his assumption of the leadership of other major committees: the new National Security Commission, which has jurisdiction over the army, police, and all foreign-related national security agencies; the new Central Leading Group on Comprehensively Deepening Reform, which has primacy over the government's State Council (led by the regime's official Number Two, Premier Li Keqiang), which traditionally directed economic affairs; and the central leading groups on foreign affairs, Internet security, and information technology.

The second indication of Xi's determination to be China's Mao-like supreme leader is the personality cult that early developed around him. His works have been widely published, and his *Governance of China*, which exists in several translations, is readily available in western bookshops. (As part of Facebook's ongoing quest for a foothold in China, Mark Zuckerberg bought several copies so that his employees could learn about "socialism with Chinese characteristics.") The domestic cult of Xi Dada ("Uncle Xi") seeks to endear him to the man in the street, while political junkies can regularly find his name in numerous headlines in the *People's Daily*. His stylish and attractive wife, Peng Liyuan ("Peng Mama"), a popular folk singer and a major general to boot, adds to the image of a power couple running China. In the post-Mao era, no leader's wife has had comparable publicity. Xi's personality cult will never reach the absurd heights of Mao's during the Cultural Revolution; thirty-five years of reform and opening up have surely inoculated most of the population against blind worship of any leader. But Xi will probably be satisfied with unquestioning obedience based on fear.

The second key element in the Maoist state was, of course, the party through which Mao and his colleagues ruled China. In their early headquarters in Yanan, before coming to power, cadres were educated in how to be good communists through the works of veteran leader (and later president) Liu Shaoqi, whose watchword was "serving the people," with the ultimate aim of emulating the "rustless screw" of the party machine, the heroic 1960s soldier, Lei Feng. Corruption certainly existed under Mao, but it was kept in check by campaigns and probably did not affect the leaders. As members of what the Yugoslav dissident theorist Milovan Djilas called "the new class," they had easy access to whatever luxuries were available. The trashing of the party machine, and the physical and mental battering that its members had to endure during the Cultural Revolution, undermined their Liuist training. Why serve the people if this was one's reward? Better to adopt the slogan of the reform era: "To get rich is glorious." The result, according to those who have led the CCP in the reform era, is massive and widespread corruption in the ranks of the bureaucracy, a phenomenon that has damaged the Party's prestige and legitimacy in the eyes of the Chinese population who grapple with it on a daily basis. The objective of Xi Jinping's thoroughgoing anti-corruption campaign is to restore the Party's reputation, reclaim popular support, and fend off any potential threats to its continued unfettered rule.

But the anti-corruption campaign is a two-edged weapon, which reminds one of the saying that used to circulate in China: "If we don't wipe out corruption, China may be finished, but if we do wipe out corruption, the party may be finished." If the campaign continues to target "tigers" like Zhou Yongkang, the Politburo member responsible for internal security, Xi may be threatened by a backlash among the elite who do not want their reputations or families thrown in the dustbin of history, nor to be jailed and deprived of their ill-gotten gains. As for the rank and file of the Party, the "flies" of this campaign, already there are indications of inertia, as humble cadres shy away from any action that might trigger accusations of corruption. Will recruitment be maintained if the financial perks of CCP membership are withdrawn?

The third element of the Maoist state, uniting leader, party, and people, was ideology: Marxism-Leninism, supplemented, in due course, by Mao Zedong Thought. There is no indication that Xi wishes to imitate Mao by making China a shining revolutionary beacon on a hill. Nor, in all his talk of a China dream, is there any suggestion that he foresees reviving Confucianism. Rather, he will reemphasize Deng's delineation of Marxism-Leninism and Mao Zedong Thought as components of the nation's four cardinal principles that cannot be questioned. Whereas, in Deng's time, this effectively meant putting ideology aside, Xi sees a need to revive communist ideology as a vibrant bulwark of China's exceptionalism, to inoculate its citizens against Western democratic ideas. It was presumably in response to Xi's concerns that, in autumn 2015, Peking University held a world conference on Marxism, inviting some seventy foreign Marxists (and at least one non-Marxist foreigner, this chapter's author) to participate. The funds are already in place for a follow-up conference. And yet, as one participant vouchsafed, *sotto voce*, "Marxism will do nothing for the Chinese, but they are stuck with it."

Indeed, Xi has an unenviable task. In 1949, the Chinese may not have been "poor and blank" as Mao once described them, but with a new regime firmly in power, they were at least persuaded that the regime's ideology had to be respected. Afterward, however, the

Chinese had to endure the ridiculous lengths to which the study of Mao Zedong Thought was emphasized in the Cultural Revolution, only to witness the demotion of ideology when Deng proclaimed that "practice was the sole criterion of truth," opening the country to all sorts of foreign ideas. The reform era has now lasted nearly forty years, almost a decade longer than the Maoist period. The impact on young Chinese has been enormous.

In particular, the demand for education in the West has skyrocketed. The number of Chinese studying in the United States alone in 2005–2006 was over 62,500; by 2015–2016, the number had climbed to over 328,000. There are many thousands more studying at campuses set up by foreign universities on Chinese soil. Most Chinese families sending their children to foreign schools can meet the cost through their own funds and are thus not dependent on government scholarships. How will Xi stop this stampede away from Chinese colleges? A few years ago, he instructed officials to remove their children from foreign schools. At the time, Xi's daughter was midway through her undergraduate studies at Harvard. She did not withdraw but finished her degree. What kind of example does this set for other official families, let alone families with no ties to public office?

Of course, Chinese students today are very different from those who pioneered study abroad in the aftermath of the Cultural Revolution, when some students looked to the West for new ideas of governance that might lead China out of the chaos of Mao's last years. Today, Chinese students come from a proudly resurgent nation, very conscious of its economic and diplomatic clout. Most are patriotic and probably see a Western education as providing an excellent basis for their careers, rather than as exposure to the ideals of democracy. Nevertheless, it is unlikely that, back in China, they will embrace the creed, based on an analysis of early industrial Britain, of a mid-nineteenth-century German philosopher. Xi's

China may trumpet Marxism as its unifying ideology, but it will be window dressing. The Thought of General Secretary Xi will effectively take its place, as Mao Zedong Thought did under the Chairman.

The final element of the Maoist state was the People's Liberation Army (PLA). Mao was always careful to ensure that the majority of the generals would back him, especially when he clashed with such revolutionary heroes as Marshals Peng Dehuai and Lin Biao. Xi Jinping obviously cannot claim Mao's revolutionary laurels, and so he has had to employ more overt means of indicating PLA support. Early in his administration, he persuaded eighteen generals to write short articles in the *People's Daily* pledging loyalty. More recently, he has assumed a new military title: Commander-in-Chief of the Central Military Commission's Joint Battle Command Center. Xi appeared in military fatigues at the new center on the occasion of the announcement of this title, suggesting that, unlike any of his predecessors, he would be a battlefield commander if the occasion arose. But whether the PLA generals will be prepared to rescue Xi in a political crisis, as they did Mao during the Cultural Revolution and Deng Xiaoping at Tiananmen, remains to be seen.

Xi Jinping has moved China back to the future at an amazing pace. Maoist institutions and values are being restored, though, in one respect, Xi's politics mark a sharp break from late Maoism. Whereas the Chairman deliberately unleashed the youth of China to make revolution, in Xi's China, no vigilantism will be tolerated, even in the cause of fighting corruption. Whistle-blowers are likely to find themselves imprisoned. Nevertheless, Mao is the lodestone of the Xi regime, the ultimate legitimation of Xi's policies and personal role in state and society. So the Chairman's portrait will continue to hang in Tiananmen, and citizens will continue to be shepherded into his mausoleum. Mao does still matter.

4 | WHAT IS THE SOURCE OF ETHNIC TENSION IN CHINA?

Mark Elliott

NOT SO LONG AGO, it was common for most educated Westerners, including many scholars, to assume that China was an ethnically homogenous nation. As such, it differed from other countries seeking to reconcile the expectations of modern nationalistic ideology with the realities of governing populations that include ethnic or religious minorities because it had no "ethnic problem." And it had no ethnic problem, for the simple reason that everyone was "Chinese."

To be charitable, there were some grounds for this assumption. With a population overwhelmingly dominated by the Han majority—91.51 percent, according to the 2010 census, down from about 94 percent in the middle of the twentieth century—with no non-Han among the national-level leadership, and with the overwhelming concentration of non-Han groups outside the frequently visited eastern urban centers, it was easy to overlook the fact that alongside China's Han people live a very sizable group of so-called "national minorities," today totaling roughly 112 million individuals, classified by the state into fifty-five distinct categories.

By any measure, 112 million is a large number—almost the same size as the population of Japan, the world's eleventh most populous nation. That the land they occupy today constitutes over two-thirds of China's national territory and encompasses nearly all of China's continental borders (including with North Korea, Russia, Kazakhstan,

Pakistan, India, and nine other countries) makes it even clearer that the complex ethnic profile of the modern Chinese state is a non-trivial aspect of its makeup. Indeed, it may be regarded as a defining feature. The official expression of this status quo since the mid-1980s is that "China is a unified multi-ethnic country," a mantra that is routinely repeated in the thousands of writings on ethnic affairs that appear annually.

Tragic events of recent years have disabused even casual observers of the Chinese scene of this misperception of China's ethnic homogeneity, making plain the existence of considerable tension between the government and some—though certainly not all—of the country's many ethnic groups. These events include the violence in Tibetan regions in 2008, followed by more than one hundred incidents of self-immolation in succeeding years, all of which join long, sad memories that reach back to the bloody protests of the late 1980s, the decimation of monasteries during the Cultural Revolution, and the suppression of revolt in Lhasa in 1959. Other recent evidence that China does, in fact, have an "ethnic problem" include occasional protests in parts of Inner Mongolia as well; but after 2009, without question, the bombings and attacks in Urumqi and other cities around the country, including Beijing, have been in the headlines. Nearly all these incidents, which have claimed hundreds, and perhaps thousands, of lives, are ascribed to Uyghur "terrorists" based in what the Western media now routinely calls China's "restive" (or "unruly") "Far West," meaning mainly the oasis towns and cities of the Tarim Basin in southern Xinjiang.

THE PROBLEM OF ETHNIC TENSION

Independent journalists are generally forbidden from working in Xinjiang and Tibet, and tight controls are placed upon print and online media throughout China. It is thus next to impossible to verify the specific details of any incidents or to know much about the motives of those involved. This, in turn, makes it hard to answer the obvious question that emerges from this sorry record: What are non-Han people—mainly Tibetans, Uyghurs, and Mongols—so unhappy about?

Difficult as it is to answer, it's a key question for the future of the country. The answer, not surprisingly, depends greatly upon who is being asked.

For the majority of PRC citizens, including nearly all Han Chinese, the reply would be that Tibetans, Uyghurs, and Mongols are unhappy because a small number of "troublemakers" among them has raised false hopes of complete independence and the supposed benefits that would follow separation from the PRC. Those who espouse such hopes—or who are believed to espouse them—put themselves and the country at great risk. Not only are dreams of independence doomed to end in disappointment, but because they threaten the integrity of the country, they deserve to be struck down.

Most Han residents would argue further that, if only they were to take a good look around them, Tibetans, Uyghurs, and Mongols would realize their great good luck in being part of the PRC. Though condemned by history to a benighted condition, these people have, at long last, been lifted out of their previous misery. Over the last few decades, non-Han communities have seen unjust forms of human exploitation ended, poverty eradicated, diseases eliminated, life spans extended, education expanded, transportation and infrastructure enhanced, and the standard of living in general quite significantly raised—all thanks to the CCP's attention and the government's generous investment of resources. For that reason, this view holds, the non-Han populations owe the country an enormous debt of gratitude. The refusal of some to acknowledge that largesse, preferring instead to cry out against perceived injustices done to them—and going so far as to commit violence in the name of rebellion against party and country—is, in the eyes of most ordinary men and women, perverse and unreasonable.

To ask this same question—Why are you unhappy?—of the Tibetans, Uyghurs, and Mongols will usually elicit a very different answer. Most, in fact, would acknowledge the material improvements in their lives thanks to the incorporation of their historic lands into the PRC. But, they would add, consider the price we have paid. Despite the guarantees made by the government—guarantees in many cases made personally to our leaders by the founders of the PRC—our way of life is disappearing, our languages are vanishing, and we are not free to practice our religion as we wish. Although we live in what are called "autonomous" areas, in practice, we have little or no power over local affairs. We cannot teach our children our language in school or even protect the right of our own people to dress or wear their hair or name their children as they like. If we ever dare to raise a grievance of any kind, we are immediately labeled as "terrorists" and "splittists," picked up, intimidated, and jailed.

Some Uyghurs might go on to note that they are treated as second-class citizens, denied equal pay and equal access to jobs even in Xinjiang, forced to carry special identity papers, and subject to what Americans would call racial profiling. If you lived here as we do, many would say, you might conclude that Chinese rule is in fact a type of internal colonialism, and that knee-jerk Islamophobia in the post–9 / 11 world is creating the very sort of polarizing hatred the CCP claims to want to eliminate.

The tension is palpable, not only between ethnic minorities and the security apparatus (which has long been the case), but—which is more worrisome—also between ethnic minorities and the Han majority, something that was comparatively rare before the mid-2000s.

No one pretends there is no problem, not even the government. There are entire bureaucracies devoted to trying to defuse the situation, and still others devoted to containing it. Countless articles appear in political and academic journals discussing things from every (permissible) angle, though open discussion of the problem in popular media is nearly non-existent. A few brave souls, such as the writer Wang Lixiong and blogger Woeser, a married couple, have come forward publicly to bemoan what appears to be a steadily deteriorating situation, as ever greater repression, tighter surveillance, decreased liberties, and heightened penalties appear to drive resistance underground and contribute to a worsening of ethnic relations that not only dooms cultures but puts at risk the safety and security of all Chinese citizens, Han and non-Han alike. They propose an end to what they consider hopeless government tactics and the introduction of more tolerant policies and a greater measure of self-rule. However, there seems to be little evidence of any shift in that direction, at least for now.

A HISTORICAL PERSPECTIVE

Ethnic tension has been an intractable problem for nearly all of China's modern history. In the early twentieth century, the KMT (Kuomintang, or Nationalist Party) saw the non-Han peoples as all originally "Chinese" and expected them ultimately to assimilate to a single, Han norm. The paternalist attitudes that went with this view did little to win the KMT regime much favor from non-Han groups. Sensing an opportunity, the CCP rejected "Sinicization" and promised far more autonomy to non-Han peoples, at one time even offering the right to secede. Though this proviso was dropped long before the first post-1949 constitution was written, still, that document included a wide range of protections for minority religions, cultures, and languages.

Mao Zedong—whose revolution would likely never have happened had he not secured the support of non-Han communities during the Long March—officially decried the negative effects of the KMT's "great Han chauvinism" and made a point of showing respect for the dignity of the non-Han groups. This more tolerant stance was temporarily set aside during the Cultural Revolution period (1966–1979), but was revived in the 1980s, when comparatively liberal policies toward minority groups prevailed. Most of these policies were dialed back in the 1990s because of fears among Party leaders of growing demands of autonomy, principally those coming from the Tibetan community, led by the Dalai Lama. The situation in Xinjiang was in turn complicated by the emergence of transnational terrorist organizations like Al Qaeda in the early 2000s.

As the transition from empire to nation continues to unfold in the twenty-first century, twentieth-century solutions, such as they were, appear to have failed. Ethnic tension on China's frontiers is now an irrefutable fact of life, for the Han-dominated Chinese state as well as for non-Han peoples. Both sides look at the past and see history on their side. The Chinese Communist Party looks at the USSR and its disintegration, a fate it seeks at all costs to avoid, and which it blames in large measure upon "erroneous" Soviet nationality policies that devolved too much authority to local, non-Russian actors. Tibetans, Uyghurs, and Mongols—few of whom seriously espouse separatist goals—point to the examples of the United States, Australia, and Canada, fearing that they face a fate similar to that of indigenous peoples in those countries, whose way of life has been extinguished, and whose sanitized, hollowed-out cultures are preserved in museums for tourists. Neither side is very keen to state these analogies openly (the very notion of "native peoples" is taboo in China), but it is not hard to see the fears that motivate different parties in this increasingly tense standoff.

ETHNIC TENSION: TWO EXPLANATIONS

Communist ideals served to provide a common purpose and foster a shared sense of citizenship among Han and non-Han alike. Over time, however, the CCP appears to have forgotten what it owes China's frontier peoples, just as many Han Chinese accuse non-Han groups of failing to recognize everything they owe the Party. Neither capitalist desires nor the "China Dream" seem to be able to bring the two together; nor does the rebirth of Chinese nationalism hold much promise. The reasons are clear when one considers some of the underlying causes of the present malaise that affects ethnic relations in China.

Some of the blame for the cracks in the edifice of the "united multi-ethnic country" goes to the opening of formerly small and autarkic provincial economies under CCP guidance and the introduction of powerful market forces into society. Since 1979, and especially since the mid-1990s, this has brought increasingly more Han Chinese out to the frontiers, where opportunities to get rich have beckoned, many tied directly to the government-sponsored "Open Up the West" campaign announced in 1999. The arrival of large numbers of Han immigrants—few of whom bother to learn the local language—to Uyghur, Tibetan, and Mongolian cities and towns means that non-Han peoples are gradually becoming outnumbered in their own homelands. For instance, in 1949, only 6 percent of Xinjiang's population was Han, whereas by 2015 the number had risen to 38 percent. The Tibetan Autonomous Region is still predominantly Tibetan, but the Han population in mainly Tibetan and Mongolian Qinghai has risen from under 40 percent in 1982 to 53 percent in 2010.

Most of the new wealth being generated in cities like Urumqi and Lhasa is going to its Han residents, a point made by Chinese social scientists, who, while noting that language is often a barrier to employment in the city, also criticize the racism inherent in awarding contracts and making hires. This means not only higher levels of income and educational inequality, but also that inequality is now closely tied to ethnic identity. Such socioeconomic stratification contributes to the sense many non-Han have that the benefits of China's economic transformation have gone disproportionately to the Han. Few of us need to be reminded of the risks to society when class and ethnicity become linked in this way.

The other most important explanation for ethnic tension in China today lies in the radically different ways that Han and non-Han groups position themselves with respect to the modern Chinese nation. Put simply, people in the Han majority think of themselves first and last as Chinese, whereas non-Han groups largely see themselves first as Tibetan, Uyghur, Mongolian, Zhuang, Korean, etc., and only secondarily as "Chinese," meaning essentially "citizens of the PRC." For this reason, today's revived Chinese nationalism—which, since its origins has been fundamentally about ensuring that the Han people remain masters of the Chinese nation—offers nothing to most non-Han groups and is no replacement for communism when it comes to inclusivity in the national project.

WHAT'S THE SOLUTION?

As the ethnic problem in China has intensified in recent years, a range of different ideas has been put forward to address it. One of the bolder proposals, advanced by Ma Rong, a Beijing University sociologist, is to eliminate "national minorities" altogether and replace them with "ethnic minorities." This would involve removing references to "nationalities" in the constitution, striking ethnic identity from individual identity cards, and following an American cultural-pluralist model in which everyone is free to assume his or her own identity in a variation of the so-called melting pot. While Ma's proposal has received much attention, skeptics worry that, given China's weak judiciary system, it would leave little in terms of legal protections for minorities. They also point to the limitations of this model even in the United States.

Another solution—which, as noted, is already underway—is to alter the demographic landscape so that the non-Han groups become minorities in their own lands. Given that, of the total 112 million non-Han, only a little over 10 percent (twelve million) belong to those groups with significant complaints (Tibetans, Uyghurs, and Mongols), from the government's standpoint, this is not an entirely unrealistic option, especially if combined with incentives to encourage intermarriage between Han settler men and non-Han local women, which some officials have lately suggested. The ultimate (unstated) outcome of such transformations of the population would be the virtual disappearance of entire peoples. Things may not come to such a pass, however, because data now show that the Han population in these regions is showing signs of decreasing.

In the end, so long as the policies being pursued are seen by the non-Han peoples as enforcing oppression, advancing a Han-centered agenda, and undermining the long-term viability of local languages, customs, religious institutions, and lifeways, it is hard to imagine how a solution to China's ethnic problems will be found. The problem will likely get worse, until one day the conflict gets out of hand, or there are no more Tibetans, Uyghurs, or Mongols to protest.

If, on the other hand, sufficient political, cultural, and economic space can be made for people to have the freedom to be simultaneously full-fledged citizens of China and ethnic Tibetans, Uyghurs, or Mongols, then some way out of the present dilemma should be possible. In fact, the blueprint exists for a modus vivendi that would be acceptable to the vast majority of the country, Han and non-Han alike, and that would preserve the great cultures of China's non-Han peoples before they are lost forever. It is already written in the Chinese constitution.

5 | WHAT SHOULD WE KNOW ABOUT PUBLIC OPINION IN CHINA?

Ya-Wen Lei

CHINA IS INFAMOUS for censorship—it has been constantly ranked by international organizations as one of the countries with the least freedom of press and speech, as well as one of the top "enemies" of "Internet freedom." Not surprisingly then, even people relatively unfamiliar with China assume political and civic life there is bleak and suffocating. Yet contrary to this popular image—and despite very real government repression—political discussion, contention, and engagement is, in fact, prevalent in China. Furthermore, since the mid-2000s, expressions of public opinion have been on the rise. From time to time, contentious events, or what Chinese people call "public opinion incidents," burst into existence, capture widespread public attention, and lead to heated debates. For example, in 2003, Sun Zhigan, a 27-year-old man in Guangzhou, died in police custody after being wrongly detained and beaten by police in a detention center. His death triggered strong criticism of the government, eventually leading to the overhaul of unconstitutional detention regulations. In these public opinion incidents, Chinese people often discuss social problems and demand that the Chinese government be responsive and accountable. In turn, that government now increasingly, if reluctantly, views public opinion as a political and social force to be reckoned with. The emerging court of public opinion has rendered the Chinese government more responsive, but it has also triggered severe crackdowns on actors seen as contributing to public opinion incidents.

What does public opinion mean in the Chinese context? To what extent is it a "new" phenomenon? How and why do public opinion incidents emerge? How can we explain the rise of public opinion as an influential political phenomenon, given ongoing state censorship and political control? And how has the Chinese government responded to public opinion, especially under Xi Jinping's leadership?

It is critical to recognize that public opinion generally means different things in China and in the United States. In the United States, the notion of public opinion is often understood—particularly by social scientists and media outlets—cumulatively, as the aggregate of individual opinions, measured through polls, which have particular weight during US elections. In comparison, public opinion is understood more holistically in China as publicly expressed opinion or public discourse. The very phenomenon of public opinion is considered more discursive and communicative in nature, with Chinese people articulating and sharing their viewpoints through media, the Internet, and by participation in public protests. Academic institutes, the media, and government agencies in China do conduct public opinion polls or surveys, which are used primarily for research and policy making. Public opinion polls as such do not give rise to contentious events, nor do they constitute important social or political forces in China, as they do in the United States.

Public opinion is not entirely new in the Chinese context, but the recent growth of public opinion is distinct in certain ways. Public opinion became increasingly salient in the late 1980s in response to problems associated with the country's economic reform, but this growth of public opinion was interrupted by the 1989 Tiananmen incident. After a decade of post-Tiananmen decline, public opinion began to rise again around 1998, when the state forced newspapers to turn commercial, keeping them under state control but also making them dependent on revenues to survive. As newspapers became more active in facilitating the formation of public opinion, the central government began to acknowledge and respond to public opinion on a regular basis for the first time in the history of the People's Republic of China.

Between 1998 and 2005, public opinion was relatively safely contained, but with the introduction of the Internet, public opinion became increasingly unruly, capable of at least occasionally escaping government control and setting the public agenda. Whereas the power and visibility of public opinion prior to 1998 generally rose and fell with large-scale mobilization and collective actions, such as the Democracy Wall movement of 1978–1979 and the Tiananmen democratic movement in 1989, Chinese people no longer have to mobilize extraordinary resources in order to express their voice and have their concerns heard by their government.

Public opinion incidents usually develop along a defined trajectory. First, an event or issue is exposed by a few mass-media outlets or individuals on the Internet. Then, the event or issue is discussed, interpreted, and amplified by netizens (Internet users) through the mediation of Internet forums, blogs, or major operators such as Weibo and WeChat. Next, the discussion leads to wider mass-media coverage and heated discussion among a broader public, eventually culminating in a public opinion incident. Throughout this process, a range of actors—mass-media outlets, major Internet companies, individual citizens (including those with legal grievances), netizens, journalists, lawyers, NGOs, activists, public intellectuals and opinion leaders—participate in shaping the public agenda and producing public opinion incidents. For instance, in the Sun Zhigang case mentioned above, the editor-in-chief of the *Southern Metropolis Daily* newspaper worked closely with editors at Sina—one of China's largest Internet companies—to create the initial report. Sina then widely circulated the *Southern Metropolis Daily*'s report online immediately after it was published, in order to increase the event's national visibility. The public exposure of the incident led to heated discussion in online forums and many follow-up media reports. Public attention and the participation of legal scholars ultimately led to the overhaul of unconstitutional detention regulations.

The kinds of issues that have triggered contentious events or public opinion incidents have shifted over time. In the late 1990s, nationalist concerns and sentiments were often responsible, but over time, domestic issues and grievances came to figure prominently. Issues related to law—particularly citizen rights protection, illegal government practices, and legal disputes—have generated the most incidents. For example, grievances regarding housing demolition and relocation, pollution, food safety, or government corruption are particularly likely to provoke outbursts of public criticism. Around one-third of the public opinion incidents between 2003 and 2014 were associated with peasants and workers—two groups rendered particularly "disadvantaged" or vulnerable through the loss of land and jobs, respectively. In response to these public opinion incidents, netizens have voiced support for, and demanded government recognition of, the rights and interests of such vulnerable groups.

It is often assumed that authoritarian states only repress public opinion. Yet, in addition to engaging in suppression and control, the Chinese government has also facilitated the growth of public opinion in both intentional and unintentional ways. The unfolding of China's economic reform led to severe problems, particularly corruption, in the 1980s. The Chinese government began to see public opinion as a critical instrument through which it could oversee local government officials and business actors. Zhao Ziyang, then General Secretary of the Chinese Community Party, promoted these ideas as "legal supervision" and "supervision by public opinion." "Legal supervision" meant overseeing government and market actors in accordance with the law, while "supervision by public opinion" meant giving the masses and the media the power to monitor government and market actors through the formation and dissemination of public opinion. Zhao argued such supervision could help the CCP "resolve conflict at the grassroots level and nip [problems] in the bud." After the events in Tiananmen in 1989, it was decided that Zhao had been too lenient, and he was kept under house arrest until he died. Crucially, however, the CCP did not repudiate his idea of supervision. Indeed, top CCP leaders still refer to the notion of "supervision by public opinion" when they want to make a democratic gesture.

Two points should be clarified here. Even when the state has actively encouraged the formation of public opinion, it has sought contained public opinion—the kind of public opinion that is controlled and guided by the Chinese government. Second, as one might expect, government rhetoric has often outpaced reality. The central government might acknowledge public opinion, but individual officials and government agencies at both local and central levels still try to censor or suppress public opinion for their own political or economic reasons.

It is, arguably, the state's unintentional facilitation of public opinion that has been most significant. Through its own actions and policies, the Chinese government has inadvertently contributed to the growth of public opinion and rendered it increasingly unruly. The state introduced a formal system of law, a commercial media, and the Internet as parts of a broader campaign to modernize the country. At the same time, the state sought to contain these instruments and the potential risk each posed for empowering citizens and destabilizing its political authority. Once set in motion, however, the various processes unleashed by the government soon escaped its control.

The development of a modern legal system required informed citizens, capable of following the legal order, to participate in a market economy and keep local officials and market actors in check. Using the media, the government sought to disseminate legal knowledge and the concept of rights. This process increased widespread legal and rights consciousness across social groups and opened key opportunities for capable lawyers and legal scholars—many of whom put much greater emphasis on protecting citizen rights and public interests. Meanwhile, forcing the media to rely on market forces transformed the profession of journalism, leading more and more journalists to see themselves as spokespersons for citizens. Allowed by the government to network and collaborate for the first time—ostensibly to ensure the dissemination of law—journalists and legal professionals began to cooperate in new ways. Together, they were able to exploit already existing state fragmentation, bypass certain forms of censorship, and produce critical news reports that uncovered social problems and demanded government accountability. As key journalists and legal professionals became public opinion leaders, their critical practices then influenced ordinary citizens through the diffusion of the Internet. Chinese netizens themselves had also developed their own contentious practices. Airing and encountering grievances and building a sense of community were among the most salient aspects of netizens' activities between the 1990s and 2000s. As noted earlier, discussing problems and grievances through the lens of law and rights was one of the most common ways of sparking a public opinion incident.

How has the Chinese government responded to these developments? Whereas the earlier Hu Jintao and Wen Jiabao leadership was similar to that of Xi Jinping in their attempt to contain public opinion, the Hu-Wen leadership had a relatively more open and responsive approach. The Xi regime, by contrast, has tied the issue of public opinion more firmly to issues of social stability and national security in order to justify increasingly combative measures. Law and technology have been used to strengthen censorship and surveillance, as manifested by the continued effort to legalize controversial practices and penalize undesirable behavior, such as declaring the vaguely termed activity of "making trouble" to be a crime. In addition, promoting the use of big data science and cloud computing aided in the pursuit of social control. The Chinese government has also cast a wide net to attack key actors who have contributed to the rise of public opinion incidents—public opinion leaders, "the disadvantaged," lawyers who defend civil rights and the public interest, journalists, and activists. Meanwhile, the government has tightened its control of media, NGOs, and Internet companies, while also asserting China's own cyber-sovereignty.

The Chinese state's effort to contain public opinion has yielded mixed results. On one hand, it has largely dismantled the key social networks comprised of lawyers, journalists, activists, and public opinion leaders that enabled previous, nationwide public opinion incidents. The targeting of such networks has greatly undermined the mobilization of social forces in producing such incidents. Although certain pro-liberal legal and media professionals and intellectuals have been very critical of the crackdown, they have not yet found effective means of countering the intensifying control. On the other hand, the state's crackdown has not completely silenced critical voices and mobilization. Frictions within the Party-state can still be exploited, creating opportunities for the media to speak up and challenge censorship. In addition, a highly educated middle class, not yet targeted for crackdowns, has retained its capacity to unite and make its voice heard. Things looks less promising for more vulnerable groups in

China, who will encounter enormous difficulty in mobilizing public support without concerted help from lawyers, NGO activists, and journalists who have been repressed. Given no other outlet for expression or redress, "the disadvantaged" in China could develop a more extreme and radical response to their grievances, threatening social stability—precisely what the Xi regime seeks to fortify. However, if discussion of societal problems significantly decreases, public opinion could become dedicated primarily to the expression of nationalism.

6 | WHAT DOES LONGEVITY MEAN FOR LEADERSHIP IN CHINA?

Arunabh Ghosh

By many accounts, the 19th People's Congress in autumn 2017 may mark a historic transformation in how the elite leadership in China is structured. Since the events of the summer of 1989, a system has evolved in China that has allowed the peaceful and smooth transition of power from one generation of leaders to the next. Dubbed "authoritarian resilience" by the political scientist Andrew Nathan in 2003, this system, whose features include limiting the president and prime minister to two five-year terms and enacting a form of expanding collective leadership, now appears under threat. There is concern that China's current president, Xi Jinping, may break with these sets of formal and informal rules and attempt to continue in the position or, at the very least, attempt to stay influential in elite politics well after 2022, when his second five-year term ends.

That Xi seeks such enduring influence is not surprising. While his immediate predecessor, Hu Jintao, who served as president from 2002 to 2012, has receded from the political limelight, Xi's patron, Jiang Zemin, together with the most influential leader in the reform era, Deng Xiaoping, continued to exercise power and influence well after stepping down from formal leadership positions. Indeed, Xi's own promotion to the presidency in the fall of 2012 occurred under the influential gaze and sanction of the octogenarian Jiang. Long since retired, and officially no longer active in politics, Jiang nevertheless cast a long shadow that was evident in the elevation of several of his protégés to the Politburo Standing Committee in 2002 and 2012. Jiang's predecessor Deng Xiaoping exercised even more far-reaching influence after his official retirement from active politics in the late 1980s. One need only recall that Deng had stepped down from all posts except the chairmanship of the Central Military Commission by November 1987. Yet, it was under his sanction that People's Liberation Army troops entered Tiananmen Square two years later, in June 1989, to disperse protestors. Similarly, it was his Southern Tour in 1992, during which he re-emphasized his pro-reform economic agenda, that reignited Chinese growth. Jiang and Deng are merely the most high-profile examples of the wider phenomenon wherein elder statesmen have continued to exercise influence without formally holding government positions.

Whether Xi upends the existing system of elite succession, chooses to follow Jiang and Deng's example, or simply steps aside, remains to be seen. From a comparative historical perspective, it does, however, draw attention to not only the age of a leader when he or she is in power, but also to their longevity per se. Longevity is perhaps less important in political systems where leaders typically withdraw from elite politics when their term limits are reached (such as in the United States) or where parliamentary forms of governance can shift the burden of incumbency rapidly and in frequently unforeseeable directions (think the United Kingdom, India, and the broader world of coalition politics). While the PRC has indeed adopted term limits, the fact that leaders who step down continue to possess decisive and direct influence on future generations means they retain far more influence than is true in countries such as the United States, United Kingdom, or India. For the historian, it also raises an intriguing comparative question: Have China's top leaders lived longer lives than their international counterparts?

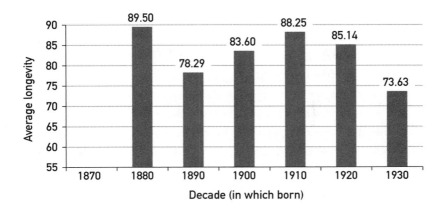

Figure 6.1. Chinese Communist Party leadership longevity by decade of birth

Data collected in 2012 by the *New York Times* on former and current members of the Politburo Standing Committee, as well as the Eight Immortals (Mao Zedong's close associates, who may not have been members of the standing committee but whose influence and contribution over the last sixty-odd years has been just as significant), shows that, over the past six decades, sixty-one people have exercised authority and influence from the pinnacle of political power in the PRC. As of 2012, these leaders had an average age of 79 years and a median age of 78.

In fact, as Figure 6.1 shows, for China's top leadership born from the 1880s to the 1930s, average longevity is in the mid-to-high 80s. The lower average for those born in the 1890s can at least partially be explained by the purges of the Cultural Revolution (1966–1976), which affected many top leaders as well. Six of the eight leaders born in the 1930s were still alive in 2012, and thus one can expect this average to rise over time. Leaders born in the 1940s have an average age of 67, including former president Hu Jintao and most of the current Politburo Standing Committee. While the simple average of 79 for the entire group already suggests a long life span, longevity is even higher once we account for younger generations, many of whose members remain living. Indeed, if we exclude the fourteen leaders born after 1940, we would arrive at a figure of 82.

How does the longevity of Chinese leaders compare with that of their peers in the former USSR, the United States, and India? The overall average longevity for leaders born in each decade from the 1870s to the 1930s is, at 82, highest in China and only marginally lower—80—in India. While the common men or women in India and China have lived, and continue to live, shorter lives on average than people in the United States and the former Soviet Union, their leaders do not fit the same pattern. What is additionally striking is that several leaders in both countries lived through periods of intense social and political turmoil, and often experienced tremendous personal physical hardship (incarceration, hunger strikes, long marches, and war, to name a few). Longevity averages 79 for US leaders and 71 for those of the former USSR, whose number is again lower on account of the large number of leaders purged in the 1930s.

The longevity of leaders seems to have no direct relationship with average life expectancy in any of these four countries. For much of the twentieth century, life expectancy in India and China was below 60. According to World Bank data, in 1960, Indian and Chinese life expectancy were 42 and 43, respectively. Both numbers have risen steadily over the last fifty years and are in the neighborhood of 66 and 75, respectively, today. American and Soviet life expectancy were around 70 in 1960. While the American number has experienced a steady increase and is approaching 80 today, the Russian one has stayed level. Life expectancy, in any case, has its limitations when looking at such a select group of individuals as national level leaders, who typically enjoy access to better health care. What does appear to be true, however, is that national leaders tend to live longer than the people they govern.

How much of an outlier is China? The percentages of leaders who have lived beyond 50, 60, and 70 are roughly comparable across the four countries; however, interesting things start happening in the next two age brackets. As one would expect, a significantly lower percentage of each nation's leaders have lived beyond 80. China enjoys a small lead here, marginally ahead of the United States and India. The gap widens somewhat when we look at the over-90 segment. China pulls away from the others: nearly one-in-five Chinese leaders has lived beyond 90. In comparison, only about one-in-seven leaders in the United States, one-in-nine in India, and one-in-ten for the USSR, has lived past 90.

When looking only at leaders born before 1940 (thereby excluding the current crop of younger leaders), we see that in the PRC well over half (63.8 percent) of those born before 1940 lived beyond 80. This is almost 10 percent higher than next placed United States. Indian and Soviet leaders do not cross the 50 percent mark. The gap is even more telling for the above-90 bracket. Nearly one in four (23.4 percent) PRC leaders lived beyond 90, compared to a little less than one-in-six for the United States, one-in-eight for India, and less than one-in-ten for the Soviet Union.

Chinese leaders do indeed live longer lives than their counterparts in the United States, India, and the former Soviet Union. Put differently, national leaders live longer in the one country where it matters that they live longer: China.

That Chinese leaders live long lives has many implications. Locally, their influence can be felt in the continuity in styles of leadership and in the mentoring of specific, younger leaders. General ideological preferences and policy commitments can therefore persist for a lot longer than elsewhere. This may also explain the longer-term perspective that leaders can take when engaging in negotiations with leaders from other countries. Longevity also has implications for the hardening of factional boundaries within the Communist Party and for the creation of loyalties that cut across multiple generations and levels of government. In the absence of several strong leaders at the top, the persistence of one faction backed by one long-lived leader can effectively stymie debate and discussion at the highest levels of the state.

At a broader level, longevity also has implications for how well leaders can grasp trends within the population and respond to them effectively. While it is no longer as young a nation as it was a decade ago, China remains younger than most developed countries. About 70 percent of all Chinese are aged 50 or younger; a little less than one-in-five is under 15. And it is the youth that were a major force for change throughout twentieth-century Chinese history. Whether it is the New Culture and May Fourth movements during the 1910s and 1920s, or the Democracy Wall and Tiananmen Square movements during the 1970s and 1980s, it is the young who have been among the most vociferous in their calls for progressive reform. The leadership, increasingly older, has consistently pushed back. Since the reform era, the continued promise and delivery of stunning economic growth has largely overwhelmed this reformist fervor. But indications are that the near double-digit GDP growth of the past fifteen years is no longer sustainable. Under such circumstances, the prospects of an older leadership tied to relatively inflexible policy agendas, increasingly out of touch with the people they putatively serve, does not offer much confidence for political or social stability.

Earlier this year, Andrew Nathan noted that "China's fairly recent ability to renew and upgrade its political leadership over the course of several decades is unique among authoritarian systems."

And yet, if the concerns about Xi are well-founded, it would appear that China is indeed reverting to some kind of authoritarian "norm." Under such circumstances, the fact that its elite leaders tend to live longer has implications not just for China's future economic, social, and political prospects, but for those of the world as well.

7 | CAN THE CHINESE COMMUNIST PARTY LEARN FROM CHINESE EMPERORS?

Yuhua Wang

IN 1912, at the age of 19, Mao Zedong's high school teacher gave him a book that became his lifelong favorite. He read it during the Long March, in his cave house in Yanan, and during his train rides across China. A copy of the book could always be found on his bedside table so he could read it before sleep. He told people that he had read it seventeen times, and he frequently referred to the book during conversations with Party officials.

The book is *Comprehensive Mirror in Aid of Governance,* which was edited by Sima Guang, an intellectual and politician in the Northern Song dynasty, and published in 1084. It is a 294-volume, three-million-word chronological narrative of China's history from 403 BCE to 959 CE. The emperor asked Sima to write this book to examine the lessons learned from previous emperors, so that future emperors could learn from them, avoid their mistakes, and become better rulers.

Why was Mao so obsessed with a book written almost a thousand years earlier? China under Mao was certainly different from its ancient past: the economy was rapidly industrializing, the state was tasked with more complicated functions, and, with the rise of the

Western world and Japan, China was no longer the "Middle Kingdom" at the center of the world. However, the core challenge Mao faced was very similar to that faced by Chinese emperors: How to stay in power?

China today is even more different from its ancient past. Its traditional agrarian society has gradually collapsed, and more people now live in urban than in rural areas. Once a secluded empire, China is now the world's largest exporter and second-largest destination for foreign direct investment. Wealthy merchants, once despised in ancient China, can now sit in the Great Hall of the People and are worshipped by the public. However, top Communist Party officials still keep asking themselves: How to stay in power?

Their worry is justified. Around the world, sixty-seven autocracies have collapsed since 1972, including many military regimes in Latin America, personal dictatorships in Africa, and the communist regime in the Soviet Union. During the Arab Spring, some of the most durable authoritarian rulers, including Libya's Gaddafi and Egypt's Mubarak, were overthrown, then killed or put in prison. Francis Fukuyama, an American political scientist, has even claimed the rise of liberal democracy as the final form of human government.

How can the Chinese Communist Party survive these worldwide "waves" of regime changes? The experiences of other communist regimes are not very informative. Cuba and North Korea have been ruled by the same families, Castro and Kim, respectively, since their founding, while Vietnam and Laos are trying to follow China's steps to maintain communist rule with a market economy.

Perhaps the CCP can follow Mao's wisdom to learn from history. From the Qin dynasty (221–207 BCE) to the Qing dynasty (1644–1911), China has been ruled by 282 emperors across forty-nine dynasties. The ups and downs of these ancient rulers and polities might instruct the Party what it needs to do to stay in power.

What are the key lessons from over two thousand years of Chinese dynastic rule? Fortunately, we don't have to read *Comprehensive Mirror in Aid of Governance* seventeen times to learn the lessons. With digitized data and modern statistical techniques, we can now systematically study the patterns behind the rise and fall of historical rulers.

Analyzing a dataset of dynasties and emperors compiled from a variety of historical and biographic sources, I draw four key lessons from Chinese history.

Lesson one: no dynasty can rule forever. The forty-nine dynasties lasted for an average of seventy years, with a wide-ranging variation from the Heng Chu (403–404), which lasted for less than a year, to the Tang dynasty (618–907), which ruled China for 289 years. Assuming the Chinese Communist Party is still in power in 2019, it will reach this seventy-year average.

Lesson two: elite rebellion is the most important cause of dynastic fall. Most dynasties were overthrown not by foreign enemies or the masses, but by political elites who were part of the old regimes. For example, the founder and first emperor of the Han dynasty (206 BCE–9 CE), Liu Bang, served as a patrol officer in his hometown, Pei County, before he joined the rebels against the Qin government. Along with Liu Bang, another rebel group led by two peasants never made it to the capital. The Tang dynasty (618–907), one of the strongest dynasties in Chinese history, was founded by Li Yuan, a governor in the preceding Sui government. Meanwhile, many of the rebels led by peasants in the late Sui dynasty were either defeated by the Sui army or eliminated by Li Yuan. Even the 1911 revolution that ended China's dynastic rule was led by a group of elites, many of whom were local military leaders in the Qing government, rather than peasants. Peasant leaders, such as Zhang Jiao in late Han, Li Zicheng in late Ming, and Hong Xiuquan in late Qing, never seized the crown despite their fame in folklore. Statistical analysis reveals the same pattern: it was neither the nomads nor the masses; over time, political elites have posed the greatest threat to China's various regimes. Elites have more resources and knowledge to mobilize the masses, and they are more familiar with how the political system works. They also know where the garrisons, arsenals, grain warehouses, government files, maps, and treasuries are. While the state capital seems like a maze to peasant rebels who have never visited big cities, political elites can easily find their way to the emperor's bedroom. Xiao He, one of Liu Bang's chief advisors and previously a magistrate's secretary in a Pei County administrative office, managed to seize all the maps stored in the Qin palace immediately after Liu's troops entered the capital.

Lesson three: only half of the emperors left office naturally. Table 7.1 shows the method of exit of the 282 Chinese emperors. While half of the emperors descended by natural death, another half exited office unnaturally. Among these unnatural exits, about half were deposed by the elites (murdered, overthrown, forced to abdicate, or forced to commit suicide). The next big category is death or deposition in civil wars, while very few emperors (seven) were deposed by, or in, external wars. The cause of ruler exit is similar to that of dynastic collapse: the biggest threat was from within the regime rather than from the society or foreign countries.

Lesson four: emperors who designated a competent and loyal successor lived longer. Among the 282 Chinese emperors, 130 (46 percent) designated a crown prince as their successor, and more than half did so in the first five years of their reign. And because there was no religious control of royal marriage in ancient China, the emperors could choose a successor from a large number of male heirs, so the chosen son was usually the most competent rather than the oldest. My statistical analysis shows that emperors who had a designated successor were 64 percent less likely to be deposed than those who did not.

Table 7.1   Exit of Chinese Emperors (221 BCE—1911)

Cause	Method of Exit	Frequency	Percent
Health	Natural death	152	53.9
Elites	Murdered by elites	34	12.06
	Deposed by elites	24	8.51
	Forced to abdicate by elites	17	6.03
	Committed suicide under pressure from elites	1	0.35
	Subtotal	76	26.95
Civil War	Deposed in civil war	20	7.09
	Died in civil war	10	3.55
	Forced to abdicate facing internal threats	1	0.35
	Committed suicide during civil war	1	0.35
	Subtotal	32	11.34
External War	Committed suicide during external war	4	1.42
	Forced to abdicate facing external threats	3	1.06
	Subtotal	7	2.48
Family	Murdered by son	5	1.77
	Murdered by concubine	1	0.35
	Subtotal	6	2.12
Other	Elixir poison	4	1.42
	Volunteered to abdicate	4	1.42
	Accident	1	0.35
	Subtotal	9	3.19
	Total	282	100

Those who did not designate a crown prince either did not have a son or relied on other rules of succession. For example, the Mongolians relied on a combination of lateral successions (principles of seniority among members of a dynastic clan) and elections to choose a new leader, the great khan. As a consequence, only 33.33 percent of

Mongol emperors were the sons of their predecessors, and Mongol emperors' average tenure was 10.8 years, much shorter than their Han counterparts' 17.8 years in the next dynasty, the Ming.

Why was having a designated successor helpful for the emperors? As the economist Gordon Tullock argues, the benefit of appointing a successor is that the elites begin planning their own maneuvers on the assumption that they will spend much more of their life under the rule of the successor than under the rule of the current dictator. However, appointing a successor also comes with a risk. As Tullock points out, the basic problem that the dictator faces in this context is that if he formally anoints a successor, this gives that successor both a strong motive to assassinate him and reasonable security that he will get away with it. This is often dubbed the "crown prince problem," and Mao Zedong learned this lesson the hard way when his designated successor, Lin Biao, tried to blow up his train. Tullock therefore suggests that hereditary succession provides regime stability during and beyond the ruler's lifetime because the son is wise to simply wait for his father to die.

These four lessons are certainly not the only ones we can draw from the rich accounts of Chinese history. They do not inform us how to develop the economy, how to manage natural disasters, how to alleviate poverty, or how to build a strong army. However, they provide two important insights that help answer the question of how to stay in power.

First, the biggest challenge to regime durability is neither foreign enemies nor the masses, but elites within the regime. Political elites have both the knowledge and resources to organize a coup against the ruler. And even during so-called mass revolts, the elites usually play a leading role in mobilizing the masses. The Communist Party does not seem to fully appreciate this historical pattern. While it is paranoid about foreign influence and mass protests, the current regime under Xi Jinping is obsessed with an anti-corruption campaign to agitate the elites.

Second, succession is an extremely important issue. Although modern autocrats can rarely bequeath their rule to a son (the North Korean Kim family is an exception), it is critical for the incumbent leader to choose a successor who is both loyal (so he can patiently wait) and competent (so the elites can rally their support). The turmoil in Chinese politics in the 1970s can be interpreted as the consequence of Mao's choosing a disloyal successor (Lin Biao) and then an incompetent successor (Hua Guofeng). The post-Mao leadership has handled the succession issue with great care. Deng was believed to have chosen both his own successor, Jiang Zemin, and his successor's successor, Hu Jintao, and Jiang Zemin seems to have played a role in choosing Xi Jinping. It remains unclear who will succeed Xi Jinping. His handling of the succession issue will be a good indicator of what the political landscape in China will look like in the next ten to fifteen years.

On his seventy-third birthday, Mao convened a meeting of some of his closest allies and told them that the easiest way to capture a fortress is from within. Without a viable son, Mao struggled with the succession problem, but he clearly got the message from reading *Comprehensive Mirror in Aid of Governance* that the people around him were the most dangerous. Has the CCP learned the same lesson?

II | INTERNATIONAL RELATIONS

8 | WILL CHINA LEAD ASIA?

Odd Arne Westad

OVER THE PAST forty years, China has gone through a transformation beyond anything seen in its long and complex history. In the 1970s, the country was dirt poor and falling ever further behind the West, and even parts of Asia, in terms of industry, technology, education, and agricultural output. Today, it is the number two economy in the world and the biggest trading nation. It is the world's largest producer of cars, ships, computers, and cell phones. There are, it is reported, now more billionaires in China than in the United States.

This restless superpower-in-the-making has raised understandable concerns among its neighbors and the existing global superpower, the United States, about the purposes of its rise. For the United States, these concerns have been about loss of economic preeminence and international predominance. As President Donald Trump's election shows, an increasing number of Americans are worried about jobs moving overseas and their country losing its economic edge in competition with others. China is often listed as the main beneficiary of ongoing adjustments in the global economy, in spite of the fact that the economies of many other countries, too, are growing faster and therefore attracting more investment than the US economy.

Americans are also uneasy about the shift to a more multipolar world, in terms of influence and power. The United States has been predominant since World War II. After the end of the Cold War in the 1990s, its supremacy seemed more secure than ever. But, in the 2000s, following the wars in Iraq and Afghanistan and the Great

Recession, the United States suddenly appeared a less effective superpower. Many events, from Russian aggression in Ukraine to civil war in Syria and the creation of new terrorist organizations, appeared to take place without the United States stepping in to prevent unacceptable consequences. China, meanwhile, was becoming more assertive in its policies toward neighbors in eastern Asia and less intent on cooperating with the United States in global affairs. By the late 2010s, the United States seemed much less the "indispensable nation," as former Secretary of State Madeleine Albright had called it in 1998, and more one giant power in a world of great powers.

If this trend toward global multipolarity continues, eastern Asia is the region in which it will have the most immediate effect. China's rise is one key reason for this. But other countries, too, have become more preoccupied with asserting what their leaders see as national interests. Japan is intent on standing up to its bigger neighbor, China, and refuses to give in to Chinese maritime territorial demands. An increasing number of South Koreans view China as a main obstacle to Korean reunification. In South Asia and Southeast Asia, nationalist leaders are likewise preoccupied with standing up for their countries' international positions. If a sense of American retrenchment from the region takes hold, these attitudes will become more potent in setting the future course for all states in Asia.

The world in which China's newfound significance will manifest itself may therefore be a much more complicated one than Chinese leaders were accustomed to during the age of American hegemony. It is quite likely that they will be called upon to deliver solutions to world problems much sooner than they believed only half a decade ago. If US involvement in regional affairs, or in setting the parameters for international trade and investment, declines rapidly, no other country will feel the burden of leadership more quickly than China. In the first part of the last century, the world's experience with multipolarity was an unhappy one, leading to two global wars and an economic depression. China's role in avoiding such scenarios in the twenty-first century will be crucial.

But is China equipped to lead, regionally or globally? The indications so far are unencouraging. Like the rest of eastern Asia, or indeed the world at large, China has seen an upswing in the emphasis on self-interest and nationalism. The period between 2010 and 2015 in Chinese regional foreign policy was mainly a lesson in how to make enemies and alienate potential friends. The focus on the territorial dispute with Japan over the Diaoyu / Senkaku Islands helped weaken thirty years of Sino-Japanese détente, a process that had been useful to both countries. Surveys show that only 9 percent of Japanese today view China favorably. The weak Chinese reaction to North Korea's provocations—including its nuclear weapons and missile program, the attack on Yeonpyeong Island and the sinking of the South Korean naval vessel *Cheonan* (both in 2010), as well as several attacks across the demilitarized zone—have convinced many South Koreans that China's real aim is to keep their country divided and weak. There are also those who believe that, long-term, Beijing's purpose may be to integrate North Korea as a part of China, forever ending the Korean dream of reunification.

Further south, the situation is not much better. Although links between China and Southeast Asia had been improving steadily for almost three decades, quarrels over sovereignty in the South China Sea have recently undermined these relationships. The result is increasing suspicions among China's southern neighbors that Beijing wants to dominate and control them, while forcing solutions to regional issues through economic influence and military power. The seven new artificial islands that China still has under construction in disputed waters signal to its neighbors that Beijing is unwilling to accept multilateral negotiations or decisions by international courts.

Some analysts argue that China is now so powerful that it will succeed in forcing neighbors to accept its preferred solutions to territorial issues and other conflicts. No power can oppose it, especially if the United States becomes less engaged in the region. In addition, almost all countries in the region have a strong interest in cooperating with China economically. There are undoubtedly leaders in eastern Asia who would like to test China's true capacity for cooperation by pulling closer to their big neighbor. But they have to be very careful with regard to their own populations. It is not only in Japan that the vast majority fear China's influence. The populations of Vietnam and the Philippines fear China almost as much as the Japanese do, despite the fact that, for economic reasons, the leaders of these countries would like to cooperate more closely with Beijing. The situation today is far from what it was in the eighteenth century, when the Chinese hold on its region started to decline. China then was widely admired, and most other countries did not have a strong sense of their own identity. Now China is feared, and popular nationalism is as strong a factor elsewhere as it is in China itself.

Others believe that China will modify its international behavior as its power grows. After all, the United States, when its influence grew in the nineteenth century, threw its weight around and was a pain in the neck both for its neighbors and further afield. However, when it came of age as a superpower late in the twentieth century, its approach was more collaborative (or at least integrationist) for as long as it was at the peak of its influence. Why should China not be expected to follow this pattern?

While it is possible that China will follow a similar trajectory to the United States, it is not very likely, at least not any time soon. This is not just because great powers need time to be socialized into a community of states. It is also because today's emphasis on bellicosity, self-interest, and narrow nationalism is a by-product of the way China is governed under its current regime. China lacks the mechanisms for political self-adjustment that the United States and many Asian countries have. Until China improves its domestic governance and installs a leadership more attuned to principles of cooperation, its international role is unlikely to improve. In fact, it may join the United States in seeing its capacity for delivering solutions to regional and world problems reduced. While its current leaders are certainly capable of striking bargains and making deals in their own interest, it is doubtful whether they are capable of more long-term compromise, in forms that also encompass the interest of others in the region.

On the whole, current Chinese policies are therefore more likely to lead to regional conflict than supremacy. Japan and Vietnam today are very dissimilar to America's neighbors, Mexico and Canada, which in the nineteenth century were weak states with limited opportunities to resist American aggression. In the twenty-first century, China's neighbors have reasonably well-defined interests and the capacity to pursue them, sometimes jointly, even in the face of Chinese pressure and threats. The position of other countries in Asia would of course be stronger if the US presence remained at the levels we see today. But even with a diminished US role, it is highly unlikely that China would achieve regional dominance through the political or economic means it currently employs.

Chinese leadership in Asia will therefore be slow in coming. China will become an increasingly important country, unless severe domestic unrest, produced by unresolved tensions, sets it back. But regional predominance will have to be gained through engaging neighbors in ways that are more collaborative and integrationist than what China seems capable of today. Such changes in policy are definitely possible in the future. Chinese scholars and officials are discussing them today, at least when they are safely out of earshot of senior leaders. Another China, which stands up for common values and not just its own core interests, may be in the making, and such a China would indeed become indispensable for its region and the world. Do not bet on it happening anytime soon, though.

9 | HOW STRONG ARE CHINA'S ARMED FORCES?

Andrew S. Erickson

TODAY, China has the world's second-largest economy and defense budget.* It boasts the world's largest conventional missile force, the world's largest coast guard, and virtually the world's only maritime militia charged with advancing sovereignty claims. If not already the world's second most powerful country, with the second-largest blue-water navy, it is on the verge of achieving those ranks; this is thanks in part to the largest, fastest shipbuilding expansion in modern history. Hence, it is only natural for observers to ask: How strong, exactly, are China's armed forces? And how would they compare with those of other nations, particularly those of the United States—undisputably the world's strongest—including in conflict scenarios that one hopes will never materialize but, with respect to which, peacetime perceptions can nevertheless influence geopolitical calculations and, thereby, the regional and global order?

A comprehensive net-assessment, however, requires all elements of complex, multivariate campaign equations, including information unavailable in open sources. Outright comparison of Chinese armed

* The analysis here is derived solely from open sources, which may be found at the suggested reading site hosted on the Fairbank Center website http:// fairbank.fas.harvard.edu/china-questions/. It reflects the views of the author alone. It does not represent the estimates or policies of the US Navy or any other organization of the US government.

forces with American (or any other) counterparts is misleading because their respective force structures differ significantly, and the two sides have very different objectives and missions. Bi-directional analysis is, likewise, essential. China is clearly expanding its inventory of weapons systems capable of targeting US and allied regional bases, platforms, and systems. But this says nothing of the countermeasures that the targeted forces might employ, nor of the ways in which they might successfully target their Chinese counterparts. This essay therefore considers both the most critical dynamics affecting the relevant equations, particularly vis-à-vis China itself, and the authoritative judgments offered by the latest unclassified US government reports.

KEY DYNAMICS

Understanding China's national security policies and power requires consideration of all three major components of China's armed forces: the People's Liberation Army (PLA), the paramilitary People's Armed Police (PAP), and the Militia. The United States is exceptional in its enviable combination of resources, innovation, decentralized governance, peaceful neighbors, oceanic access, and lack of sovereignty disputes. These factors enable expansive external security policies and operations by clearly defined military forces. Chinese national security is far more geographically confined, continuous, complex, and contested. While the PLA is the primary tool for combat operations far from China, elite maritime units within China's militia participate in sovereignty promotion operations vis-à-vis regional features and waters claimed by Beijing, and the PAP underpins domestic and border security.

China's armed forces, and the policies that inform their construction and use, have been shaped by Beijing's evolving hierarchy of national security interests. Having consolidated political, domestic, and (the vast majority of) border security, at least for now, the CCP is operationalizing its security priorities externally in progressively diminishing "ripples of capability" beyond China's mainland. Now, and likely for years to come, the area of most intense development concerns the Near Seas (Yellow, East China, and South China Seas), home to all China's outstanding island and maritime sovereignty claims.

To this end, Beijing is developing its armed forces with a view to targeting vulnerabilities in the forces of the United States and its regional allies and security partners to radically raise the risk they would face in intervening in Chinese sovereignty disputes. It is doing so in part by emphasizing missiles and other land-based, counter-intervention systems that are considerably cheaper and easier to build and employ than to defend against, bringing new relevance to the traditional PLA concept of "using the land to control the sea." Beijing's goal is to "win without fighting" and achieve deference to its "core" security interests, perhaps in part by becoming the preponderant East Asian power.

It pursues this end in a twofold manner: (1) at the high end, deterring foreign military intervention in the first place through a combination of demonstrating capabilities (ideally not using them lethally) in a way that intimidates the United States and its allies with the prospect of paying unacceptable costs; and (2) at the low end, achieving incremental progress below the threshold of war through "gray zone" coercion of rival claimants using primarily its coast guard and maritime militia. To enhance China's prospects for realizing these objectives, President Xi Jinping, who is also Chairman of the Central Military Commission, has charged the PLA with ambitious reforms to strengthen its ability to wage modern wars, while bolstering China's other two armed forces.

ESTIMATES AND PROJECTIONS

US government publications draw on comprehensive, robust, carefully vetted data and analysis that is largely unavailable to outside observers until long after their release. They have demonstrated their merit over time by the great degree to which their findings correspond to verifiable facts. Reports by US government-affiliated think tanks and their analysts are less demonstrably authoritative but offer greater diversity and specificity of insights. To these may be added Chinese government and open sources, which rarely provide detailed net-assessments but offer useful context when considered critically.

These sources conclude collectively that, in recent years, the PLA has greatly increased its ability to conduct operations in support of Beijing's objectives vis-à-vis the Near Seas, but that these capabilities diminish sharply beyond that margin. Given China's priorities and capabilities, the two leading Near Seas contingencies commonly analyzed by US government and related sources concern Taiwan and contested Chinese claims in the South China Sea's Spratly Islands. Assessments generally conclude that, over the next fifteen years or so, US forces will retain their ability to prevail over the PLA in a protracted war, but that the PLA might temporarily achieve superiority in specific sea- and air-spaces, and US victory would be far costlier than it would have been years ago.

A Taiwan scenario remains the PLA's leading high-end planning factor. It is widely regarded as able to engage in militarily significant operations, such as seizing a Taiwan-held offshore island or launching missile strikes on Taiwan proper. Such actions would almost certainly be counterproductive politically, however. A more sophisticated blockade would likely fail if opposed forcefully by Washington, making American intervention a decisive factor. An outright amphibious invasion of Taiwan's main island remains unrealistic, given both PLA force structure limitations and Taiwan's ability to exploit its formidable natural defenses.

The South China Sea is a far more permissive environment for China's armed forces. At stake is not a sophisticated society of 23.5 million that Beijing claims as Chinese compatriots but, rather, isolated islands and reefs that are sparsely inhabited at most, and sustain few, if any, indigenous people. Given the relative weakness of neighboring countries with whom China has disputed claims, China's coast guard and maritime militia can engage in multifarious "gray zone" operations, to significant effect. Regarding potential major combat operations, the PLA could likely prevail over rival militaries absent American involvement. Were US forces to intervene, for example, to support Washington's Philippine ally in a crisis or conflict with China, both sides could face significant operational challenges. The PLA would have difficulty deploying adequate forces to the highly vulnerable Spratly Islands and resupplying them there. Should it somehow succeed in massing sufficient forces with some element of surprise, however, it might confront Washington with unappealing alternatives.

Further afield, spurred largely by growing overseas interests, as encapsulated in part by Xi's "One Belt, One Road" initiative (which proposes to extend China's economic and political influence along the former Silk Road to Europe, as well as by sea), China is weaving an outer layer of substantive and influential but less intensive capabilities. These are enabling selective forays to protect Chinese citizens and assets abroad, including through evacuations from Libya and Yemen and anti-piracy escorts in the Gulf of Aden. The last, together with growing UN peacekeeping participation, offer welcome examples of growing international security contributions. Chinese developments enabling more formidable maritime power projection—including aircraft carrier operations and enhancing access to overseas facilities, possibly in part by developing further naval support-points beyond the initial one materializing in Djibouti—are progressing more gradually.

IMPLICATIONS

The aforementioned dynamics are poised to shape the capability of China's armed forces for the foreseeable future. Geography will remain foremost among them, making it imperative to view Chinese national security prospects "through the lens of distance." China has already arrived as a great power with formidable armed forces. Close to home, to the extent that the CCP retains favorable conditions domestically, it will retain and likely build on powerful synergies and advantages vis-à-vis the sovereignty claims that it prioritizes along its contested maritime periphery. Even as China's armed forces advance substantially overall, however, the Party-state that guides and supports them may face an economy with significant downside risks, an overall slowing in the growth rate of all elements of national power, and perhaps mounting challenges from within. The result is almost certain to be more complex national security tradeoffs and policy choices than Beijing has faced since the late 1970s, with the possible exception of domestic instability in 1989. Given the likelihood that national narratives and prioritization concerning unresolved sovereignty claims will persist, external security debates and policy adjustments will probably moderate plans regarding some of the more demanding high-end combat capabilities specific to long-range power projection.

Farther afield, Chinese military progress—beyond the emerging basic capabilities of presence and non-traditional security operations—toward growing ability to contest other capable militaries will come with a steep price. Increasing convergence will bring China the same rising costs and diminishing returns that notoriously plague established

Western militaries as they struggle to maintain their relative standing amid competing national priorities and evolving competitors. All three of China's armed forces will face escalating personnel-related costs. Structural and organizational reform will require intensified investment and impose associated demobilization costs. As with Western militaries, rising salaries and benefits to attract, educate, train, and retain capable professionals will consume an increasing portion of the budget. Growing entitlements will likewise impose a mounting burden, particularly as more retirees draw benefits that are already quite generous in some respects.

As China's most sophisticated armed force, the PLA will additionally face particularly significant technological requirements and attendant challenges. The closer it approaches leading-edge capabilities, the more expensive and difficult it will be to advance further, or even to retain a stable position vis-à-vis foreign competitors. Cutting-edge innovation is difficult and expensive—a burden that has long plagued the United States. Weapons systems and associated infrastructure will become progressively costlier to build, operate, and maintain than their simpler predecessors. China's cost advantages decrease as military equipment centers less on labor and more on advanced materials and technology. The more sophisticated and technology-intensive PLA systems become, the less relative benefit China derives from acquiring and indigenizing foreign technologies, and the less cost advantage it will have in producing and maintaining them. Additionally, propulsion, electronics, and other complex systems-of-systems hinging on the precise interaction of demanding apex technologies remain a key Chinese weakness—in part because they defy China's preferred approach of combining domestic and foreign technologies piecemeal.

Nevertheless, Beijing already enjoys formidable means to promote its Near Seas objectives without approaching American technological sophistication; such leading-edge accomplishment is far more essential to long-distance warfare. Again, geography matters.

Such are the unrelenting undercurrents of China's meteoric military-security development, which faces meaningful constraints from the prospect of US opposition as well as long-range challenges, just as surely as it enjoys short-range opportunities and is working hard to exploit them.

10 | WHAT DOES THE RISE OF CHINA MEAN FOR THE UNITED STATES?

Robert S. Ross

THE RISE OF China presents the United States with an unprecedented foreign policy challenge. For the first time since World War II, the United States faces a great power competitor that possesses both economic and military capabilities that may soon rival US capabilities. China is also the first great power since prewar Japan to challenge US maritime supremacy, a post–World War II cornerstone of US global power and national security. The rise of China challenges US security in a region vital to security. The United States waged World War II and the Cold War in East Asia to preserve a regional balance of power that assured American security.

The rise of China requires US-China policy to fulfill two strategic imperatives. First, US policy must balance the rise of China by enhancing its military forces in the region. Failure to offset China's improved military capabilities with increased capabilities of its own will undermine the ability of the United States to sustain its strategic partnerships in East Asia, and it will erode its regional presence, weakening US ability to preserve the balance of power.

Second, the United States must promote US-China cooperation and regional stability. The United States possesses many bilateral and global interests that require US-China cooperation. The United

States would incur significant costs should these interests become hostage to US–China strategic conflict. Heightened US–China strategic competition would also impose significant costs on US security and the US economy.

US-CHINA POLICY: SECURITY WITHOUT STABILITY

Since 2010, there has been a downward spiral in US–China relations. The US–China strategic relationship is now not only worse than at any time since 1972, but the US strategic position in East Asia is also worse than it was at the end of the George W. Bush administration.

During the Obama administration, the United States and China were on opposite sides of increasingly militarized territorial disputes involving China and Japan, and China and the Philippines. The US and Chinese militaries frequently challenge each other's presence in the air and at sea in Southeast Asia, with an increasing likelihood of an intended or unintended military incident. There has also been heightened US–China military competition. Washington and Beijing have each developed and deployed weapons with the explicit purpose of defeating the other in a war. Meanwhile, after reclaiming territory in the Spratly Islands, China now has maritime facilities in the southern reaches of the South China Sea, contributing to its ability to pressure US allies and carry out much enhanced surveillance of US naval operations.

The United States has responded to Chinese activism with expanded maritime strategic presence, seeking to consolidate its strategic partnerships and contend in the regional balance of power. It has strengthened its alliances with Japan, Australia, and, under President Benigno Aquino III, the Philippines. During the Obama administration, the United States also increased its military presence in the Philippines, Australia, Malaysia, and Singapore, and it has deployed a growing share of its most advanced military technologies to East Asia.

Many US strategic partners in maritime East Asia welcomed expanded cooperation with the US Navy. The Obama administration had been "pushing at an open door." Similarly, the US Navy has had little difficulty deploying additional defense platforms in East Asia and challenging Chinese maritime activities. The challenge for the United States is to balance China's rise while contributing to regional stability and US-China cooperation. But, regardless of its intentions, US policy signaled that the US strategic objective is containment, seeking to counter any Chinese action that alters the regional status quo, thus contributing to heightened US-China conflict. Simultaneously, in significant respects US policy also has failed to advance US security.

Over the past decade, there has been no erosion of robust US–South Korean deterrence of North Korean use of force. Nonetheless, since 2010, the United States has increased its ground forces presence in South Korea and expanded military cooperation. In 2016, it pushed Seoul to allow deployment of the US Theater High Altitude Area Defense (THAAD) anti-missile defense systems in South Korea. Yet missile defense cannot contribute to South Korean security. North Korean missile launchers are too close to South Korean targets to enable intercepts by THAAD. But the preferred US missile defense radar for South Korea can cover Chinese territory. Thus, expanded US–South Korean defense cooperation and efforts to deploy US missile defense systems signal to Beijing that the United States intends to contain Chinese influence on the Korean Peninsula and degrade China's nuclear deterrent.

As a result of the US–South Korean agreement to deploy THAAD, China has refused to cooperate with the United States in constraining North Korea's nuclear weapons program. Yet any possibility of success in restraining North Korean proliferation requires Chinese cooperation. Moreover, the agreement has caused tension between China and South Korea, contributing to North Korean confidence. Finally, the agreement contributed to the 2017 victory of Moon Jae-in as president of South Korea. During the presidential campaign Moon criticized the agreement. After becoming president he quickly suspended deployment of the THAAD system and moved to improve relations with China.

Since 2010, the United States has increased naval cooperation with Vietnam and, in 2016, lifted its ban on arms sales to the country. But Indochina is a continental theater in which China possesses substantial superiority over the United States. Should Vietnam risk meaningful defense cooperation with the United States, Chinese ground forces can, at minimal cost, apply effective coercive military pressure on Vietnam's northern border. The United States would have no effective response, lacking the interest and capabilities to counter Chinese pressure in this region. Despite US efforts to improve relations with Vietnam, Hanoi has reassured Beijing that it will not challenge Chinese security. Thus, rather than contributing to US security, defense cooperation with Vietnam merely suggested the United States' intent to contain China's rise.

Regarding the East Asian maritime territorial disputes, none of the disputed islands have strategic significance for US–China relations. Even after Chinese reclamation, the islands are too small to support wartime operations or provide facilities to obstruct trade or strategic sea lanes. There are no significant mineral deposits in the disputed waters of the South China Sea, the economic significance of which is limited to fishing.

US declaratory policy is that the United States takes no position on these maritime sovereignty disputes. Nonetheless, US policy supported its allies' efforts to challenge China's claims. In 2012, after the Japanese government ignored US advice and purchased disputed islands in the East China Sea, President Obama publicly guaranteed US treaty support for Japanese defense of the islands. Similarly, during the Obama administration, the United States strengthened defense cooperation with the Philippines and publicly warned China not to escalate tension with the country, but the United States did not publicly caution the Philippines, which could have helped reassure China of US intentions.

The United States encouraged the Philippines to challenge Chinese maritime claims at the United Nations Permanent Court of Arbitration (PCA), hoping to establish US resolve to support its allies and to use the "moral high ground" to isolate China in Southeast Asia. The Philippines won a victory at the PCA, but the ultimate outcome was a victory for China. Rather than isolate China, Manila's challenge to Chinese sovereignty isolated the Philippines in South East Asia as it encountered coercion from China, the region's rising power. Thus, new Philippine president Rodrigo Duterte quickly sought rapprochement with China. He announced that the Philippines' legal victory would have minimal effect on its negotiations with China and that the Philippines would hold bilateral discussions with China, rather than "internationalize" the issue, which had been China's original demand. He also signaled that he would scale back the level of US–Philippine defense cooperation. China rewarded the Philippines with infrastructure and military aid and eased restrictions on Philippine fishing in disputed waters.

US Navy fanfare around its exercises and its freedom of navigation operations in East Asia similarly contribute to Chinese perception of US containment. If the navy's purpose were simply deterrence or support for international law, low-profile operations would suffice. But the extensive publicity surrounding US Navy exercises suggests an effort to deny China greater naval presence in the South

China Sea and to bolster active regional resistance to Chinese territorial claims. US policy has only strengthened Chinese resolve to resist US pressure.

The US response to the rise of China has failed on two counts. First, it failed to develop improved security ties with South Korea, the Philippines, and Vietnam, and it failed to constrain expanded Chinese naval presence in the South China Sea, principle objectives of the administration's East Asia Policy. Second, US policy failed to manage Chinese perceptions of US intentions. US initiatives toward South Korea, Vietnam, and in the South China Sea persuaded Chinese leaders that US intent is to thwart the rise of China.

A POLICY OF RESTRAINT

The rise of China ensures that US-China relations will become more difficult and contentious, no matter how accommodative or confrontational US policy is. The military competition will intensify as China continues to develop advanced naval capabilities and the United States expends increasing resources to balance the rise of China and sustain its East Asian alliance system.

But deterministic arguments that say war is the mechanical result of shifting structural dynamics are wrong. Leaders and policy choices matter. They contribute to the extent and cost of conflict, including the likelihood of hostilities. The United States and China may not be able to avoid conflicts with one another, but they do have some control over the duration, intensity, and escalatory aspects of such conflict.

US foreign policy does not require maximizing power. Nor does it entail an uncompromising strategic posture. These objectives are neither realist nor pragmatic. Rather, they are nationalist impulses. A realist foreign policy values negotiations and compromises as essential elements of a restraint that seeks to protect American security at minimal cost in blood and treasure.

America's security interests lie in maritime East Asia. It is not helpful to US security for the United States to expand its military presence on the Korean Peninsula or to build military cooperation with Vietnam. If North Korea is not deterred by existing US and South Korean capabilities and the risk of massive conventional and nuclear retaliation, then it is undeterrable. No amount of US military assistance to Vietnam can offset China's conventional superiority on the Sino-Vietnamese border.

In the East China Sea and South China Sea, the United States can publicly restrain its allies' activism in sovereignty disputes and quietly deter Chinese belligerence without undermining US security. It can expand its military presence in its maritime East Asia strategic partners and thus reassure its partners of its commitment to collective defense, while constraining its allies from actively defending their territorial claims. In so doing, it can contribute to a shelving of this dispute by all of the claimants, rather than contribute to ongoing tension.

Regarding freedom of navigation operations, the United States should prioritize security over principle. Highly public and frequent freedom of navigation operations do not contribute to US security. In peacetime, such operations have no significance for intelligence collection. In wartime, access to disputed waters is determined by US capabilities, not by legal principle. Similarly, highly publicized naval exercises are not necessary either to reassure our allies or deter China.

TOWARD A BALANCED CHINA POLICY

China's contribution to US-China tension is clear. Since 2009–2010, Chinese policy has suggested impatience to transform the regional order. In 2009, Chinese government ships expanded patrols of disputed waters in the South China Sea. In 2010, China seemed to support North Korea after it had sunk a South Korean Navy ship and shelled a South Korean island, killing civilians. That same year, China announced sanctions on US companies contributing to Taiwanese defense and threatened retaliation against Japan's arrest of a Chinese fisherman who had rammed his boat into a Japanese Coast Guard ship in disputed waters. In 2011 and 2012, Chinese government ships harassed Vietnamese fishing boats and government survey ships operating in disputed waters.

China exhibited even less restraint from 2012 to 2014. In September 2012, the Chinese Coast Guard challenged Japanese sovereignty in the East China Sea and Philippine sovereignty in the South China Sea. In 2013, China announced, with minimal international consultation, its air defense identification zone for the East China Sea and began land reclamation activities in the South China Sea. In May 2014, China began oil drilling in disputed waters in the South China Sea. Throughout this period, China increased its surveillance of US air and naval operations in East Asia.

This was all too much, too soon. China's multiple initiatives have suggested that it will exercise limited restraint in defense of its sovereignty claims and to challenge US alliances and naval presence, even at the risk of hostilities. Chinese leaders cannot be surprised that their policies have elicited heightened concern for Chinese intentions in the United States and throughout East Asia, as well as an unwelcomed US response.

China may respond to US selective accommodation with continued assertiveness, but the United States does not have to sacrifice security to test Chinese intentions. By signaling strategic engagement while strengthening its strategic presence in maritime East Asia, the

United States can revert to overt, coercive diplomacy against an impatient and coercive China from a position of strength.

The US–China relationship is at a strategic crossroads. China's increasing maritime power has contributed to destabilizing foreign policy activism. But US concern for its alliances and credibility to defend the balance of power has contributed to its resistance to compromise and to its military expansion on the East Asian mainland. For the United States, this trend in US–China relations has led to unnecessary and costly escalation of tension, strategic competition and regional instability, and diminished US security in East Asia.

The challenge for the United States is to respond to Chinese foreign policy with measures that signal to Beijing its interest in engagement and conflict de-escalation, all without undermining US security. This is also the challenge for the Trump administration. It has the opportunity to contribute to greater US–China cooperation and a more stable East Asia, as well as promote US security through the maintenance of the regional balance of power. It should grasp this opportunity while it still exists.

11 | IS CHINESE EXCEPTIONALISM UNDERMINING CHINA'S FOREIGN POLICY INTERESTS?

Alastair Iain Johnston

ONE OF THE MOST deeply ingrained beliefs in China is that the Chinese are a uniquely peaceful people who draw from a philosophical and cultural tradition that stresses harmony. As a result, the belief contends, Chinese rulers across time have generally avoided violence and invasion when dealing with external threats, unless given no choice. Chinese commentators will often summarize this uniquely peaceful orientation by citing the line from Confucius that, for Chinese people, "peace / harmony is the most valued," or the famous phrase in military strategist Sun Zi's *Art of War* that "not fighting and subduing the enemy's army is the best of the best."

Over the last ten years or so, this meme of unique peacefulness has received greater attention in the official *People's Daily* newspaper than during previous years. Premier Li Keqiang said that the phrase "peace / harmony is the most valued" expresses the essence of traditional Chinese culture, while President Xi Jinping has said the Chinese people are by nature "peace-loving." He has even stated hyperbolically that there is "no gene for invasion in Chinese people's blood." These identity claims are used by Chinese leaders and analysts alike to argue that China's rise as a great power will be different from those of other great powers in the past.

This self-description is not unique to China; the people of many countries believe in their own exceptionalism. Indeed, they often criticize those whom they feel are discounting national exceptionalism. Belief in American exceptionalism—seeing the United States as a "shining city on the hill"—is a litmus test for politicians. Some right-wing critics of former US president Obama accused him of not believing in such exceptionalism.

Of course, Chinese claims about their own culturally unique peacefulness are empirically problematic. There is plenty of historical evidence that in both pre-modern and modern China, Chinese leaders have often used force against other kingdoms and countries. There is also evidence throughout Chinese history, including in the Mao Zedong period, of the large-scale killing of Chinese by other Chinese.

Moreover, a vast and robust literature in social psychology, sociology, political science, economics, and the social neurosciences shows that perceptions of ingroup uniqueness are often linked to perceptions of outgroup inferiority, particularly when the ingroup perceives a threat to its cohesiveness. Under these conditions, outsiders are often identified not only as normatively inferior but also as threatening competitors. This contributes to perceptions of danger and fear, which in turn leads to an emphasis on seeking relative gains as opposed to absolute or joint gains when dealing with outsiders. Such a worldview can bring skepticism about the benefits of cooperation in such areas as free trade, arms control, or other expressions of mutual benefit.

The paradox, then, of the belief in the Chinese people's uniquely peaceful identity is that such a belief is in fact related to realpolitik worldviews and policy preferences. That is, the more peaceful Chinese people believe themselves as a people to be, the more their own foreign policy preferences tend toward realpolitik or hard-line options.

This relationship between how Chinese identify themselves as a peaceful people on the one hand and more realpolitik policy preferences on the other is supported by my analysis of the 2015 Beijing Area Study (BAS), a survey conducted by the Research Center for Contemporary China at Peking University. The BAS uses a random sample of some 2,600 people living in Beijing. One series of questions asks respondents to rate the Chinese people on a seven-point scale ranging from "peaceful" to "warlike" and, additionally, how they would rate Japanese and Americans on this scale. Other questions ask about certain foreign policy preferences.

The survey data show that respondents who consider Chinese people to be extremely peaceful express significantly lower levels of amity toward Japan and the United States compared to those who believe Chinese people are not so peaceful. Those who believe Chinese people to be extremely peaceful also express a much stronger perception that the United States is trying to contain China's rise. Greater perceptions of Chinese peacefulness are associated with a greater focus on traditional state-focused security threats to Chinese national security (for example, Japanese or American military power) and with less focus on non-traditional global security threats (for example, global economic decline and climate change). In other words, beliefs in Chinese peacefulness are associated with a narrower, China-centric threat perception, rather than with a more global, shared threat perception.

It is therefore not surprising that a strong linear relationship exists between perceptions of the peacefulness of the Chinese people and support for increasing military spending. In Figure 11.1, the y-axis measures respondents' perceptions of the Chinese as a people. The bars indicate where on this scale supporters of different policies toward military spending are found. Respondents were asked whether they supported increasing military spending, keeping it unchanged,

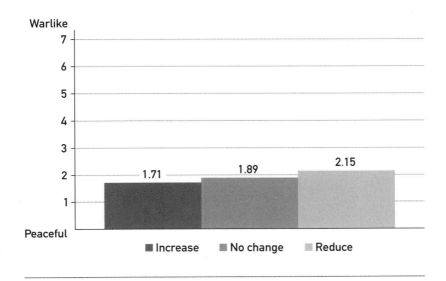

Figure 11.1.   Relationship between beliefs about Chinese peacefulness and position on military spending. Source: Beijing Area Study, 2015

or reducing it. The figure shows a linear relationship between belief in Chinese peacefulness and support for military spending. In other words, supporters of increasing military spending believe Chinese people are more peaceful than do supporters of reducing military spending. This relationship is statistically significant.

These results tend to be stronger when examining respondents' comparisons between Chinese and Japanese traits. That is, the wider the perceived gap between Chinese peacefulness and Japanese belligerence, the more hawkish respondents tend to be. The more respondents believe Chinese and Japanese to be different (with Chinese as more peace-loving than Japanese), the lower the level of amity toward Japan. Similarly, the more peaceful respondents believe Chinese people are compared to Japanese people, the more likely respondents are to see Japan as the primary national security threat to

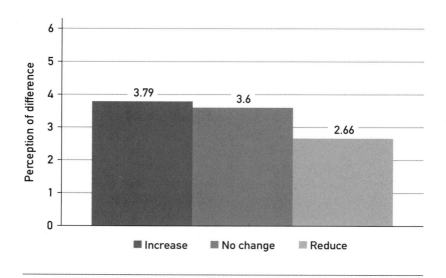

Figure 11.2.   Relationship between perceptions of difference between
Chinese and Japanese people and position on defense spending.
Source: Beijing Area Study, 2015

China, instead of a range of other state-based or global and non-
traditional security threats. And the greater this perception in Chinese peacefulness and Japanese belligerence, the more likely respondents are to favor increasing military spending. In Figure 11.2, the
y-axis increases from 0 (no perceived difference between Chinese
and Japanese people) to 6 (maximum perceived difference between
"peaceful" Chinese and "warlike" Japanese). The bars show a linear
relationship between this difference and support for change in military spending. That is, those who support increasing military spending
have significantly higher perceptions of difference than those who
want to reduce military spending.

I want to stress that this is not a claim that Chinese people are
inherently less peaceful than others, even as Chinese themselves be-

lieve the opposite. My analysis of these data reveals clear variation within Chinese society in the strength of these beliefs. For example, those who are urban, young, well educated, and have traveled abroad generally demonstrate less support for exceptionalist beliefs than those without these traits. Moreover, the belief in Chinese peacefulness may simply be one element in a more complex mixture of exceptionalist beliefs, such as that the Chinese people are uniquely civilized, sincere, or modest.

None of this is surprising. Strong believers in Chinese exceptionalism are like strong believers in American exceptionalism: they both tend to hold hard-line policy preferences that are inconsistent with their self-image (in the Chinese case, of their inherent peacefulness; in the American case, of their inherently virtuous, law-abiding, and just nature). According to a study by the Public Religion Research Institute, believers in a religious-based notion of American exceptionalism are more militarist and more likely to support torture than non-believers. In an analysis I conducted using a 2012 Pew survey of American perceptions of China, I compared the attitudes of Tea Party supporters with those of non-supporters. The Tea Party supporters—who are very strong believers in US exceptionalism—have significantly more hard-line foreign policy preferences, including with respect to China. Tea Party supporters are more likely to see China as an enemy and a threat across a range of policy domains. And compared to non-supporters, including other Republicans, they were more supportive of tougher foreign policies toward China, including the use of force to defend Taiwan. In short, Chinese and American beliefs about their own exceptionalism may have different outward expressions, but they appear to have similar effects on foreign policy preferences.

While it is likely that China's leaders genuinely believe in China's unique peacefulness, it is also likely that deliberate promotion of this belief serves the purposes of the Communist Party. It leads both ordinary citizens as well as elites to believe that conflicts with other countries are caused by those countries, and that China is blameless.

The effects of this are paradoxical, however. On one hand, the promotion of Chinese exceptionalism helps shore up the domestic legitimacy of the ruling party. On the other hand, it may also hinder the CCP's efforts to enhance its external legitimacy through developing better international relations. One important theme of Beijing's "soft power" diplomatic offensive is that China is a uniquely peaceful nation. Yet this argument may actually undermine the diplomatic effort in two ways. First, emphasizing China's uniquely peaceful nature can imply that others are inferior, making China appear arrogant or hypocritical. For example, the 2015 China National Image Global Survey, conducted by a government-controlled media outlet, found that only 8 percent of developed country respondents believe China is a peaceful, cooperative, and responsible major power. In contrast, 65 percent of Chinese respondents believe this to be true about China. China's leaders have their work cut out for them if they want to improve China's image as inherently peaceful. Ironically, stressing the Chinese people's allegedly exceptional peacefulness may well be counterproductive. This is particularly the case given counter-narratives of China's rise created by massive increases in military spending in recent years and the increase in domestic political repression in China. The more salient these narratives, the more hypocritical or delusional the claims about China's inherent peacefulness appear in the eyes of others.

This relates to a second implication: Chinese leaders' perception of Chinese exceptionalism may also reduce their ability to understand the perceptions of other countries. Strong beliefs in one's own unique traits tend to be associated with a strong rejection of the legitimacy of criticisms of one's behavior. One question in the 2013

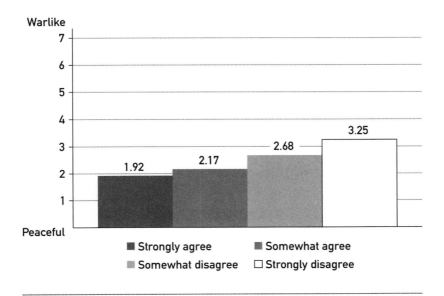

Figure 11.3.   Relationship between perceptions of Chinese peacefulness and the personalization of criticisms of China. Source: Beijing Area Study. 2013

Beijing Area Study survey asks Chinese respondents whether they agreed with the statement: "When others criticize China it is like they are criticizing me personally." As Figure 11.3 shows, there is a linear relationship between beliefs about the unique peacefulness of Chinese people and personalizing foreign criticisms (the relationship is statistically significant). If this relationship holds for China's leaders as well, then it is likely that their beliefs in Chinese exceptionalism are in fact obstacles to empathetic understanding of the concerns other countries have about China's rise.

In short, the belief in, and promotion of, Chinese exceptionalism can lead to outcomes—criticisms of China's arrogance and hypocrisy, and discounting external criticisms—that may well help intensify rather than reduce security competition with other countries.

But there is some good news: although beliefs about identity are sticky, they can change. There is evidence from laboratory experiments and surveys that increased contact with other societies and cultures—through tourism, education abroad, and consumption of foreign cultural products—as well as higher levels of education can help turn black-and-white views of identity into grey ones that are associated with mutual understanding. In a psychology experiment conducted at Peking University, Professor Wang Dong, Ph.D. student Wang Baoyu, and I found that even when students imagined casual social contact with a Japanese person, this improved their overall assessment of Japanese as a people and Japan as a country, compared to those who did not imagine such contact. Moreover, the Beijing Area Study surveys show that those Chinese citizens born in the 1980s and after generally have more positive views of Japan and Japanese, and of the United States and Americans, than older generations. This is consistent with the fact that, compared to older generations, younger, urban Chinese are more skeptical of extreme views of Chinese peacefulness. In short, more internationalized Chinese youth may be relatively less likely to buy into Chinese exceptionalism.

Here's the rub: if China's leaders are interested in moderating security competition with other countries, they should stop promoting perceptions of China as uniquely peaceful and exceptional. Rather, they should stress the common or universal elements of Chinese identity. But like nationalist politicians around the world, including in the United States, it seems unlikely that they will be willing or able to engage in this kind of self-reflection.

12 | (WHEN) WILL TAIWAN REUNIFY WITH THE MAINLAND?

Steven M. Goldstein

For the past six decades, tensions between Taiwan and China have threatened to spark an armed conflict. The leaders of the People's Republic of China (PRC) on the mainland see the island as an inseparable part of China ruled by a defunct regime supported by the United States. Those on Taiwan maintain that they are the legitimate rulers of the island that enjoys separate, equal sovereign status from the mainland. During the past three decades, dramatic changes in the area have prompted speculation that some form of the resolution of cross-strait differences is possible.

This essay explores this possibility by first presenting a discussion of how relations across the Taiwan Strait looked sixty years ago. It then contrasts that with the situation today and concludes by speculating whether the passing of sixty years has helped to diminish the salience of the issues dividing the two sides.

COLD WAR AND STALEMATE

In 1957, any discussion of China-Taiwan relations would have begun with the civil war origins of cross-strait tensions. In 1949, the defeated government and armed forces of the Republic of China (ROC), dominated by the Nationalist Party (Kuomintang, KMT), fled to Taiwan and other small islands off the China coast. The KMT did not view itself as a government exiled in some foreign land. It considered itself to be the legitimate national government of China, including Taiwan, that was still fighting a rebellion of "communist bandits" on the mainland. The island was a "bastion," a place for preparations to retake the mainland. To prepare for the struggle to come, martial law was declared, and the ethnic Chinese population that had lived under Japanese occupation since 1895 was subjected to authoritarian rule and enforced indoctrination in mainland values at the expense of Taiwan's history, culture, and language.

Across the strait, the Chinese Communist Party (CCP) declared the founding of the People's Republic of China. Its view was the mirror image of the KMT's in that it, too, claimed to be the legitimate national government of China, entitled to the rights and privileges of a sovereign state in the international system. It maintained that Taiwan was a part of China that had to be "liberated" to restore the nation's territorial integrity and dignity. In short, two sides did not differ over whether Taiwan was a part of China, but over who ruled China. With little likelihood of either surrender or military victory, the civil war between the cross-strait rivals resulted in a stalemate that created two Chinas in the world.

In 1957, there was no pressing need for Taiwan to concede. Its economy was healthy, and it was a member of the United Nations, with roughly twice as many countries recognizing it as the legitimate government of China than recognized the PRC. Moreover, despite a recent military confrontation in the Taiwan Strait, there was little indication that the ROC, which enjoyed US support, could be easily defeated.

Indeed, American support was essential to Taiwan's resistance to the mainland. At the Cairo Conference in 1943, President Franklin Roosevelt insisted that Taiwan be returned to China after Japan's surrender. This condition was confirmed in subsequent Allied statements and put into effect following Japan's defeat in World War II. Soon afterward, the United States became entangled in Chinese politics, attempting to mediate the CCP-KMT differences before full-scale civil war broke out. By January 1950, against a background of disillusionment with the ROC and a desire to leave options open for dealing with the new communist Chinese government, President Harry Truman affirmed the validity of the Cairo Declaration stipulating the return of Taiwan to "China's" communist government and denied that the United States had either "predatory designs" on the island or any desire to intervene in China.

When the Korean War broke out, Truman reversed himself. He declared that the occupation of the island by the PRC would be a "direct threat to the security of the Pacific area," stating, "The future status of Formosa [Taiwan] must await the restoration of security in the Pacific, a peace settlement with Japan, or consideration by the United Nations." Washington had reneged on the Cairo Conference pledge and declared the status of Taiwan to be undetermined.

This was the first of a number of decisions that reversed Washington's withdrawal from China and pursued policies promoting the stalemate in the Taiwan Strait, as well as the "two China" situation. After the summer of 1950, relations with the ROC were restored and a Mutual Defense Treaty took effect in 1955, just as the United States came to Taiwan's assistance in a cross-strait conflict. Moreover, American international support sustained the fiction that the ROC was the legitimate government of all China.

This support became an essential element in Washington's Asia policy. Despite the KMT's authoritarian rule, it was held up as a "democratic" alternative to "Communist China" and an example of American commitment to Asia during the Cold War. However, Taiwan was not given a blank check. The objective was to maintain a posture in the area that would be supportive enough to secure Taiwan by deterring the mainland while, at the same time, not being so supportive as to encourage the ROC to provoke the mainland and entrap the United States in a conflict with China. In the long run, Secretary of State John Foster Dulles's goal was a divided-country solution similar to the situation in Germany. In the short run, Dulles sought to maintain the status quo of stalemated civil war and two Chinas. In 1955, cross-strait relations were triangular, with the United States in the middle of the civil war again.

NEW IDENTITY AND ONE CHINA

In 1979, the United States recognized the People's Republic of China. From the American perspective, the ROC was now a non-government on an island the status of which had been declared undetermined in 1950. Washington's rapprochement with the mainland also dramatically reduced the ROC's international standing, beginning with expulsion from the United Nations in 1972 and followed by a steady stream of nations shifting their recognition from the ROC to the PRC.

Taiwan's domestic politics changed in response. By the end of the twentieth century, it was transitioning toward democracy. All island-wide political institutions became subject to popular election; an independence-oriented opposition party dominated by local Chinese emerged; the restrictions on political freedoms implemented during the civil war were repealed; and an economic relationship with the mainland was begun.

Democratization had a profound effect on the identity of Taiwan and its people. The end of wartime restrictions was an implicit acknowledgment that the civil war for control of the mainland was over. Moreover, the election of legislative bodies and the president only by the people of Taiwan undermined the myth that the ROC represented China and suggested separation. How could a government claiming to rule all China elect its rulers from only one province?

Moreover, democracy allowed the expression of once-forbidden topics, such as the different histories of Taiwan and the mainland, allowing previously disfranchised local Chinese an opportunity to claim an identity different from that imposed by the mainland authorities. Elected leaders now needed to be responsive to this change.

The results of these changes were striking. On the issue of individual identity, a survey showed that between 1992 and 2015, respondents who identified themselves as "Taiwanese" increased from 17.6 percent to 59.5 percent, while those considering themselves to be "Chinese" declined from 25.5 percent to 4 percent. In addition, in a poll taken in late 2015, the largest percentage of those surveyed (69.3 percent) favored the depiction of the relationship with the mainland as "one state on either side [of the strait]," while only 16.2 percent supported the mainland position that "two sides of the strait both belong to one China." In contrast to the views of the defeated leaders in the civil war, who yearned to return to the mainland, public opinion today suggests strong identification with Taiwan (both the island and its government) as an entity apart.

And contemporary politicians are responsive to this mood. Both major political parties in Taiwan affirm that the government which rules Taiwan (the ROC) is a "sovereign independent state" entitled to international participation as well as negotiation with the mainland on the basis of equality. For example, Taiwan's President Tsai Ing-wen has, to date, refused to recognize the somewhat contrived definition, one that made cross-strait talks since 2008 possible, of Taiwan as a part of China, recently signing a guest book as the "President of Taiwan (ROC)" on a foreign trip. The sequence of identification was no coincidence.

In contrast to these changes in Taiwan, the PRC's position has changed little in sixty years. Beijing adheres to the "One China Principle" that affirms "there is only one China in the world; the mainland and Taiwan both belong to one China and China's sovereignty and territorial integrity are indivisible." Proceeding from this, the PRC's solution for the controversy is based on a proposal made by Deng Xiaoping in 1983 (later implemented in Hong Kong), known as "One Country, Two Systems." This would incorporate Taiwan as a "Special Administrative Zone," where a domestic system different from the rest of China could be established with "only the People's Republic of China . . . [representing China] in international affairs." The mainland has committed to peaceful modes of achieving this goal, although it has retained the option to use force.

In other words, the mainland has apparently stated the solution before any talks begin: namely, restoring China's territorial integrity and fulfilling the Communist Party's pledge to allow no compromise. However, what makes this position even less attractive to Taiwan is the fact that the PRC insists that the essence of the final resolution, acknowledgment of the "One China Principle," is a necessary prerequisite to future talks, a requirement rejected by the ruling Democratic Progressive Party that not only dismisses the principle but also the ambiguous formula that had allowed earlier talks to proceed.

In response to this resistance, the mainland has also sought to use economic incentives to bypass the government and win over the people of Taiwan. Prominent among these has been the development of economic ties with various strata of society, through policies ranging from favorable tariffs for farmers and investment and trade opportunities for corporations, to employment for young graduates. However, despite the growth and improvement in economic ties, little has been achieved in creating a receptive response to mainland conditions.

Because of this, Beijing has focused on deterring further separation from the mainland and its acceptance as a sovereign state. The PRC has been aggressive in its insistence that Taiwan be excluded from international organizations (even non-governmental) without its consent or under any designation that suggests such sovereignty. Moreover, it has not been shy in stating the rationale and developing the capacity to use force should all else fail. In 2005, the rationale was codified in an Anti-Secession Law that stated that if there were any actions to cause Taiwan's "secession from China," or if "possibilities for peaceful reunification should be completely exhausted," force could be used to "protect" China's territorial integrity. To meet such an eventuality, the PRC has developed a modern military force with army, air force, naval, missile, and cyber capabilities that far exceed those of Taiwan. These constitute a potent deterrent to acts by the ROC interpreted by Beijing as approaching or seeking independence.

However, should it choose to use force, the PRC will have to contend with possible American intervention. As was the case in 1957, the United States remains in the middle of the cross-strait conflict, and its policy is the principal reason cross-strait relations have remained stalemated. If analyzed as a whole, the American stance, seeking to take a middle position on the approach, is riddled with contradictions.

In respect to the Chinese stance on the nature of cross-strait relations, Washington officially "recognizes" the People's Republic of China as the government of China, but only "acknowledges" the PRC claim that Taiwan is a part of China. In fact, although not often publicly stated, the American position has not changed since 1950: the status of the geographic island is "undetermined." Moreover, in response to Chinese threats to use force, American statements have consistently expressed the necessity of peaceful resolution.

As for Taiwan, the United States no longer supports the status of the ROC as a sovereign state in the international system or maintains official diplomatic relations with it. In 1995, this stance was encapsulated in President Bill Clinton's "Three Noes": no support for Taiwanese independence; no support for either "two Chinas" or "one Taiwan and one China"; and no support for Taiwan's participation in an organization requiring statehood. In other words, the implication of the present American position is that Taiwan is in a kind of international limbo as a non-existent government ruling an island, the status of which remains undetermined.

However, this does not mean the United States has no contacts with or obligations toward the ROC. According to the negotiated terms for the recognition of the PRC and the Taiwan Relations Act (TRA) passed by Congress in 1979, the United States retained the right to have "unofficial relations" with the ROC and to sell it defensive arms. In addition, the TRA provides for the treatment of Taiwan as a foreign government in American courts and continuation of certain treaties. However, the most important part of the TRA is the stipulation that Congress and the President should consult on possible action if there is "any threat to the security or the social or economic system of the people on Taiwan and any danger to the interests of the United States arising therefrom." Moreover, the legislation requires that the American military be prepared to act in such a case if it is called upon.

Finally, since 1979, there has been a steady increase in the intensity and scope of the relationship between Taiwan and the United States. This has ranged from a significant intensification in defense coordination to economic cooperation, mutual visits at higher levels of government, and Washington's support for Taiwan's efforts to enter international organizations that are consistent with the "Three Noes" policy.

It is from this posture that the United States seeks to maintain the current status quo in the Taiwan Strait (peaceful stalemate) until there can be a negotiated resolution of differences. Of course, this is a status quo that is unsatisfactory to both sides. Taiwan seeks to gain recognition as a sovereign entity, and the mainland seeks the island's incorporation into China. However, the effect of the posture maintained by the United States is to deter either side from realizing its ultimate goal by, on one hand, threatening to withhold support from Taiwan should it provoke the mainland by seeking independence or, on the other, to defend Taiwan should the PRC seek a coerced solution. In this way, each side is expected to act with restraint, knowing that the other side is deterred. At present, this policy, called "dual deterrence" by one scholar, is playing a central role in keeping a tenuous peace in the Taiwan Strait.

After sixty years of cross-strait relations, it is tempting to cite the aphorism that "the more things change, the more they stay the same." The two sides still hold irreconcilable positions, and the United States is still in the middle, seeking to preserve a peaceful status quo until such time as the two sides can peacefully arrive at an agreement acceptable to both.

Yet, appearances are deceiving. It seems that the passage of time has made the differences more intractable, rather than less so. The most significant change in the situation is the democratization of Taiwan that has transformed its identity from a staging area for the build-up of one side in a civil war to that of a sovereign state demanding international representation, and declaring that its status as a part of China is not to be assumed. Moreover, this status has been practiced for at least two decades and has apparently taken hold among the population of the island—especially among the young. In short, in contrast to the civil war period, there is no longer a shared assumption across the Taiwan Strait that either the island, or the regime that governs it, is a part of China.

This complicates the task of the mainland as it seeks to woo Taiwan. However, this has not resulted in a fundamental change in

Beijing's Taiwan policy. It approaches a transformed Taiwan with a depiction of the relationship ("One China") and a solution to the differences ("One Country, Two Systems"), as in the past. Such an approach has gained very little traction in Taiwan.

Of course, one could think of several compromise solutions to this new situation, such as shared sovereignty or federation. However, it would be difficult today for a leader in China to accede to the giveaway of sovereign Chinese territory, or for a leader of Taiwan to be willing to diminish the sovereignty of the island that has become an accepted, practiced fact in the eyes of so many on the island.

There are other possibilities that have been suggested, such as the natural pull of economic forces toward the mainland (about 40 percent of Taiwan's exports and 75 percent of its foreign investment go to the mainland), or the costs of Taiwan's isolation at a time of the emergence of regional economic networks. Moreover, it seems that many on Taiwan would be open to an agreement with the mainland, should it become more prosperous or democratic. However, as yet, none of these eventualities seem to be developing in a direction that might change the present situation.

Finally, there is the possibility that either side might simply lose patience with the present stalemate. For example, a politician on Taiwan might provoke the mainland by pushing toward formal independence, or a Chinese leader might decide that maintaining the status quo is creating the gradual, peaceful separation of Taiwan from the mainland and resort to force to settle the differences.

Naturally, much depends on the details of the scenario, but there is little doubt that the United States, being in the middle, would be involved. Such involvement could range from attempts to secure a cease-fire to actual military intervention. Whatever course it might take, all sides are aware of the danger of a rapid escalation of the conflict with its inevitable economic and reputational costs. This is clearly a "solution" that none of the three sides in the cross-strait conflict would like to see.

So for the foreseeable future, peace in the Taiwan Strait will exist along with the stalemate and tensions that are now present in the regional status quo. It is a status quo that none of the three sides is satisfied with, but that all must accept—and, for the present, work to sustain.

13 | CAN CHINA AND JAPAN EVER GET ALONG?

Ezra F. Vogel

THERE CAN BE no stability in East Asia, and indeed no stability in the world, if China and Japan, the world's second- and third-largest economies, cannot find a way to work together. It is in the interest of the people on both sides that the two nations avoid a clash and work together to promote economic exchanges, prevent global warming, improve the environment, respond to natural calamities, and share advances in medical science. And yet relations between the two nations are brittle, their militaries confront each other over disputed islands, their leaders, and even their high level diplomats, rarely meet and have not held serious discussions for years.

In the latest Pew public opinion polls, only 7 percent of Chinese hold a positive impression of Japan, and only 6 percent of Japanese hold a positive impression of China. Chinese overwhelmingly believe that Japan has not properly acknowledged the horrors that it committed in World War II. Japanese overwhelmingly believe Japan has apologized for its aggression but that Chinese people are largely unaware of these apologies, and that it is ridiculous to criticize people for not apologizing enough for acts that occurred before they were born. Chinese criticize Japanese leaders for visiting Yasukuni Shrine, where the spirits of war criminals are commemorated, and for allowing the Japanese government to purchase disputed islands (which the Japanese call Senkaku and the Chinese call

Diaoyu) from a private owner, when the islands are disputed territory. Japanese explain that their country gave up militarism at the end of World War II, that Japan has pursued the path of peace, that it spends only 1 percent of gross national product (GNP) on military matters—far less than China, the United States, and many other countries. Japanese believe that they have been generous to China in recent decades and that the Chinese public is unaware of the extent of their contributions. Discussions over possible joint exploration of the seabed in disputed areas for mutual gain terminated several years ago and have not resumed.

Since coming to office, President Xi Jinping and Prime Minister Shinzo Abe have never had lengthy, serious discussions, compared with those between Xi and Presidents Barack Obama and Donald Trump. Xi and Abe met only briefly at side meetings during multilateral conferences. When they and high level officials from the two sides do meet, they express accusations about the other country's actions.

The greatest risks of conflict derive from a group of tiny islands of little intrinsic importance. Japanese and Chinese both claim the territory of the Diaoyu / Senkaku Islands, but Japan has administered the islands since World War II, and the Japanese claim there is no territorial dispute. China sends ships and planes to areas near the islands, and Japan sends out ships and planes to warn them.

Relations between the two countries have remained at a very low state ever since 1992. Before then, when China was trying to break out of sanctions from Western countries that followed the June 4, 1989, crackdown on Tiananmen Square, the country that was most helpful to China was Japan. The Japanese were more willing than Western countries to increase trade with China, and they supported the efforts of President George W. Bush to reduce sanctions. For the three years between 1989 and 1992, China and Japan had considerable contact, and officials of each country were restrained in their criticism of each other. Relations between the two countries were sufficiently good in 1992 that, for the first time in history, the Emperor of Japan visited China and was received graciously by his Chinese hosts.

But after that visit, relations deteriorated rapidly. From 1978 until 1992, China had received more help from Japan than from any other country. At that time, following the disastrous Great Leap Forward and Cultural Revolution, China had very little money and badly needed outside help to promote economic growth. The Japanese government, through JETRO (Japan External Trade Organization), responded with technology and industrial advice, and JETRO in turn called on Japanese officials and even Japanese firms, which dispatched officials to China to provide assistance. By 1992, China was no longer in such desperate need, and other countries had begun to remove the sanctions imposed in response to the 1989 Tiananmen incident. Thus, Japan was no longer unique, and there was less need for China to refrain from criticizing it.

By 1992 as the Soviet Union was breaking apart and the Cold War was ending, it was no longer necessary for China, Japan, the United States, and other countries to cooperate against the Soviet Union.

By 1992, the Chinese were also gaining more confidence in an economy that was growing rapidly. It was growing so fast that they could project that, within two decades, it would exceed that of Japan. Ever since Japan had defeated China in the Sino-Japanese War of 1894–1895, the Chinese, who considered their civilization to be far ahead of Japan's, resented the need to accept the humiliating Shimonoseki Treaty of 1895 that had caused China to yield Taiwan to Japan and pay such a large indemnity that China had to seek funds from many different countries. It had been humiliating to pass along parts of Shandong Province that had been occupied by Germany to the Japanese during World War I. For many Chinese who were shamed by the "century of humiliation," China was now resuming its proper place at the top of the hierarchy in Asia. It was not just the immediate political and economic issues but a matter of broader national pride, and it seemed only fitting and proper that Japan should acknowledge that China was now the leading power in Asia. But while the Japanese acknowledged that China was larger, they still believed Japan was a more modern and successful nation.

Another cause of deteriorating relations was the growing separatist movement in Taiwan under Lee Teng-hui, the first Taiwan-born president. He was very close to Japan, causing the Chinese to worry that Japan would support the Taiwan independence movement that they so strongly opposed. In 1992, Lee Teng-hui held the first Taiwanese national elections, and populist pressure for an independent Taiwan grew, especially after Lee returned from a visit to his alma mater, Cornell University, in 1995. For half a century before 1945, when Taiwan was under Japanese rule, local people had used the Japanese language in schools and imbibed Japanese culture. Since the Japanese continued these close relations after 1945, Beijing officials, after 1992, worried that Tokyo was supporting Taiwan's powerful independence movement.

In 1992, Chinese leaders, concerned about the loyalty of China's young people, started a patriotic education campaign. Among the campaign's themes, the one that had most resonance among Chinese youth described the cruelty of the Japanese invasion and occupation from 1931 to 1945. Chinese officials used modern methods for conveying the message, such as showing televised movies of Chinese fighting heroically against the Japanese. These proved popular, leading movie companies for commercial reasons to make even more of them. Hand-held electronic games for youth that show Chinese fighting off Japanese invaders also proved to have a continuing commercial dynamism. The images conveyed by these films and games helped reinforce the negative attitudes toward the Japanese even though, as time passed, the percentage of Chinese who personally experienced World War II was declining.

The impact of these issues was reinforced by some awkward political moves that could have been avoided if the two countries had a higher level of communication and deeper mutual understanding. In 1998, when President Jiang Zemin visited Japan, he mistakenly thought that applying more pressure would cause Prime Minister Obuchi Keizo to sign a statement apologizing for the horrors Japan caused in World War II, as he had for Korean president Kim Dae Jong a few weeks earlier. But, unlike Kim, Jiang had not made statements about future cooperation between the two countries, and Prime Minister Obuchi, aware of Japan's public reaction to Jiang's pressure, refused to sign, thereby heightening tensions between the two countries. In 2012, when Tokyo governor Ishihara Shintaro offered to buy the Senkaku Islands, Prime Minister Noda Yoshihiko, without fully appreciating the serious problems it would cause with China, decided that the Japanese government should buy the islands to avoid issues that would arise if Governor Ishihara should arrange for ownership of them. Chinese officials exploded in anger, further heightening tensions.

Is there hope that relations between the two countries can dramatically improve? Not in the short run. No leader of either country could show that he or she is caving in to pressures from the other. Any leader who wants to remain popular must show strength by standing up for the national interest.

Is there hope that China and Japan can develop good relations in the long run? Yes. As former premier Zhou Enlai said years ago, and as national leader Deng Xiaoping repeated later, China and Japan

have had some two thousand years of relations, and the really trou-
bled relations involved only half a century, from 1894 to 1945. Well
over a millennium ago, during China's Sui and Tang dynasties
(contemporaneous with the Nara and Heian periods in Japan), the
Japanese acquired their basic culture—including written language,
Buddhism, Confucianism, architecture, governmental organization,
city planning, and art—from China. Having similar cultures did not
prevent armed conflicts between the United States and Great
Britain, but sharing culture does provide a broad base of understanding that can be drawn on to create positive ties.

Following Deng Xiaoping's successful trip to Japan in October 1978, there was a fourteen-year period of relatively good relations.
In 1980, there was not yet public opinion polling in China, but in
polls in Japan at the time, 78 percent of people expressed positive
feelings toward China. Deng and his Japanese counterparts talked of
mutual cooperation. During this period there were many exchanges
of groups from both sides, including young people, and movies and
TV serials of ordinary Japanese life were popular in China. Japanese provided help in modernizing Chinese industry, giving advice about management and governmental planning.

What should be done now? Although no leader of either country
can suddenly withdraw all pressure on the Diaoyu / Senkaku Islands,
a determined leader could gradually reduce the pressure, and if the
other side reciprocated, the two could gradually take more steps.
They could resume efforts to find projects in the region where they
could cooperate. Japanese experience in improving the environment
and managing an economy as it moves from higher to lower growth
rates could be taught to Chinese on a larger scale. Leaders and officials of the two countries could meet more often, and those who have
deep understanding of the other country could be given important
positions. Youth exchanges and preparation of young leaders who

have deep knowledge of and friendships with the other country could be promoted. An increase in Chinese tourism could help promote understanding, as tourists can present a more accurate picture of contemporary Japan than that supplied by some of the media. Much more could be done to make it attractive for Japanese tourists to visit China. In short, there are plenty of opportunities to improve relations.

The year 2018 is the fortieth anniversary of the signing of the Treaty of Peace and Friendship between the two countries, and of Deng Xiaoping's enormously successful visit to Japan. There would be no better way to celebrate that anniversary than for the two countries to take serious steps to improve their relations.

III | ECONOMY

14 | CAN CHINA'S HIGH GROWTH CONTINUE?

Richard N. Cooper

CHINA HAS EXPERIENCED the greatest reduction in poverty in the history of mankind: between 400- and 600-million people moved out of poverty, depending on the exact definition used. Its economy grew at nearly 10 percent a year for thirty years, a sixteen-fold increase, which, after allowing for population growth, yielded the country a twelve-fold increase in per capita income. This gave families real choices in life for the first time, not only for themselves but especially for their children. The change has been literally fantastic; if one had forecast in 1980 what China's economy would be like in 2018, both Chinese and foreigners would have dismissed the forecaster as living in a dream world. Yet it happened.

What were the sources of this unexpected growth, and can it continue? This chapter will identify seven sources, and contend that six of them will disappear or be greatly reduced. This means China will see a significant decline in growth during the next decade that, while garnering headlines, should not be interpreted as a policy failure. The slowdown will be for fundamental reasons. Some policies may well fail, but slower growth by itself will not signify failure.

In the jargon of economists, growth requires increased labor supply (including higher levels of education and experience), more capital, and a residual called total factor productivity, which includes everything else. Most studies find that during the post-1978 period, capital accumulation in China accounted for much of the growth, with increases in labor providing only 10 to 20 percent, implying a significant increase in total factor productivity. But what caused that? I identify seven reasons, and no doubt others could be found.

The first was a significant change of how the government allocated resources. It moved gradually from the top-down, central planning common to socialist systems, which involve government-directed production quotas and extensive rationing of supplies, to a more market-based approach. This meant that both households and companies could make their own consumption and investment decisions on the basis of prices, which, in turn, were strongly influenced by supply and demand, product by product. In addition, domestic prices became more closely linked to those in the world economy.

The second reason was a national shift from near-isolation to engagement with the world economy. Exports were encouraged, initially through tax- and regulation-favored special economic zones (SEZs), later more generally. In contrast to Japan and South Korea, inward foreign direct investment (FDI) was also encouraged, partly through the SEZs, but partly also for the domestic market. This came initially through joint ventures, and later through fully foreign-owned domestic enterprises. The initial goal was to earn scarce foreign exchange and, later, to bring foreign technology (including marketing and management skills) into China.

The third growth factor was exploitation of the extensive overseas Chinese diaspora, whose members were highly knowledgeable about dealing with foreigners and could act as a bridge between the isolated mainland and the rest of the world. Chinese businessmen in other countries knew what goods and services would sell well, especially in the United States and Europe, and were familiar with marketing channels and other technical aspects of carrying on foreign trade successfully. Much of the initial investment in SEZs came from people in Hong Kong, Taiwan, and other overseas Chinese communities.

The fourth factor was what analysts call a demographic dividend: the ratio of mainland Chinese of working age (15 to 64 years old) to total population rose significantly, from 66 percent in 1990 to 74 percent in 2012. If they could be employed productively—and, in fact, they were—it would augment total economic growth and per capita income. China's one-child policy, of course, contributed to this dramatic "dividend" before serious aging set in.

The fifth factor was a dramatic movement of workers from agriculture into more productive activities. This is a fundamental aspect in all poor countries, which initially are overwhelmingly agricultural, and in which productivity is low except possibly during planting and harvesting seasons. This movement from farms to factories (or service jobs) brought large increases of per-person output. In 1980, 70 percent of China's labor force was in agriculture; by 2016, this had dropped below 30 percent. One important study estimates that this shift alone accounted for 1.1 to 1.3 percent a year in GDP growth.

The sixth factor was an especially high (by international standards) rate of savings and investment—approaching half of the nation's production in some years. Some investment was by state-owned enterprises, and some by local authorities. But much of it came from new entities that were not owned by the central government, such as those started by local towns and villages. These were followed by purely private investments, including some by foreigners, under the new rules that Beijing put into effect. Perhaps 65 percent of total investment came from private sources by 2012, providing buildings and equipment for the rapidly growing non-agricultural labor force. But much of it also provided new and improved housing for a rapidly growing urban labor force with rising incomes. Much also went into infrastructure, partly for such urban needs as water supply, sewers, roads, lighting, transportation, and partly for ports, airports, and inter-urban transportation such as highways and railroads.

The seventh factor was education. Back in the 1950s, the newly installed Communist Party made the strategic decision to provide free primary education to all young Chinese, bringing a minimum level of literacy to the peasantry. This decision served China well, as more young adults, familiar with the discipline of attending school regularly and following instructions from teachers, moved into regular factory jobs. Free public schooling was extended to nine years from the mid-1980s, and upper-middle (high) schools and universities expanded their enrollment to the point that, by 2016, around 30 percent of young adults were getting some university education, up from only 2 percent in the early 1980s.

These major factors determined China's high growth rate during the three decades following initial economic reform. Of course, advances in technology, mainly acquired from abroad, also played an important role. But new technology largely came from the factors mentioned above: foreign investment (and advice), the contribution of the Chinese diaspora, the high rate of investment, and increased education, including training by foreign firms.

What, then, of the future? Can these seven factors continue to play a significant role? If not, are there plausible substitutes? Unfortunately, the likely answer is negative for all of them except, possibly, education. Let us take them in turn.

China has largely completed the transition to a price-based market economy. There are still some exceptions, especially in banking, petroleum, and telecommunications, so there is still some way to go. But as a source of future growth, further changes in the rules of resource allocation—further economic reforms—are likely to be much more limited than during the 1980s and 1990s.

Foreign direct investment continues to flow into China at a pace second only to the United States. Some modern technology will flow with it, and its future contribution may be similar to the past. But foreign trade, another dimension of globalization, will surely make a more limited future contribution. Chinese exports, measured in dollars, grew by an extraordinary 17 percent annually during the three decades from the 1980s to the 2010s, moving China from a negligible role to the world's largest exporter. Thus, future export growth can no longer give the country a major boost; gains will be more or less comparable to growth of the world economy—perhaps 5 to 7 percent a year in dollar terms (including some inflation). Overseas Chinese continue to be important, but no longer as a major source of growth. Mainlanders have now learned (mostly) how to deal with foreigners directly. That adjustment was a once-and-for-all catch up and has now passed into history.

The demographic dividend ended in 2012, when the ratio of working age to total population reached its peak. It is now projected to decline, slowly at first, then more rapidly in the next decade, returning to the mid-sixties as China's population ages rapidly. The birthrate may pick up now that population policy has shifted to a two-child limit, but aging will be the most important factor. The median age is expected to rise from 35 years in 2010 to 47 years in 2040—an extraordinary rate exceeded only by South Korea. Natality is likely to remain low, as in other East Asian economies, despite the change in policy.

China's agricultural labor force has dropped below 30 percent of the total—still high by standards of industrialized countries. So some contribution to future growth can continue from this source. But the most mobile farm workers have already moved, and the average adult age in the countryside has risen rapidly. Also, land tenure and urban registration policies (known as the *hukou* system) inhibit families from giving up their agricultural land completely, since they would likely see it reassigned to others. Thus, the continuing movement out of agriculture will likely be less dramatic than in the past, making a lower contribution to growth. In addition, labor productivity in agriculture has risen and will rise further, thus reducing economic gains from this reallocation.

It is a stated policy of recent Chinese governments to "rebalance" the Chinese economy from reliance on exports and investment to greater reliance on private and public consumption—that is, to create a consumer society. In addition, the rate of return on new investment—especially on public investment (infrastructure) and investment by lumbering, state-owned enterprises—has declined during the past decade, implying that even large new investments would make a smaller contribution to growth than in the past. On both counts, therefore, the decline in the rate of investment (relative to GDP) and the decline in the rate of return suggest a smaller contribution to overall growth than in prior years.

Thus, these six factors will do less for future growth than they did in the early post-reform period. These changes are fundamental, not readily influenced by policy, so a decline in China's future growth should not be called failure. Only the seventh factor, education, may contribute as much as in the past, given the rapid expansion of the educational system—provided the graduates can find good jobs.

The Chinese government, conscious of these slowing factors, has spoken of a "new normal" growth rate of around 7 percent, well below the 9 or 10 percent rate of the recent past. This is an attempt to bring public expectations into line with reality. Thus, the 13th Five-Year Plan (for 2016–2020) assumes average annual growth of 6.5 percent. The government also emphasizes the importance of "innovation" as a key source of future expansion, but it is far too early to judge how much success it will achieve. The educational system, with its emphasis on rote learning and single correct answers to every question, is not conducive to extensive innovation. China's level of technology use is below standards of the developed world in many areas and can still benefit from importing more from abroad. But it has been doing so for thirty-five years, and there is no assurance that it can increase its rate of absorbing foreign technology and increase domestic innovation as well.

If it cannot, China can expect its national growth rate—even with no serious policy mistakes—to fall well below the 6.5 percent target set for the next decade, probably to less than 5 percent a decade hence. Yet while such a decrease may bring alarmed headlines, it would not signal a fundamental failure. Both Chinese and foreigners need to understand that.

15 | IS THE CHINESE ECONOMY HEADED TOWARD A HARD LANDING?

Dwight H. Perkins

IT IS NOW widely accepted that China's three decades of high-speed, catch-up growth has ended. Catch-up growth ends in all countries long before they reach the income levels of the most advanced economies, and China has been no exception. The migration of surplus labor from low productivity jobs in the countryside to higher productivity jobs in urban areas has largely ended, except for the children of migrants who were left behind with their grandparents. The rapid expansion of China's exports has also come to an end, partly because of the world recession, but mostly because China has saturated the markets for goods dependent on cheap labor—which in fact are no longer cheap. China's future growth will depend increasingly on its own ability to innovate and compete internationally in sectors such as automobiles, where others have a long head start.

Over the past year or two, this economic slowdown has stoked fears that China could be headed toward a "hard landing." That term is seldom defined but, if it means anything, it presumably refers to a fear that China is heading for a recession for several quarters or longer. These fears seem to multiply every time something unexpected happens in the economy—for example, a small percentage-point drop in the *renminbi* exchange rate, or the collapse of a large stock market bubble, to mention recent events. In and of themselves, these events had little impact on China's overall economic performance, but there was concern that they signaled the beginning of what could become a much wider crisis. Fears of a crisis usually begin from the rapid and unsustainable buildup of debt, particularly corporate debt, or the expansion of the largely unregulated shadow financial markets, such as moneylenders who operate outside the regular banking system.

The unsustainable debt expansion and the problems of the shadow financial markets are real enough, but the possibility of these leading to a financial collapse and a major recession is not very realistic. The real danger facing the Chinese economy lies elsewhere and is caused by current trends in Chinese policy that involve much more than just the financial sector.

The reason a financial collapse is not likely to result in a sharp recession starts from the fact that almost all of China's debt is owed to other entities in China, notably but not exclusively the large state-owned banks. These banks, among others, have begun to experience a rise in bad loans (called non-performing loans), and it is widely believed that their share of total bank assets could rise further by a large amount. Formally, many of these banks could become bankrupt if the non-performing loans exceed their total capital, which is possible and perhaps likely. But China in the 1990s had an even worse situation with non-performing loans, which officially equaled a quarter of total state bank assets (and unofficially may have reached 40 percent). The government formed asset management companies to take over all bank non-performing assets, followed by a government refinancing of the banks.

More recently, the government has reduced the non-performing assets by trading bank debt for equities. In essence, these and other methods involve the government restoring banks to economic health by printing and distributing money. It has done this in the past, and it is unthinkable that it will not do it in the future, given that a financial collapse or a sharp recession would have major implications for political stability. Printing money could lead to unwanted inflation but, in the context of a threatened recession without a bail-out, that does not seem likely.

The one way a financial crisis in China could lead to an unpreventable recession is if much of the debt were owed internationally and denominated in foreign currencies. Even this would not be much of a threat if China's foreign-exchange reserves stayed near the $4 trillion level of the recent past. However, a decline of Chinese reserves of more than $700 billion during the past year suggests that China might not always have such a robust foreign-exchange total. In all likelihood, that particular decline mainly involved corporations and others that had for a long time held large *renminbi* reserves in hopes that the Chinese currency would continue to rise in value. With the partial liberalization of China's international capital flows, it appears that the currency is now more likely to fall (devalue) than rise (revalue), and it no longer makes sense to hold large *renminbi* reserves. But in the future, China could experience a currency run for other reasons that, in turn, would reduce its reserves to dangerously low levels, causing a sharp devaluation. If at the same time China had accumulated a large foreign debt denominated in foreign currencies, there could be widespread bankruptcies that the Chinese government could do little about. That happened in Thailand, Indonesia, Malaysia, and Korea in the 1997–1998 financial crisis. China today, however, is far from any such danger. Its reserves remain large, and its foreign debt is small.

The real danger for China is not a hard landing but a significant slowdown in growth to well below the 6.5 percent rate projected in the 13th Five-Year Plan covering the years 2016–2020. Poor lending policies and more bad bank loans could cause such a slowdown, but the major threat is only indirectly related to the financial sector. China's major structural problem is that its investment rate, as a share of gross domestic product (GDP), is much too high. Total investment peaked in 2011 at 47.3 percent of GDP, but it was still at 44.1 percent in 2015. There are no readily available statistics on how much investment is required to produce all of the goods that China consumes and exports (and to produce the machinery to make those goods), but it is not likely to be much over half of what China actually invests each year. In order to maintain full employment of its resources, China must find additional investments amounting to roughly 20 percent of GDP.

Until the last year or two, China had little problem finding productive investments to fill this gap in aggregate demand. The Soviet-style investment policies of the pre-1978 period had largely ignored investment in both housing and transport. The result was that urban housing in China was wholly inadequate (only 7.2 square meters—about seventy-two square feet—per capita in 1978), and the transport system was straining to handle the comparatively modest traffic volumes of the early 1980s. In the late 1990s, and particularly since 2000, the Chinese government and the private sector began a massive investment drive to overcome this neglect. This investment drive was further reinforced by China's use of large government-stimulus measures to avoid being dragged down by the world recession of 2007–2009.

These massive investments transformed the Chinese transport system. High-speed limited-access highways did not exist prior to 1988, but there were 16,000 kilometers (slightly less than 10,000 miles) of these highways by the year 2000 and 123,500 kilometers (77,200 miles) in 2015, longer than the interstate system of the United States. Passenger cars rose from 1.6 million in 1990 to 141.3 million in 2015 (127.6 million privately owned). Most of the two-lane roads that reach into many remote towns and villages are now paved all-weather roads. Every large city, including all provincial capitals, has a large modern airport, and the number of commercial aircraft has reached over 1,900. The high-speed rail system is also now the longest in the world, crisscrossing the country. No doubt some portions of the transport system still could be improved, but the country's major needs have been met at first-world standards, and the major expenses ahead will be for maintenance rather than new highways or airports.

The housing experience has been similar. Investment in housing already was large before 2010, but between 2010 and 2014, China built 6.78 billion square meters of housing space, or enough for sixty-seven million three-person families, each in apartments of one hundred square meters. By 2010, there were 31.6 square meters per capita, and that figure rose over the next several years. Demand could not sustain this level of building and inventories rose, particularly in second- and third-tier cities. China might be able to continue adding one-billion square meters of residences a year if a major effort were made to house cities' rural migrants, but the 1.36 billion square meter pace of 2010–2014 was not sustainable. Prices in all but the largest cities fell.

Compounding the problems created by this enormous transport and building construction boom was that key supplier industries kept expanding capacity, apparently on the assumption that the boom would go on indefinitely. China, by 2014 and 2015, had the capacity to produce over half of the world's steel and cement, far more than domestic demand needed. Steel producers tried to solve the problem by rapidly increasing exports, leading to worldwide anti-dumping actions to curtail them and keep North American and European steel mills operating. There was also excess capacity in sectors such as shipbuilding, in both private and state-owned enterprises.

Table 15.1 Supply Side Sources of Growth in China

	Growth Rate (%)				
Period	GDP	Fixed Capital	Raw Labor	Education Enhanced Labor	TFP
1953–1957	6.5	1.9	1.2	1.7	4.7
1958–1978	3.9	6.7	2	2.7	−0.5
1978–2005	9.5	9.6	1.9	2.7	3.8
2006–2011	11	15.1	0.4	2.1	3.3
2012–2015	7.4	11.9	0.4	2.1	1.1
1953–2005	7	7.7	1.9	2.6	2.1

Sources: This table was used by the author in a meeting of the Chinese Economists Society in Shenzhen in June 2016. The estimates through 2005 are from Dwight H. Perkins and Thomas G. Rawski, "Forecasting China's Economic Growth to 2025," in Loren Brandt and Thomas G. Rawski, *China's Great Economic Transformation* (Cambridge: Cambridge University Press, 2008), pp. 829–886. The 2006–2011 educated labor figures were compiled by Dr. Zhang Qiong using the same methodology as the earlier figures, and the capital stock and total factor productivity estimates for 2006–2015 were completed by the author of this chapter using the same methodology.

These investments were profitable for many years, and the argument was sometimes made that the construction boom was not becoming a dangerous bubble. But, as Chinese researchers have reported, the extraordinary investment rates from 2010 caused profits, or the national rate of return on capital, to fall from over 10 percent to 6.6 percent by 2012 and likely has fallen further since. Of equal importance, the overall rate of productivity growth (total factor productivity or TFP) fell sharply in 2012–2015 (see Table 15.1). A decade ago, it appeared that China would need total factor productivity growth of at least 3 percent per year, if the country were to sustain an annual economic growth rate of 6 percent after 2015, and that a higher rate was probably not attainable because it would require an unlikely total factor productivity growth of well over 4 or 5 percent. As it turned out, China achieved only a 1 percent growth rate in total factor productivity from 2012 to 2015, though its impact was somewhat offset by large increases of capital investment.

There are future investments the government could make usefully, notably to clean up the environment. These could keep up the productivity rate provided progress was measured in a way that reflected environmental improvements. China could also shift from relying on high investment rates to lower rates combined with increased household consumption as a share of the total economy. Shifting to a more consumption-based economy, however, is extremely difficult, and China has had only limited success in this regard, despite considerable effort.

Finally, a higher rate of total factor productivity could be achieved if China vigorously implemented the long list of reforms announced after the Third Plenum of the Communist Party Congress in 2013. Many reforms it announced are likely to increase productivity significantly, provided they are vigorously implemented. To date, however, despite action in such areas as the financial sector, progress overall has been slow. Furthermore, arguably the most important announced reform was to force state-owned enterprises to face full market competition. There was even some speculation that some big corporations would be cut loose to succeed or fail on their own. The evidence so far, however, is that these enterprises now play an even larger role than in the past, both at home and abroad, and will continue to enjoy strong backing from the central government that controls them. This continued reliance on state enterprises, combined with slow market-oriented reform for the rest of the economy and a continuing high rate of investment, could sustain a national 6 percent growth for a time. But it is also possible that total factor productivity and the rate of return to capital will continue to fall, and the GDP growth rate will fall with them.

16 | WILL URBANIZATION SAVE THE CHINESE ECONOMY OR DESTROY IT?

Meg Rithmire

In 2011, for the first time ever, more than half of China's population of 1.35 billion people lived in cities. On the one hand, observers are touting the emergence of a new, urban middle class in China, causing global business to look to Chinese urbanites as a source of demand and consumption. On the other hand, many point to over-investment in infrastructure, rapidly rising real estate prices in top-tier cities (think Shanghai and Beijing), and falling prices elsewhere, plus the existence of "ghost cities" as evidence that urban China is not the engine of global growth but, rather, a bubble readying to burst.

At the heart of these differing visions of the future of urban China is a fundamental economic contradiction: China over-invests in urban areas, yet China is also under-urbanized relative to other countries at its level of development and industrialization. Although now half of all Chinese live in urban areas, 200 million of these urbanites, or 17 percent of the urban population, are formally registered as rural residents and therefore lack access to urban public- and social-welfare services. Outside of urban areas, a staggering 300 million rural residents are underemployed in the agriculture sector, working around 150 days per year, yet unable to relocate to urban areas. This contradiction is a product of unique political economic institutions that govern labor, land, and capital. Understanding these institutions—and the likelihood that they will undergo major reforms—is the key to understanding the future of urban China.

A UNIQUE INSTITUTIONAL LANDSCAPE

China's institution for managing population movement—the *hukou*, or household registration system—is perhaps the most notorious of these political economic institutions. Beginning in the 1950s, the Chinese Communist Party (CCP) adopted an internal passport system in order to prevent migration to cities. Although enforcement was relaxed in the 1980s to allow labor migration to cities, urban dwellers with rural registration status suffer discrimination in what most scholars agree to be a system of second-class citizenship, which some have likened to an "apartheid pass" system. While the system has successfully prevented the kind of haphazard urbanization that has produced political unrest and social conflict elsewhere in the developing world, it has also dramatically misallocated labor, contributed to China's abnormally high savings rate, and discouraged urban consumption, not to mention the human costs of informality and exclusion.

This duality in labor markets and citizenship has a mirror in the institutions that govern land. Urban land remains owned by the state and, in rural areas, by the "collective." When rural residents migrate to cities, they have mostly been unable to sell or transfer their land rights. This both inhibits migration and leaves the countryside riddled with vacant structures and untilled land of uncertain ownership. Only the state may convert rural, collectively owned land into urban, state-owned land for construction. In urban areas, local governments represent the "state" as landowners and collect large, lump-sum fees for land they lease out. This institutional system thereby encourages local governments to expropriate land from farmers at low prices to then lease it at high market prices. Land urbanization, therefore, has proceeded faster than the urbanization of people, creating social conflict and misallocating land resources. Dwindling farmland for food production provoked the Ministry of Land Resources to declare a "red line" of 120 million hectares of farmland necessary for national food security, producing conflict among levels of government as they compete for their quota of construction land while maintaining this red line.

Chinese fiscal and financial systems also contribute to local government hunger for land and for urban investment. While local governments are responsible for the lion's share of social and physical expenditures in urban areas, they are entitled to far less tax revenue than the central government and have been barred from borrowing directly. The result is what political scientist Lily Tsai has called "local government on a shoestring," meaning governments must depend on land revenues and central transfers to meet even basic expenditure burdens.

If fiscal institutions push local governments to over-supply urban construction, China's financial system generates demand for investment in real estate. As mentioned above, Chinese savings rates are incredibly high (49 percent of gross domestic product, one of the highest rates for any country for which we have data), and domestic demand very low (36.5 percent of GDP, one of the world's lowest rates). Many factors contribute to high savings, including insecurity about health care and old-age insurance, China's upside-down population pyramid and rapidly aging society, or a conservative outlook based on the turmoil Chinese families experienced in previous generations. Whatever the causes, household savings have to go somewhere. Decades of capital controls have prevented ordinary families from investing abroad, and bank deposit rates are low, leaving domestic equity markets and real estate as primary venues. Many middle-class Chinese families have purchased second and even third homes as investment properties, hoping to pass them on to married children or simply to see savings appreciate as property prices rise.

These institutions channel flows of people and capital in specific ways, and it becomes easier to understand some of the more dramatic and contradictory phenomena in urban China: a rapidly urbanizing country without the kinds of informal settlements that pervade urban landscapes elsewhere in the developing world; empty satellite developments outside of major Chinese cities with few occupants, and cities eager to expand even more; and 300 million underemployed farmers, even as wages are rising in major cities along the east coast.

CHINA'S URBAN FUTURE

Inarguably, the state of urbanization in China is riddled with undesirable outcomes and significant distortions—an assessment with which the CCP itself agrees. The question is whether these distortions will be resolved in an orderly way, say through significant economic and institutional reforms, or in a more disorderly and chaotic fashion, through economic or political crisis. While an acute crisis—for example, a sudden collapse in real estate prices precipitating major economic turmoil—seems unlikely, so too does a completely painless resolution. The sustainability of urbanization, as well as the future of economic growth and social stability in China, rests on how, and indeed whether, the CCP carries out its own plans to accelerate urbanization and transform its process.

Understanding unique Chinese institutions and the economic patterns they produce underscores how some phenomena in urban China should not be viewed through a Western lens. For example, when an average American sees empty housing developments and rapidly rising real estate prices, she is apt to fear a real estate bubble vulnerable to the same explosive debt dynamics that began with mortgage market defaults in the United States in 2007. Yet most Chinese families invest in real estate with savings rather than debt. Chinese real estate markets are vulnerable to price adjustments, but worries about debt should be directed at local governments and developers, who borrow with land as collateral, rather than at home-buyers themselves.

Debt concerns in the public and corporate private sector are serious. In 2015, China's government debt was a little more than half of GDP, which is low, but total debt exceeds 250 percent of GDP. Estimating total private and public debt is difficult because many debt instruments and borrowing organizations were designed to obscure such information, for example, "Local Government Financing Vehicles" (LGFVs), which are semi-public, semi-private corporations designed to circumvent rules barring local governments from borrowing from banks. These borrow on behalf of local governments, with implicit (but not official) government backing, using land as collateral. The central government only discovered the extent of LGFV activity in 2010 and has since made some attempts to rein them in, yet it has so far seemed unwilling to truly do so or, more importantly, find a fiscal arrangement that doesn't leave local governments to rely on land- and debt-based financing.

Given Beijing's apparent intolerance for financial turmoil (it intervened heavily in stock markets in 2015), it is hard to imagine an acute debt crisis because the central government likely will support local governments and developers whose hardships could endanger the overall economy. In any case, property prices in major cities remain high, suggesting that any price collapse may be localized in lower-tier markets unlikely to engulf the economy overall.

If chaotic unwinding is unlikely, a sustainable resolution relies on the CCP's own plans for reform, most of which were outlined between 2012 and 2014 in what is called the plan for "New-Style Urbanization." The plan calls for the creation of 250 million new urban citizens by 2030. Many of these new urbanites will be normalized migrants already living in urban centers, and the rest will comprise new migrants channeled into urban centers with reforms to land management and the household registration system. According to the National Development and Reform Commission (NDRC), China's most powerful economic guidance group, the "new urbanization" is more than just a plan for human migration; it is additionally a plan to transform both the rural and urban economies to create environmentally and economically sustainable growth.

By creating urban citizens rather than informal urban residents, and conducting social welfare reform, the plan aims to create a secure urban middle class who will pursue the kind of consumption that the Chinese (and indeed the global) economy so desperately needs. The CCP itself estimates that consumption as a share of GDP will increase to 66 percent by 2030 as a result of the reforms (with investment decreasing to 30.9 percent). Critically, these new urban residents will be directed to smaller towns and cities and deterred from settlement in major urban centers. The *hukou* institution allows the CCP to control how many migrants resettle and where; cities with fewer than one million residents will experience full *hukou* liberalization; medium-sized cities will experience some liberalization; and cities of more than five million residents will experience no *hukou* liberalization.

Land reforms proposed to accompany *hukou* reforms will allow rural residents to transfer some of their land rights, both inducing migration and rationalizing land use in rural areas. These reforms, piloted in the major cities of Chengdu and Chongqing, appear in some form in twenty-nine of thirty-one provincial-level units. They allow a rural resident to sell development rights to his rural homestead land to a developer or the city government itself, receiving capital in return and usually an urban *hukou*. (To clarify: rural residents may not sell their share of collectively owned farmland, only the land on which their own homes sit.) The developer may then develop a similarly sized parcel of land closer to the city center and turn the former homestead into arable farmland, thereby having no effect on a local government's quota of land for urban construction. Part of the goal of the "new urbanization" is to transform the countryside and agricultural sector. Migration will allow upscaling of rural farms, which now average one hectare in size, and leave only "professional farmers" behind, thereby correcting distortions in labor markets and, hopefully, resulting in greater agricultural efficiency.

Understanding these plans for state-managed urbanization, one begins to see "ghost cities" in a different light. Many, such as the much-photographed city of Ordos in the desert of Inner Mongolia will remain ghost cities, physical testaments to a failed model of investment-driven urban growth. But others, especially those large developments on the outskirts of cities and in third- and fourth-tier cities, may be sites of the new urban normal in China in several years. In this sense, the CCP's approach to urbanization is a sort of unintentional "if you build it, they will come" strategy: the over-supply of urban infrastructure and development can be met with an increase in demand as the CCP draws on its unique instruments of population and land control.

Both population control and land reforms aim to formalize the process of rural-to-urban migration by using existing institutions rather than replacing them. These are reforms around the edges of the household registration system and public ownership of land rather than steps en route to their complete transformation. Significant reforms in other areas—such as social welfare and inter-government fiscal relations—are notably absent. Without substantial reforms to how local governments raise revenue, especially if populations are to swell in the most vulnerable, smaller cities, it is hard to imagine how reliance on land finance and debt can be abated.

Ultimately, the urbanization plans are most associated with Li Keqiang, the current premier, widely seen to be China's weakest premier of the last thirty years. In the present political climate, dominated by the politics of intra-party cleansing and by President and Communist Party leader Xi Jinping himself, very little progress has been made on these reforms as discussion of urbanization has fallen by the wayside. Although Xi has stated that markets should allocate resources, his administration has demonstrated a firm refusal to subject itself to market forces. The administration's excessive focus on politics, loyalty, and anti-corruption efforts has put the CCP in what seems to be a "reactive" mode of economic management, neither letting markets take the lead nor taking up proactive reforms to ameliorate the many problems of China's growth model.

The best path would be something in between the status quo stalemate and a vigorous implementation of state-directed urbanization. If markets fail to direct migrants to places where opportunities are most plentiful, we may also hope that China avoids the more socially, politically, and economically disastrous consequences of state-led population movements: concentrated poverty, broken social networks, communities of new urbanites with few jobs, and political coercion. The CCP would do best to proceed with the next wave of economic and urban reforms in the same manner it has carried out reforms over the last generation: through experimentation, open channels for feedback and criticism, and policy adjustment based on local successes and failures.

17 | IS CHINA KEEPING ITS PROMISES ON TRADE?

Mark Wu

ON DECEMBER 11, 2001, after fifteen years of arduous negotiations, China acceded to the World Trade Organization (WTO), the 164-nation body that regulates global commerce. By doing so, China agreed to abide by thousands of legal commitments concerning its trade practices. Is China living up to these promises? As with many difficult questions, the answer turns on one's perspective. But the fact that one has to quibble over facts highlights why trade tensions with China have become such a politically charged issue in recent years.

This much is certain: upon joining the WTO, China undertook a massive overhaul of its domestic laws and regulations to ensure their compliance with WTO requirements. New markets, previously closed to foreign firms, were opened. Processes for judicial review and transparency were strengthened in areas where this was required by the WTO. Within the government, the Ministry of Commerce assumed the role of a watchdog to ensure that other government agencies complied with China's treaty obligations.

WTO accession provided the crucial impetus necessary to break the logjam within the Chinese leadership over the future direction of economic reform. To fulfill its WTO obligations, the government transformed the Chinese political economy. State-owned enterprises underwent a massive restructuring. Market forces were allowed to play a stronger role. Increasingly, private enterprises emerged as the key driver for economic growth.

China gained tremendously from these reforms. With the legal uncertainty surrounding tariffs now resolved by its WTO membership, massive amounts of foreign direct investment (FDI) flowed into the country—more than $1 trillion worth in the following fifteen years. As production shifted to China, the country became an export powerhouse. Chinese exports grew from $266 billion in 2001 to $2.3 trillion in 2015. In 2013, China surpassed the United States to become the world's largest trading nation.

But the beneficiaries of China's WTO accession have not been exclusively Chinese. Many foreign firms gained access to the huge Chinese market, helping fuel corporate earnings. Foreign consumers, too, have benefitted from low-priced Chinese imports and cheap credit arising out of China's recycling of its trade surplus.

So why then is this not simply a happy "win-win" story about the mutual benefits of trade and globalization? Importantly, the gains from China's deepening integration with the global economy have not been shared by all. Within advanced economies, pockets of communities have been decimated by the lingering effects of the "China shock." Critics warn of China acting unfairly and not playing by the established rules. President Trump, in his 2016 campaign, went so far as to declare, "We cannot allow China to continue to rape our country."

The Trump administration came into office promising bold new policies to tackle Chinese mercantilism. Peter Navarro, the director of the National Trade Council, has described China as "the biggest trade cheater in the world." Among the trade practices considered to be unfair are China's export subsidies, intellectual property protection, currency manipulation, forced technology transfer, labor conditions, and dumping of surplus goods.

Even the mood among establishment "China hands" is shifting. A 2017 Asia Society report, written by a team consisting of several former US government officials, described the US-China trade relationship as "increasingly unbalanced and disadvantageous" for US companies. Of particular concern, the bipartisan group noted, was the "ever-more skewed playing field, particularly in high-tech sectors, where Chinese protectionism has noticeably intensified."

Is it the case that China's gains in world trade have come because it blithely ignored its WTO commitments? From 2002 to 2016, a total of thirty-eight complaints were filed against China at the WTO. On average, this amounts to a paltry two complaints per year. Compared to the thousands of commitments made by China in its WTO accession agreement, this figure does not suggest a concerted disregard of its treaty commitments.

Moreover, consider the fact that over the same time period, a total of seventy-three complaints were filed against the United States. One way to interpret the empirical evidence is to suggest that China has behaved no worse than America when it comes to breaching its WTO commitments. Furthermore, when China has been challenged at the WTO and lost, it has generally complied with the ruling, at least on its face.

All of this might appear to suggest that China, by and large, has been a responsible and respectful adherent of the status quo trade regime whose rules were largely shaped by the United States and other Western advanced economies. This certainly is how China would like for the international community to understand its treaty compliance record. But there is another body of facts that undercuts this interpretation.

First, the number of complaints is likely to be an inaccurate proxy for whether a country is compliant or not. It simply represents the times when a constituency thought that the stakes were high enough to justify spending heavily in legal fees to file a case against a country. Not all breaches necessarily result in the filing of a formal complaint. Given fears of potential retribution by the Chinese government, some companies might avoid pressing for a WTO complaint.

In addition, only in situations where evidence is available to prove one's case will one choose to file a complaint. Given the fact that elements of the Chinese system are much less open and transparent than comparable systems in advanced democracies, there also may be transgressions for which a complaint has not been filed because of the inability to obtain the requisite evidence.

Second, if one examines the nature of the complaints themselves, we discover that they cut across a much wider swath of subject matter for China than for other trading countries. Although the number of cases brought against the United States may be comparable to China, the complaints are concentrated in a relatively narrow set of categories. WTO members complain primarily about US trade-remedy practices and American subsidies for particular goods such as airplanes and agriculture products.

Complaints of this sort can also be found in the cases filed against China. But they constitute the minority of the complaints. Compared to the United States, WTO members have filed cases accusing China of breach for a much wider set of circumstances. These include accusations that China has failed to protect intellectual property rights as promised, has failed to open up certain service markets as promised (such as for films or electronic payment systems), and has applied illegal restrictions on exports of certain minerals in order to benefit domestic producers.

Third, even though China may abide by the technical letter of a WTO ruling, there is a sense that China is not always abiding by its spirit. Take, for instance, a series of WTO cases related to export restrictions imposed on China on raw materials and minerals. These restrictions benefit downstream Chinese producers at the expense of their foreign competitors and induce firms to shift production to China. In 2012, the WTO Appellate Body found China's restrictions on nine industrial minerals, such as bauxite and zinc, to be illegal in the *China—Raw Materials* dispute. Subsequently, in 2014, the WTO Appellate Body also found China's export restrictions on seventeen rare earth elements and two other metals to be illegal. Both sets of restrictions were then eliminated. This might give rise to the impression that China strongly abides by WTO law, even when it loses a dispute. But two years later, yet another complaint was filed against China, this time over its export duties on yet another set of minerals. This type of behavior gives rise to doubts over whether China is truly committed to following established principles or simply playing a game of "catch-me-if-you-can" when it comes to following certain obligations.

However, perhaps the biggest source of unhappiness over Chinese trade practices stems not from unfulfilled promises but rather from the inadequate and incomplete nature of the legal commitments. Most WTO legal obligations date back to the mid-1990s, prior to China's WTO accession. They therefore were not written necessarily with the current structure of the Chinese political economy in mind. Supporters of China's WTO accession might have harbored hopes that as China grew richer from trade, its political economy would inevitably transform to resemble those of other fast-growing East Asian economies or other postcommunist states. Those expectations have not panned out. Even if they had, the negotiators could not have anticipated how China's political economy would transform following its WTO accession.

Although market forces play a more active role today in China than they did in the 1990s, the Chinese political economy remains unique. Several factors collectively account for the distinctive nature of today's "China, Inc."—a complex, dynamic, and ever-changing entity. These factors include the Party-state's control over key strategic industries and the banking sector, the powers and role of the National Development and Reform Commission, and the formal and informal linkages between the Party-state and private enterprises.

WTO law is not necessarily well-equipped to tackle all of the problems that arise out of this type of political economy structure. For example, when a Chinese bank provides a loan to a Chinese private enterprise, is this a breach of China's promise not to provide unfair subsidies to domestic industries? The answer turns on the questions of whether the state is directing and controlling the bank, and whether the terms are favorable compared to prevailing market terms. But in a country where the mechanisms of control are opaque and might fall under the Party (as opposed to state) structure, answering this question proves difficult.

In addition, some areas are simply not covered by existing WTO rules at all. For example, WTO law, by and large, defers to the International Monetary Fund (IMF) when it comes to questions of unfair currency manipulation. The WTO's jurisdiction is confined to narrow questions of specific subsidies, whereas the IMF has jurisdiction over exchange rate issues. In addition, WTO law is not robust with respect to ensuring fair labor working conditions. Nor does it necessarily offer a mechanism to address rebates of value-added taxes (VAT) to exporters, unless the VAT rebate is contingent on the use of domestic content requirements or otherwise amounts to a subsidy as defined by WTO rules. Finally, WTO agreements were drafted long before the rise of the digital economy. They therefore often do not present a path for international litigation to address the complaints raised by the United States and other foreign technology companies.

For such areas, although China's trade practices may be problematic and inflict harm on foreign firms, it is hard to accuse China of having violated its trade promises per se. One can only go so far as to say that China may be backtracking on the spirit of its commitments to open markets and trade reciprocity. A renewed impetus must be placed on negotiating new obligations and updating trade rules for the twenty-first century. Until that is done, additional efforts to strengthen enforcement of China's trade commitments via WTO cases can only accomplish so much.

All of this is to say that the answer to the question posed above depends on the particular Chinese trade practice at issue. For certain areas, no doubt, China has not lived up to its promises. But for many other areas, it has followed through. And with certain issues, the problem is with the promises themselves, or more specifically, their incomplete scope. China has deftly managed to take advantage of the gaps in WTO law to advance particular industrial and quasi-mercantilist policies to benefit its own producers. Such practices may be helping China move up the production value chain. But they are also contributing to rising populist tensions in advanced economies and the gradual fraying of the trade ecosystem that has been instrumental to China's rise.

18 | HOW DO CHINA'S NEW RICH GIVE BACK?

Tony Saich

ONE OF THE MOST striking features of the past few years in China has been the rise of individual wealth. This is new terrain for the Chinese Communist Party (CCP) to navigate. For a party that still professes to take Marxism as a guide to understanding society, the profusion of billionaires with money to spend independent of the state sets new challenges. Ever since the CCP General Secretary Jiang Zemin put forth his significant policy change called "Three Represents" in 2002, which paved the way to allowing private entrepreneurs to join a supposedly proletarian party, suspicion has remained about how the super-rich might use their wealth. In general, the Beijing approach has been to co-opt these new elites with institutions and regulations that bind them into more traditional-looking "Leninist" structures and thus ensure their philanthropic impulses match official priorities.

This chapter looks first at the framework that the state has been developing to manage this growing wealth and then examines philanthropic activities of the new rich.

A clearer picture is emerging of how the CCP hopes to channel this new wealth and limit its potential for encouraging creation of a civil society that is independent of state patronage. Thus, the regime has passed new legislation, such as the China Charity Law, both to regulate the sector and also encourage more giving to sectors approved by the central government.

In past years, and for several reasons, Chinese individuals have not been very generous, and, in 2015, China ranked 144th in the World Giving Index that tabulates charitable donations globally. In 2013, for example, China's top one hundred philanthropists combined gave away less than did Facebook founder Mark Zuckerberg and his wife. To date, most giving has been by corporations rather than individuals, except in 2008, when the massive Sichuan earthquake caused an outpouring of sympathy. However, this enthusiasm soon subsided because of various scandals in the philanthropic sector, reports of massive corruption, and the paucity of reliable organizations to give to. For example, the China Red Cross saw its donations plummet after 2011, when a woman named Guo Meimei, who claimed to be one of its managers, published photos of her personal lavish lifestyle, leading to public questions about the Red Cross use of funds. Although her story was untrue, it raised concerns about proper oversight and the use of funds by philanthropic organizations and helped reduce public contributions. (In September 2015, Ms. Guo was fined and given a five-year jail term for running an illegal casino!)

The wariness that restricted individual giving was heightened by regulations that were either unclear or did not encourage charitable giving. Thus, when chief executive Jack Ma of Alibaba, a major e-commerce company, set up his charitable trust, he did so in Singapore, because he called the Chinese rules "not yet perfect." Further, the lack of clarity about tax relief, the very high payout rate for foundations, and the low administrative costs that are permitted all discourage giving through foundations or other charitable organizations. Charitable funds have to pay out 8 percent of their annual donations to worthy causes—compared to a typical required payout of 5 percent in the United States—while their endowments must pay 20 percent of what they collect yearly in taxes to the government. The lower payout rate in the United States enables the foundations to be more sustainable, and they are also tax-exempt organizations under US tax law.

Setting up a foundation can be costly, requiring two million *renminbi* (RMB, "people's currency") to set up a local foundation and twenty million RMB to set up a national one (one US dollar is the equivalent of 6.7 RMB). Indeed, this high payout rate, the lack of effective tax incentives, and the high starting threshold probably were designed intentionally to prevent the development of foundations not sponsored by the state. Before effective legislation was passed to control and guide the sector, the CCP was wary of any organization that could develop its own funding sources and operate with a degree of freedom that made the Party uncomfortable. As a result, even those companies that had set up foundations would still run most of the salary and other administrative costs through the corporation.

Given its origins, the Communist Party has always been suspicious of private wealth. More recently, the emphasis of President Xi Jinping's regime on fighting corruption has made local officials, rightly or wrongly, wary of taking private funds. Given the many accounts of collusion between government officials and their local entrepreneurs, this is not surprising. The official media has published many reports of close but illegal relationships between wealthy businessmen and government officials that have led to criminal convictions.

The Charity Law that took effect in September 2016 seeks to clarify the situation and ensure that giving is channeled to those areas that have official support. On the positive side, it provides a broad definition of approved charitable activities and the kinds of organizations that can engage in them. The list includes foundations, social groups, social service organizations (previously referred to as civil non-enterprise institutions), and undefined "other forms of organizations." This should open the field to a wider array of philanthropic organizations. However, the areas that receive support are limited to nonpolitical ones, such as agencies for poverty relief, care for the elderly and orphans, disaster relief, and the promotion of education, science, culture, and sports. Organizations deemed reliable will no longer have to go through a process of double registration, finding first a sponsor and then registering with the relevant bureau of the Ministry of Civil Affairs. They can now skip the first step and register directly with the relevant bureau of civil affairs. Most importantly, public fund-raising will be allowed, but only if a license is obtained in advance. Administrative costs are not allowed to exceed 10 percent of overall expenditures in any given year, thus preventing the organizations from growing too large. Finally, there will be tax incentives, but the law does not specify how these will work.

This new framework should, then, encourage greater giving. Discussions with some of the new philanthropists indicate they are, in fact, interested in questions about how to give back to the society that made them wealthy and what the most effective means may be. Some are curious about the great philanthropists of America's "Gilded Age," such as John D. Rockefeller, who used his wealth to construct the Peking Union Medical College and funded its operations until the communist takeover in 1949. Despite coming from very different societies, they find empathy in the writings of former philanthropists who have left legacies that exist well beyond their lifetimes. There is a similar fascination with the new technology philanthropists, such as Bill Gates of Microsoft and Mark Zuckerberg of Facebook.

So what are the wealthy doing? A study by Harvard Kennedy School's Ash Center for Democratic Governance and Innovation of the one hundred top Chinese philanthropists in 2015 provides some answers (http://chinaphilanthropy.ash.harvard.edu). Donating $3.8 billion, they accounted for approximately 25 percent of all giving in China, and this amounted to 0.03 percent of China's total economic output. (Overall, Chinese charitable giving equals 0.12 percent of GNP, compared to the US figure of 2.1 percent.) However, these figures may underestimate Chinese giving as they do not include local donations to temples, churches, and clan associations.

What is interesting is that the giving is overwhelmingly local, with donors giving to projects within their own locality. This means that charity does little to reduce regional disparities, a major problem in China. Thus, Tibet received only 0.01 percent of all donations, while Beijing received 15.7 percent. Because Beijing is the capital, it is not surprising that corporations based elsewhere, perhaps wishing to gain favor through their donations, contribute almost 90 percent of all monies received. This is probably because of the high concentration of academic institutions in the capital; education is a favored field for donors. In turn, those based in Beijing were the most willing to donate to organizations in other areas and gave a surprising 86.5 percent of their funds to other regions. For the donors as a whole, education proved to be the most popular field, receiving over 70 percent of all donations.

Most donors tend to support just one line of activity (71 percent) with education the most favored activity (fifty-nine of one hundred donors gave to this field, amounting to 57.5 percent of their total giving). In the United States, education support, at 15.4 percent of giving, comes second to donations to religious institutions and activities, which receive 33 percent of all giving. Only seven leading donors contributed to two different activities, while Jack Ma was the only one of the top one hundred who contributed to four different causes: education, environment, social welfare, and disaster relief. Given the attention paid to environmental degradation and the Party leadership's concern about air pollution in major cities, few philanthropic dollars have been given in support of clean air, a mere 0.9 percent of the total.

The new Charity Law gives hope that this field of philanthropic giving may expand in a more regulated way. Indeed, of one hundred top donors, about one half have already established personal or family foundations, and this total is likely to grow. Already, the first independent training center for philanthropy has been registered in the southern industrial center of Shenzhen in collaboration with the China Philanthropy Research Institute of Beijing Normal University. Yet as some American researchers have shown, wealthy private entrepreneurs have not only been co-opted by the state but in many ways have grown wealthy thanks to state policies, especially after China joined the World Trade Organization in 2001, which increased Chinese access to foreign markets. They have shown little interest in challenging Party and state power, and there is no evidence that philanthropic giving will challenge communist priorities or support causes and groups that it has marginalized.

As we look forward, it is clear that these new laws and other regulations will benefit what are referred to as government-organized nongovernmental organizations (GONGOs) or party-organized ones with close government connections. Education will remain a priority and social service providers will also benefit. The emphasis on the latter is proven by their designation in the Charity Law. By contrast, advocacy for what have been called "marginalized groups" will be closely monitored and are unlikely to benefit much from future donations. Dropping the need to have a sponsoring agency will make it easier for those individuals with good records and connections to register their foundations or charitable trusts. However, public fundraising will be closely monitored due to the need to have an official certificate. By contrast, as is shown in the new regulations governing them that took effect January 1, 2017, foreign philanthropies are likely to be subject to greater scrutiny; for them, double registration remains in place, and there is a new obligation to register with the Ministry of Public Security rather than the Ministry of Civil Affairs. The CCP is far more likely to trust its own wealthy citizens, who are products of the system they control, rather than foreign entities whose true objectives may arouse suspicions. The result might well be an expansion of the Chinese third sector (voluntary and community organizations) while space for free association, as part of a normal civil society, may well contract.

19 | WHAT CAN CHINA TEACH US ABOUT FIGHTING POVERTY?

Nara Dillon

IN 2015, the United Nations announced with great fanfare that the Millennium Development Goal (MDG) to cut extreme poverty in half had been achieved. Using the World Bank's international poverty line of $1.25 per day, the UN calculated that the number of people around the world living below this standard fell from 1.9 billion in 1990 to 836 million in 2015. This measure of poverty is designed to identify the people who have difficulty meeting their basic subsistence needs, especially having enough food to eat.

Progress toward this global goal was uneven. Altogether, fifty-five developing countries met their MDG targets, and many overshot them significantly; this performance contrasts to nineteen countries that experienced poverty increases in the same period. One of these fifty-five success stories, however, stands out from the rest. China alone accounted for more than half of the global decrease in extreme poverty. Moreover, the UN target for poverty reduction could not have been achieved if China had not dramatically exceeded its MDG target, reducing the incidence of extreme poverty by 94 percent.

How did China do it? The answer is not simple, and some Chinese policies are not easy to replicate in developing countries with different economic and political systems. But the overall Chinese strategy toward poverty alleviation holds important lessons in the global fight. This strategy consists of three key elements: data, development, and welfare.

The first element of the Chinese anti-poverty strategy is data. Unlike other communist countries (such as Cuba), the Chinese government has made an effort to measure poverty, developing its own standards and studying a range of international methodologies as well, including the World Bank's poverty line and economist and philosopher Amartya Sen's capabilities approach. Scholars debate the quality of these government statistics, but the data is collected and released to the public. Furthermore, Chinese and foreign scholars have carried out extensive surveys and experiments to study the changing nature of poverty and the impact of poverty-alleviation policies. These data play an important role in the policy process, helping Chinese officials adapt their programs and respond to poverty's changing nature.

These data also give us a picture of what extreme poverty looks like in China today. A typical Chinese person living below the World Bank poverty line is a young girl living in a mountainous region in western China. She attends primary school in her village, which is connected to the outside world by unpaved roads and is located more than seventy-five miles away from the nearest train station. Her family makes its living from agriculture, growing most of what they eat and selling the rest for their limited cash income. Her house has electricity, but no running water. School and health-care expenses are her family's biggest economic concerns. These concerns are not misplaced; her parent's health and her own education represent the family's best route out of poverty, through hard work and better employment opportunities.

The second element of the Chinese strategy to help these impoverished families is economic development. Since China's rapid economic growth has received so much media attention, this aspect of China's fight against poverty seems easy to understand, even if it is hard for other developing countries to reproduce. But in fact, the ways in which economic growth has translated into poverty reduction is a complex story. Moreover, this complexity points to the importance of policies to transform economic growth into income gains that are either widely shared or effectively targeted to the poor. Even if few countries are in a position to match the Chinese pace of economic growth, these policies can also help counter poverty at more typical growth rates.

China made its biggest gains in poverty reduction in the 1980s through a series of agricultural reforms that boosted the incomes of most rural families. For example, China's campaign to dismantle agricultural collectives in the late 1970s and early 1980s had a major impact on poverty. This land reform movement improved work incentives by giving farmers control over production. It also led to an equitable distribution of land, ensuring that the gains from agricultural production were widely shared. Combined with market reforms allowing farmers to sell their surplus in private markets, agricultural production and incomes surged.

The single most important poverty-alleviation policy in the 1980s, however, had nothing to do with market reform. The government also raised procurement prices for agricultural goods significantly, including a 91 percent increase in grain prices from 1978 to 1985. The policy behind these price increases marked a sharp reversal in economic development strategy, eliminating the "price scissors" used by central economic planners to generate the capital necessary for a Stalinist industrialization drive. By deliberately setting the prices for agricultural goods low, central planners in the Mao era kept rural living standards at subsistence levels and redirected any economic surplus from the agricultural sector into investment in urban industry. Unfortunately, these communist economic-development strategies turned out to be misguided. China's decision to end the price scissors in the 1980s proved to be a more effective approach to economic development. At the same time, this policy reversal led to the first significant gains in rural living standards since the 1950s.

On the surface, these policies only pertain to other communist and semi-socialist countries that redistribute land and control agricultural prices—and therefore have little relevance for fighting poverty in most countries today. But because so many capitalist development policies are also marked by profound urban bias, the broader principle of limiting the degree of such bias in economic development could help reduce extreme poverty in capitalist countries as well. Promoting agricultural development is complementary to industrialization. It can contribute to the goal of increasing the prosperity of society as a whole and, at the same time, address the needs of the rural poor who are most likely to experience extreme poverty.

Since the Chinese government gradually phased out central planning in the late 1980s and early 1990s, China's economy has become increasingly defined by the market. In the process, China's poverty-alleviation policies also grew increasingly similar to those used in capitalist countries. As a result, lessons drawn from the Chinese case can go beyond broad principles to more specific policies.

As industrialization accelerated in coastal China in the 1990s, employment off the farm and rural-urban migration became the most important forces reducing extreme poverty. Even with these growing opportunities for income diversification for rural households, the rate of poverty reduction slowed by more than half from the rapid pace set in the 1980s. The new jobs were not as widely distributed as the gains in agricultural production and prices had been.

The causes of poverty also grew more diverse over time. For example, the rapidly rising cost of health care became a leading cause of poverty in the countryside in the 1990s. In addition, the privatization and reform of state-owned industry led to deindustrialization and the emergence of urban poverty in China's rust belt cities in the late 1990s and early 2000s.

In response to these changes, the Chinese government sought to target special economic-development programs to the poor. A regional poverty-alleviation program adopted in 1994 provided grants and subsidized loans to 592 poor counties, where per capita incomes fell below the national average. These resources were devoted to promoting non-agricultural employment, crop diversification, and infrastructure development, especially road building projects. The program boosted economic growth rates in these counties, but in most cases failed to improve the pace of poverty reduction significantly. Part of the problem lay in the difficulties of effectively targeting the gains from these programs within these counties. Poverty reduction was significant where these resources created jobs accessible to the poor or built roads that connected them to markets. But frequently more prosperous villages and households in these counties experienced the greatest gains in income. In 2001, the Chinese government shifted the focus of the program from the county to the village level in the effort to target the poor more effectively.

In this context, the third element of the Chinese approach to fighting poverty—welfare—has also grown increasingly important. The Chinese government has created a variety of new welfare programs over the last twenty years, targeting poverty alleviation even more narrowly to focus on poor people rather than poor places.

These new safety-net programs reflect another shift in Chinese economic policy, which had long been premised on the idea that necessary trade-offs exist between welfare and economic development. Instead, Chinese policy makers increasingly seek to integrate economic and social policy, viewing welfare programs that prevent extreme poverty and boost human capital as investments in long-term, stable economic growth. For example, the government adopted a major new urban social assistance program in 1999 to facilitate the reform of state-owned industry. In 2007, the program was extended to the countryside, creating a safety net for poor families whose income falls below poverty lines set by local governments. Cash benefits provided by the program vary widely with the cost of living and financial capacity of local governments, but the goal is to meet the subsistence needs of people who cannot support themselves through their own efforts.

In addition, the Chinese government implemented a national rural health-insurance program in 2008. Although the new rural medical cooperatives provide more limited benefits than their urban counterparts, they address one of the new causes of rural poverty by covering 70 percent or more of the cost of hospital care. Another form of investment in human capital was the 2006 policy to eliminate tuition for rural schools, accompanied by new funding from the central government to close the budget gap.

The one element of China's anti-poverty strategy that is unlikely to be adopted by other countries is the one-child policy. The government has been very successful in convincing most Chinese that this policy has been a necessary sacrifice to achieve the country's economic goals, even as it quickly evolved into a one-child policy in cities and a two-child policy in the countryside. Now that the policy has ended, demographers question whether a more gradual, natural decline in fertility in the wake of economic development and urbanization might have achieved comparable results without generating the problems of such a rapidly aging society.

President Xi Jinping has set the goal of completely eliminating extreme poverty in China by 2020, mobilizing local officials to use all these programs to address the needs of families below the poverty line. This goal may be more ambitious than most developing countries are likely to contemplate, but bringing together data, development, and welfare in a strategy to combat poverty is not unique to China or communism. The same approach can be adapted to address the different problems faced by the remaining 784 million people living in extreme poverty in Asia and Africa today.

The final characteristic of the contemporary Chinese poverty-fighting strategy relevant to other countries is not a principle or policy but, rather, a conception of poverty alleviation as an ongoing endeavor. As old obstacles to shared prosperity are overcome, new sources of poverty emerge that demand new solutions. Most importantly, rising expectations and increasing inequality are redefining perceptions of poverty in China. Ensuring that young girls in remote mountain villages have enough to eat is a historic accomplishment, but these children increasingly want more from life than just avoiding the hardships their parents and grandparents have lived through. Even after China eliminates the problem of extreme poverty, it will still face the challenge of responding to the needs and aspirations of the poor.

IV | ENVIRONMENT

20 | CAN CHINA ADDRESS AIR POLLUTION AND CLIMATE CHANGE?

Michael B. McElroy

REPRESENTATIVES OF 196 COUNTRIES, parties to the UN Framework Convention on Climate Change (UNFCC), met in Paris in December 2015 to address the issue of human-induced climate change. Emission of carbon dioxide (CO_2) associated with combustion of fossil fuels—coal, oil, and natural gas—is primarily responsible for this problem. China is the single largest national source. Absent a comprehensive strategy to address the issue, China, and indeed the world, will be forced to adapt to an uncertain and potentially hazardous climate future, one defined most likely by an increase in damaging weather extremes: heat waves, floods, and droughts. At the same time, China is faced with an even more immediate problem: air pollution that threatens the health of its population. The problems are inextricably linked. Dealing with the issue of climate change will ultimately require a sea change in China's energy economy, a shift from the current reliance on fossil fuels to less hazardous options such as wind, solar, nuclear, and hydro. If China can successfully navigate this transition, air quality can be restored to its earlier pristine level. But accomplishing this transition will not be easy.

The UNFCC parties agreed to an objective limiting the increase in future global average surface temperature to no more than 2°C above the standard that applied in the preindustrial era. Accomplishing this will require challenging, in many respects unprecedented, changes in how countries meet their future energy demands. The priority must be to limit CO_2 emissions, the most important of the greenhouse gases (GHGs) that play a central role in regulating emission of infrared heat radiation from the earth to space. An increase in the concentration of GHGs, all other factors remaining equal, will lead to a net increase in solar energy absorbed by the earth, with implications not only for a rise in global average surface temperatures but also for an increase in the quantity of heat stored in the ocean. The likely result is a future with a very different climate, a prospect for which we may be ill prepared: extremes of temperature and precipitation, increases in the incidence of floods and droughts, more violent storms, and prospectively a devastating rise in sea level. Fossil fuel combustion represents the primary source of the additional CO_2 that has accumulated in the atmosphere over the past several centuries.

Analysis of air trapped in ice drilled from central regions of Antarctica indicates that the concentration of CO_2 has varied between 180 and 280 parts per million (ppm) over most of the past 850,000 years—low during ice ages and high during the warm interglacial periods that punctuated the geological record approximately every 100,000 years. The concentration took off roughly 150 years ago, departing from the long-term trend, responding to a surge in demand for energy associated with the Industrial Revolution. It increased much faster over the second half of the twentieth century, and current levels exceed 400 ppm. Accepting even the most optimistic projections for the limitations in emissions adopted at the Paris conference, concentrations of CO_2 are likely to rise over the next several decades to levels not seen since dinosaurs roamed the earth sixty-five million years ago.

A key development affecting plans to address the climate issue took place in Beijing on November 11, 2014, in advance of the Paris meeting. Presidents Xi Jinping and Barack Obama pledged to limit future emissions of GHGs from their two countries. China is currently the world's largest national source of GHGs, surpassing the United States for this position since 2006. President Xi's commitment was that China's emissions should peak by 2030, if not earlier, and that non-fossil sources should account by that time for as much as 20 percent of China's total primary energy consumption. To place this in context, coal accounted for 73 percent of China's primary energy consumption in 2012. President Obama's pledge was that the United States would emit 26 to 28 percent less carbon in 2025 than it did in 2005. Both commitments were ambitious, challenging other countries to come up with comparable plans as they prepared for Paris. As indicated in a fact sheet released by the White House, "Xi's commitment would require China to deploy an additional 800 to 1,000 GW [gigawatts] of nuclear, wind, solar and other zero emissions generating capacity by 2030—more than all of the coal-fired plants that exist in China today and close to the total current electricity generating capacity in the United States."

President Xi's announcement may be viewed as a logical extension of initiatives identified earlier in China's 11th and 12th Five-Year Plans for economic development. Targets for the more immediate term were formulated and announced subsequently. These call for a cap on coal consumption at 4.2 billion tons, natural gas to account for 10 percent of total primary energy supply, nuclear power capacity to rise to 58 GW with an additional 30 GW under construction, hydro capacity to increase to 350 GW, investments in wind systems to reach 200 GW, solar PV (photovoltaic) to increase to 100 GW, and non-fossil sources to account for 15 percent of total primary energy consumption—all of this was to be achieved by 2020. Assuming that these ambitious objectives can be realized, prospects for China to meet Xi's stated longer-term objective would appear to be reasonable.

As indicated earlier, China has important reasons beyond climate change concerns to cut back on its use of fossil fuels. China needs to address the problems posed by episodes of serious air pollution threatening the health of its population. Sources of this air pollution may be classified as either direct or indirect. Smoke emitted by burning low-grade, untreated coal provides an example of the former. In addition to the suite of carbon compounds formed as a result of incomplete combustion, referred to collectively as soot, smoke can incorporate a variety of toxic gases including sulfur dioxide (SO_2), nitrogen oxides (NO_x), and carbon monoxide (CO). The origin is usually obvious. It can be observed directly as it emerges from the smoke stacks of factories and power plants, the chimneys of coal-heated residences, or the exhaust of passing cars and trucks. The solution is also usually obvious. The problem can be addressed by taking steps to eliminate the source. Often, though, an extreme-pollution event may be required to trigger action.

More than four thousand people died in an air-pollution episode involving direct emissions in London, England, in 1952, some simply falling down dead in the streets. The disaster was triggered by the accumulation of direct emissions in the atmosphere, a circumstance that resulted from an unusual meteorological condition, an inversion of temperature as a function of altitude. This led to an unusually stable environment that inhibited dispersal of smoke and noxious fumes from the city's factories and homes over a period of four days between December 4 and December 8. The political response was immediate. Parliament banned the use of soft coal in the city, and legislation was extended subsequently to prohibit burning coal in all homes in cities throughout the United Kingdom. China is now confronting the impact not only of pollutants similar to those that caused the problems in London, but also the effect of products formed indirectly through secondary reactions in the atmosphere. Addressing this issue is correspondingly more difficult.

China's wake-up call took place in January 2013. Attention focused initially on the accumulation of small particles (under 2.5 micrometers in diameter, referred to collectively as $PM_{2.5}$, or haze) in the atmosphere. Concerns were prompted at the outset by dissemination through social media of measurements of $PM_{2.5}$ from an instrument on the roof of the US embassy in Beijing. The data suggested that concentrations of $PM_{2.5}$ were significantly higher in China than levels reported by official government sources. The problem was so severe that it was impossible in some cases to discern the identity of nearby objects directly across a street. More serious than the implications for visibility, however, was the impact this toxic mix could have on human health. The particulate matter involved is so small that it can penetrate deep into human lungs and enter the bloodstream, resulting in serious, even life-threatening, cardiovascular and respiratory problems for exposed populations and vulnerable individuals.

The situation that developed in 2013 was exacerbated by a meteorological inversion that covered a large portion of eastern China for much of January, a larger-scale and more persistent version of the conditions responsible for the disaster experienced sixty years earlier in London. Commenting on the occurrence in China, the *Los Angeles Times* reported on January 13 that the associated pollution "closed highways, caused cancellations of flights and sporting events, sending countless peoples to hospitals complaining of respiratory ailments." The *China Daily,* an official newspaper, commented that "the air quality in big cities could have been better had more attention been paid to the density of high rises, had more trees been planted in proportion to the number of residential areas, and had the number of cars been strictly controlled." The public response was immediate, prompting the central government to take aggressive steps to address the issue with a new Air Pollution Prevention and Control Action Plan (APPCAP). The number of cities in China in which $PM_{2.5}$ would be measured more than doubled, with results reported in real time on government websites. The credibility of the central government is seriously invested in the need to mitigate this high profile problem. For the general public, it clearly ranks higher than the threat of climate change.

Paradoxically, Chinese-style pollution could have a positive impact on climate. A fraction of the fine particles included in this pollution is relatively bright-colored. In addition, they have the potential to increase the concentration of the nucleating agents responsible for the formation of clouds: more cloud-forming particles lead to more reflective clouds. The net effect could be enhanced reflection of sunlight, offsetting to some extent the additional heat retained as a consequence of the increase in the concentration of GHGs. This should not, however, be interpreted as justification for a decision to postpone action to reduce the conditions responsible for producing this toxic mix of local and regional pollution.

The physical and chemical factors responsible for indirect sources of pollution can be exceedingly complex. Absent a detailed understanding of the relevant processes, actions to address specific problems run the risk of being counterproductive, harmful rather than helpful. The experience in dealing with photochemical smog in the United States in the 1950s and 1960s provides a case in point. It took time for the authorities to conclude that elevated levels of ozone were primarily responsible for the pulmonary problems experienced by citizens in Los Angeles. Indirect evidence pointed to the automobile as an important contributing factor, although ozone was not produced directly by these vehicles. Rather, it was formed as a result of the photochemical processing in the atmosphere of a mix of NO_x and hydrocarbons in the presence of sunlight, with auto exhausts supplying the primary NO_x source. Hydrocarbons are supplied from a mix of anthropogenic and natural sources, the latter including a potentially important contribution from plants and trees. The abundance of ozone depends critically on the relative magnitudes of the sources of NO_x and hydrocarbons. In one regime, reducing emissions of NO_x could result in an increase in the concentration of ozone (a condition in which the chemistry is defined as hydrocarbon limited). In another, the opposite could be the case: more NO_x, more ozone (NO_x limited). Policy makers in China could confront a similar dilemma in addressing the challenge posed by elevated levels of $PM_{2.5}$.

A diversity of chemical compounds, including organic carbon, elemental carbon, sulfate, and nitrate, is incorporated in the $PM_{2.5}$ fraction of pollution in China. The composition and density of these particles vary significantly both in time and space. Precursor emissions include gases such as SO_2, NO_x, and ammonia (NH_3). Combustion of coal and, to a lesser extent, oil and gas represent the primary sources for SO_2 and NO_x, while agriculture, animal husbandry, and, potentially, human waste are all involved in the production and emission of NH_3. A number of factors contribute to the severity of a particular pollution episode. First is the composition and intensity of the emissions. Second is the prevailing meteorological condition, which allows these emissions to be either dispersed or retained. Third is the photochemical state of the atmosphere at the time of emission, which can either enhance or retard the rate at which SO_2 and NO_x are converted to particle-forming sulfate and nitrate. If the episode is severe enough, it can begin to feed on itself. Absorption of sunlight by the aerosol component can warm the atmosphere aloft, at the same time cutting down on the intensity of sunlight reaching the surface. The net effect could be a cooler surface combined with a warmer atmosphere, leading to an increase in atmospheric stability and, as a result, more efficient trapping of pollution. The problem is evidently complex. It is essential, though, that it be addressed and at least moderated.

To return to the question posed in the title to this essay—can China successfully address the air-pollution and climate-change problems it faces—I conclude that the answer is yes. But it won't be easy. The immediate priority should be to target air pollution. Technological opportunities exist to limit emissions of conventional pollutants such as NO_x, SO_2, and particulates. They should be implemented as widely and rapidly as possible. It will be important also to promote research to advance understanding of the underlying physical and chemical processes. This can serve as an effective guide for future policy. In the long run, if we are successful in dealing with climate change, the problem of air pollution may be expected to fade into history. The bulk of the problems associated with air pollution relates to our use of fossil fuels. Transitioning to an energy system based on a combination of wind, solar, hydro, nuclear, and geothermal—rather than coal, oil, and natural gas—will go a long way toward clearing the air.

| IS THERE ENVIRONMENTAL

AWARENESS IN CHINA?

Karen Thornber

THE SIMPLE ANSWER to this question is yes, environmental consciousness is quite strong in China, and it has grown significantly in the past decade. Most notably, the nation's ever more educated and wealthy urban population is demanding a better quality of life for themselves and their children. Particularly concerning to Chinese of all classes is air pollution, which is becoming more and more disruptive and at times is so severe that cities are brought to a standstill, with airports and highways closed. Slowing if not reversing climate change is also a priority. Chinese president Xi Jinping's opening plenary speech at the World Economic Forum in January 2017 positioned China as a leader in the global fight against climate change, even as the United States appears likely to withdraw from this role.

Recent reports rank China a dismal ninety-first in the world in Internet speed, while the government restricts access to numerous segments of the Internet. Yet social media—especially Weibo (Chinese Twitter) and Weixin (WeChat)—have greatly facilitated discussion and debate in China on environmental crises. Literature also has contributed to rising environmental consciousness and activism. Creative writers such as worldwide sensation Yan Lianke ruthlessly satirize the seeming obsession of Chinese authorities with economic growth and wealth at all costs. Especially noteworthy in this respect is Yan Lianke's recent novel *Explosion Chronicles* (*Zhalie zhi*), which describes the transformation of Explosion from a small mountain hamlet into a megacity. This novel exposes and sharply critiques the relentless drive for economic dominance that has severely compromised human health, scarred China's landscapes, and contributed to devastating pollution and global warming.

Film has had an even greater impact in strengthening Chinese environmental awareness. Former China Central Television journalist Chai Jing's self-financed documentary film *Under the Dome* (*Qiongding zhi xia*), a penetrating if not entirely accurate exposé of air pollution in China along the lines of Al Gore's *An Inconvenient Truth* (2006), was viewed more than 150 million times within three days of its release in 2015. At first, *Under the Dome* escaped censorship. China's Minister of Environmental Protection Chen Jining initially praised the film, drawing parallels with Rachel Carson's monumental book *Silent Spring* (1962). Chinese officials likely promoted Chai Jing's film because it focuses on the China National Petroleum Company, a target of Chinese president Xi Jinping's anti-corruption campaign, and because, as has been reported in the press, the government viewed the film as a way to use public opinion to its advantage for promoting tougher measures for combating pollution. Yet within a week of its release, after it had been viewed more than 300 million times, *Under the Dome* was ordered removed from Chinese websites.

Despite such censorship, popular environmental consciousness probably has never been greater in China than it is today. The Chinese people are talking about environmental challenges and protesting environmental destruction more than ever before, while Chinese writers, film directors, visual artists, and other creative producers are addressing environmental degradation on a seemingly unprecedented scale. Furthermore, as historian Prasenjit Duara has noted, China's government is committed to environmental education, mandating it in the nation's public schools since 2003. To be sure, environmental courses are not always taken seriously because the material covered is not on the college entrance examinations, but this curriculum does introduce Chinese children to some of the challenges they are inheriting. Moreover, the struggles of grassroots environmentalists, often inspired by China's writers and artists, have met with some success. For instance, former president Hu Jintao in 2007 advocated that "ecological civilization" replace economic development as the nation's core focus, and in 2008 the State Environmental Protection Agency gained full ministerial status, with local environmental protection branches set up across the country.

But what about earlier environmental consciousness in China? Chinese for millennia have engaged in ecologically unsustainable practices, everything from massive deforestation to sizable hydro-engineering projects (such as canals, irrigation systems, and dams), terracing ever steeper slopes, and developing technologies that increasingly allowed communities to shape their environments. But throughout China's history, concern for the environment has accompanied ecological destruction.

Nascent environmental consciousness in China dates to well before the ancient philosopher Mencius (372–289 BCE), who famously declared: "If nets of fine mesh do not enter pools and ponds, there will be more fish and turtles than we can consume. If axes enter the hills and forests only at the proper times, there will be more wood than we can use." To give an earlier example, Guan Zhong, a prime minister during the Eastern Zhou dynasty more than two thousand years ago, cautioned Chinese "not to raise too many cattle on the grassland, lest it fail to recover from over exploitation; and not to plant crops too close together, otherwise the fertility of the soil would be insufficient." And the *Huainanzi*, an essay collection of similar vintage, declares that those who prospered were careful not to deforest, overhunt, overfish, or otherwise abuse the environment. For its part, radical environmental sentiment in China dates at least to the eighth-century writer Han Yu, who decried people who destroyed nature by plowing, felling, drilling, digging, and building; he argued provocatively that reducing the human population would benefit both heaven and earth.

To be sure, much early Chinese writing and painting does not question human treatment of the environment. Instead it celebrates the beauties of nature and provides an often distorted, idealistic view of people as intimately connected to the natural world. Some creative texts—including poems in China's first poetry anthology—even go so far as to celebrate human destruction of nature. One such poem declares that heaven created a state in the very place that people had uprooted all the oak trees and cleared the pines and cypresses. Indeed, razing the land for agriculture was an important marker of becoming civilized; peoples the early Chinese perceived as barbarians called attention to their deforesting prowess as proof of their own progress.

But in many parts of China, the consequences of so doing could be fatal. A Ming dynasty poet four centuries ago wrote:

It's easy to exhaust the pines and bamboos,
and the grasses and weeds don't grow enough . . .

When we traveled through the mountains last month,
the trees on the mountains appeared to pile up together,
but now that we've come down from the mountains,
we see afar they're sharp and bare.

The farmers have nothing to use as fuel,
so they set on fire the axles of their water carts.

This text is based on a landscape (the lower Yangzi River region) that had been subjected to millennia of human transformation and, during the seventeenth century, was consistently unable to meet human demands.

A century later, Wang Taiyue's poem "Laments of the Copper Hills" describes mines that have been exhausted and forests that are no more, warning of the consequences of continued human destruction of nature:

> The mining paths go deeper and deeper every day . . .
> What once was just a morning's work,
> now takes at least ten days.

> The lumber too has grown increasingly scarce,
> the woodlands resemble clean-shaven heads.
> For the first time they regret that all this logging, day after
> 　　day
> has left them without the firewood they need . . .

> So fertile are the hills and seas
> that it seems ridiculous to ask whether they flourish only
> 　　when protected by disaster . . .
> But if people take everything, if they have no restraint,
> then they will exhaust heaven and earth.

Read literally, the poem's concern extends beyond the woodlands to the biosphere more generally. It depicts not a flourishing environment, nor even one whose damaged areas are relatively contained, but instead a world threatened by a growing human population with ever increasing demands. The poem acknowledges that calling for caution might appear absurd, given how fertile much of the natural world remains, but it stresses that people have the capacity to wreak irreparable harm and warns that they will be left with nothing if current behaviors continue unabated.

Similar concerns were voiced in the following centuries, as Chinese authorities sanctioned, and often explicitly ordered, vast destruction of the country's landscapes. Official rhetoric surrounding the Great Leap Forward (1958–1961) and the Great Proletarian Cultural Revolution (1966–1976) was striking in its overt antagonism toward nature. As is well known, the Chinese Communist Party launched a literal "war on nature" to "defeat nature," declaring that "shock troops" were to reclaim grasslands and that wilderness was to be opened to plant grains. After the death of Mao Zedong in 1976, Chinese leaders no longer spoke so explicitly of a war on nature and in fact issued propaganda posters urging people to "green the motherland," "plant trees and make green," and "cherish greening and treasure old and famous trees." But they believed ecological protection to be incompatible with economic growth and did little to safeguard the nation's environment.

China's unchecked industrialization under Deng Xiaoping and subsequent leaders has resulted in some of the world's most polluted air, water, and land. China's sustained economic growth in the past few decades has radically improved living standards for millions, but the environmental costs have been staggeringly high. Matthew E. Kahn and Siqi Zheng provide statistics: in 2012, 57 percent of the groundwater in 198 Chinese cities was officially rated "bad" or "extremely bad," and more than 30 percent of China's rivers were labeled "polluted" or "seriously polluted." Similarly, in early 2013, smog in northern China measured more than forty times greater than what the World Health Organization has deemed healthy; only 1 percent of China's urban population lives in cities that meet the air quality standards of the European Union. China is now the world's largest emitter of greenhouse gases.

Even as China's central government signs international environmental agreements in a bid to achieve global legitimacy and, ultimately, leadership, problems persist at the municipal and provincial levels, where local officials often ignore regulations from Beijing because of their ties to local industrialists. As frequently is noted, increasing wealth remains for many the top priority, in China and globally. So the juggling act continues, with China's long-term environmental prognosis uncertain but with the environmental consciousness of its people unlikely to diminish anytime soon.

V | SOCIETY

22 | WHY DOES THE END OF THE ONE-CHILD POLICY MATTER?

Susan Greenhalgh

IN OCTOBER 2015, thirty-five years and one month after it was launched with a dramatic Open Letter to all Communist Party members, the policy advocating one child for all was quietly ended with a terse announcement from the Party's Central Committee that, as of January 1, 2016, all married couples would be allowed to have two children.

Some have seen the end of the notorious one-child policy as a momentous change for China and its people. But is it? Journalists and many scholars have treated it as simply a demographic measure, yet the one-child policy was much more than that. Designed to upgrade the "quality" of China's population as well as limit its quantity, the one-child policy was the centerpiece of a gigantic, sprawling state project that sought to transform China's backward masses into a competitive labor force and modern citizenry befitting a global power. In seeking the meaning of its demise, we need to consider this larger context.

EFFECTS, PLUS AND (MOSTLY) MINUS

The one-child policy was the harshest and most unpopular fertility policy ever imposed on a large national population. Though it was deeply flawed—it was neither demographically necessary nor politically feasible—the state was determined to enforce it, with exceptions allowing couples in certain circumstances to have two, no matter what. Not surprisingly, the policy profoundly remade China and its people.

Some of the effects were generally positive. Although the impact on fertility was relatively modest and hard to assess—the state's claim that it averted 400 million births is inflated by at least 50 percent—the quantity-quality project, working with market forces and societal changes, created a generation of well-educated, healthy, savvy global citizens able to lead China to global prominence. It also modernized Chinese society, creating a population with the social and demographic profile of a modern nation.

Yet the human costs of those achievements have been monumental. How can one measure the costs to the health and psyches of rural women whose bodies for decades bore the brunt of the policy? How does one gauge the impact of the loss of female life snuffed out through infanticide and, later, routinized abortion of female fetuses by women desperate for a son? How does one grasp the enormity of the loss suffered by parents when their hopes for a family are crushed or when their single child is lost? These kinds of damage are incalculable and irreparable.

Reproductive modernization created not only individuals who fit the new, modern, supposedly scientific norms (the "quality child," the "good scientific mother," and so on), but also deviants, so-called "backward" persons who, because they fell outside the norms, were excluded from the state's regime of social welfare and virtue. One huge category of have-nots includes couples who violated the policy and carried an unauthorized pregnancy to term. While the parents were subject to strong state sanctions, their unplanned offspring, known as "black children," suffered even more. Unless their parents managed to get them a household registration (essentially identity papers), unplanned children have been treated as nonpersons and deprived of state benefits, from schooling and health care to the right to work, marry, and even die. Another type of "unmodern person" includes those who have rejected the state's conservative norms on reproduction, sexuality, and marriage. Gay couples, unmarried mothers, and childless adults have lived lives of social exclusion and faced intense social pressure to conform.

The policy also distorted the population structure, accelerating aging, emptying out working-age members, and leaving the generation of single children, numbering over 150 million, with the burden of caring for their aging parents on their own. Reflecting many villagers' preference for sons, the policy also produced a huge gender gap among infants: 119 boys to 100 girls, among the highest in the world. While women have married up the social ladder, some twenty to forty million men, mostly at the bottom of the social hierarchy, have remained unwed, unable to marry in the culturally acceptable ways. Known as "bare branches," they are consigned to live lives beyond the pale.

MORE FREEDOM AND MORE BABIES?

What difference does it make, then, that the one-child policy has now been abandoned? Two main answers have been advanced: more freedom and more babies.

The Western media have cheered the CCP's decision, calling it the end of decades of "brutal horror" (in the words of the *Boston Globe*) and the beginning of a new era of reproductive freedom for Chinese couples. Setting aside the problematic assumptions buried in these assertions (that China is unfree and America, the implicit foil, is free, or that the policy has not essentially changed in thirty-five years), let us consider this widespread claim. A close look at how

the policy fits into China's political discourse and governance structures suggests that, without other changes, ending the one-child
policy will not enlarge the circle of reproductive freedom very much.

The official rationale for the policy shift makes clear that it had
nothing to do with reproductive rights and everything to do with
tackling demographic changes—especially the decline in the working-
age population and increase in the elderly that threaten China's plans
to move into the ranks of prosperous, highly developed countries.
Since the early 1980s, population has been deemed a "strategic area
of long-term state interest." Even if the policy were liberalized further (to include unmarried couples or to allow three children, for
example), it would not substantially expand reproductive freedom
for individuals, since population is of overriding interest to the state.
Since the early 1970s, population planning has been part of development planning. Unlike in other countries, where family planning
programs encourage couples to plan out their childbearing, under China's state birth planning program the state determines the number of
births couples should have to meet the needs of the country. (The term
"family planning" is a misnomer in the Chinese context.) Birth planning remains one of a handful of "basic state policies" to which, President Xi Jinping declared in May 2016, China must adhere for the
long term.

China has not abandoned the state planning of births. Although
the central government profile of the State Birth Planning Commission, formed in 1983, was lowered by its 2013 merger with the Ministry
of Health, the apparatus of state birth planning remains in place.
That includes state monitoring of births, social compensation fees for
violators, sanctions against officials whose localities exceed birth
limits, a national law and countless regulations on population, plus
state and quasi-state birth planning bureaucracies hundreds of millions strong. In making the policy change, the state neither redefined

the population project nor dismantled the institutional and legal structures guiding birth work; instead, it simply made an incremental "adjustment" in the rules on births, from allowing two children for couples in which one member is a single child (a 2013 innovation) to allowing two for all couples.

China's population and development planners clearly hope that the policy change will spur a baby boom to push the fertility rate—now an unsustainable 1.7 births per woman—upward. (Experts agree that a 2.1 child per mother rate is needed to avoid population decline.) China's recent history of policy tinkering suggests that any uptick in the birthrate is likely to be small. Of the eleven million couples eligible to have two children under the 2013 policy relaxation, only 15 percent opted to do so. In major metropolises the numbers were half that. Although many couples still dream of having a "complete family" of one son and one daughter, the economic demands of raising a quality single child place that dream off limits to all but the very rich. Like growing numbers of countries, which have tried but failed to raise births from rock-bottom levels, China is likely to be stuck with ultralow fertility for a long time to come.

FROM STATE TO MARKET: DANGERS AHEAD

If the policy shift will bring neither reproductive freedom nor renewed population growth, what difference will it make, and should it be cause for celebration or concern? Playing the contrarian, I want to suggest that reduced state control carries risks, for the power of the state is being replaced by the power of the market. Having the market shape reproductive ideas and practices may seem preferable, since market forces work indirectly (and mostly invisibly) by changing individual desires. Yet the market has insidious effects. In creating the policy rules, the state, for all its heavy-handedness, had to consider fairness across social sectors in order to limit collective protest. Though it was enforced raggedly and sometimes not at all, the official norm was one of equity—shared suffering—in which an entire generation was asked to sacrifice for the good of future generations. In the market, by contrast, the de facto norm is inequality based on ability to pay, and the result is a widening gap between rich and poor.

Especially since the 1990s, when China decisively embraced the global market, market forces and consumer norms have played an ever-widening role in reproduction, creating a vast gulf between the reproductive haves and have-nots. Many of these trends are actively opposed by the state, but to little avail. One thing money can now buy is "excess" children, which have become major status symbols. Even as the poor must comply with the birth rules to avoid heavy fines, the new class of wealthy celebrities—football star Hao Haidong and filmmaker Zhang Yimou are among the most visible—have openly violated the one-child rule, happily paying the fines to get the number of children they desire.

Another thing money can buy is top-of-the-line health care for young mothers. If, in the 1980s and 1990s, the good mother was one who sacrificed herself to give birth to a quality child, today she is one who spends heavily to pamper herself while receiving customized reproductive health and beauty services at one of China's new maternal spas. Traditional postpartum practices of "sitting the month" have also been recast as an arena of class competition. While the rich may pay $30,000 to spend their twenty-eight days of confinement in opulent maternal palaces with round-the-clock care, the middle class must settle for nannies who help out at home, and the poor may get no postpartum rest at all.

For the rich, money can also solve the problem of infertility, which has risen rapidly in recent years. Although surrogacy is illegal, parents able to pay up to $240,000 and willing to accept the risks have the option of hiring a surrogate to carry their child. Money can also buy an American birth. Birth tourism is big business, especially in California, and couples willing to pay $60,000 and fortunate enough to escape the police crackdowns can give birth to an American citizen, gaining the promise of green cards in the future. With the end of the one-child policy, the motor force behind reproduction will shift even further in the direction of the market, widening the already large class divides in health care, family size, and social status.

OPPORTUNITIES TO DEMONSTRATE GLOBAL GOOD CITIZENSHIP

Much of the world has viewed China's compulsory birth policy as a blatant violation of the international ethical norm that a couple has the right to freely choose the number of children it has. Those creating the one-child policy saw things differently. By quickly reducing the growth rate of the world's largest population, they thought, China would contribute importantly to the welfare of the world, gaining respect as a responsible and ethical member of the community of nations. Those hopes were soon dashed, however, as news spread of widespread human rights abuses in the early 1980s, and concerns about the constructive ends of fertility control were drowned out by concerns about the intolerable means used to achieve them.

Little known outside China, since the mid-1990s, program leaders have been working hard to remove abusive practices and improve the program's legitimacy by gradually bringing it into line with internationally accepted practice. Childbearing preferences have fallen to historic lows, making coercive methods increasingly unnecessary. Although the one-child policy is now gone, ethical concerns persist because the adverse social legacies of the birth program have not been addressed, or even acknowledged. By taking steps to undo some of the policy's worst social effects, China has an opportunity now to demonstrate global good citizenship and earn the praise it believes it deserves. Among the many meaningful steps it could—and should—take, three stand out.

First, the Party-state should move quickly to right the wrongs done to those born outside the birth plan by giving them household registrations and ensuring they have access to all the benefits of citizenship. Second, it should ease the problems of the "bare-branches" by recognizing them as victims of the one-child policy (or, in state discourse, "sacrificers for the nation") and providing the social and economic assistance they need to participate fully in social life. Third, the regime should abandon the rigidly conservative posture toward family structure that underlay the one-child policy, in which only heterosexual married couples were recognized as worthy of official reproductive support. By expanding the circle of those deserving reproductive care to include gay couples, single women (and men), and others of non-normative genders, sexualities, and family structures, the state could take important steps in the direction of social progress and equity, and perhaps even raise the birthrate. By such action, the state would not only ensure that the end of the one-child policy was more than symbolic, it also would send a message about new social priorities, finally earning the international recognition it has long sought for its work on reproduction and population.

23 | HOW ARE CHINA AND ITS MIDDLE CLASS HANDLING AGING AND MENTAL HEALTH?

Arthur Kleinman

By 2040, an extraordinary condition will materialize in Asia: societies will reach a new demographic reality never experienced before in human history. Japan will be the first society in which adults aged 60 years and older will comprise 40 percent of the total population. China will not be far behind at 25 percent, and growing fast. But whereas, at present, more than seven Chinese workers support each retiree financially, by 2040, that number will be less than two, creating a crisis in social welfare support. Moreover, as in the United States, one quarter or more of all Chinese will (and nearly now already do) suffer from depression, anxiety, substance abuse, dementia, or some other mental health condition in the course of their lives. And to respond to these problems, China is now making and will continue to create entirely new social policies and health programs: policies and programs not only of social significance but of economic and political importance as well. Hence, these two interrelated global conditions—aging and mental health—will come to play a large and influential role in how we understand Chinese society and the Chinese, both in themselves and in the world.

Consider the present Chinese context for such challenging social problems and responses, and how China appears whenever we make these issues more central to Chinese studies. As China has become a wealthier, more urban, and more globalized society, it has impressed many that the building of a new middle class is one of the truly transformational developments that is most influential yet still poorly understood. Numbering somewhere between 200 million and 350 million, this group of business people, professionals, technicians, high skilled workers, and other reasonably well-educated and well-traveled individuals is at the forefront of a nationwide movement demanding higher standards and better quality in everything from food and drugs to professional and business ethical practices. It is no surprise, then, that this orientation is especially salient when it comes to the aging and mental health fields.

Aging, to begin with, is associated with higher rates of chronic noncommunicable diseases such as diabetes, cardiovascular disease, cancer, and depression. Causing pain, serious disablement, and death, these diseases are a major burden on health-care systems and families. People in the older adult age-bracket use health services at a substantially higher rate, which costs them and their families time, energy, and money. In addition, middle-class older adults are particularly concerned with the quality of care they receive. And their criticisms, based on common experiences of poor care and doctors who are more interested in earning money than relieving suffering, have helped fuel the distrust of doctors that has reached crisis proportions in China today. This distrust pressed the Chinese government to rework health insurance and the health system itself.

The eldercare conundrum for the lives of millions of middle-class Chinese is: how to provide quality care for aged and disabled parents when both husband and wife work, home health-care aides are untrained and in short supply, and assisted living facilities and nursing

homes are limited and of dubious quality? This latter problem is ac-
centuated and made more difficult in cases of dementia, because only
now has China embarked upon building high-quality dementia care
facilities. The moral and emotional problem of institutionalizing the
elderly is made more troubling still because of the influential Confucian norms of revering and caring for the elderly at home. Commentators often point to eldercare as a test of traditional values in
modern society.

Many of the problems facing social welfare agencies in China result from this core conundrum of caregiving being caught between
family and institutions. Resolving this vexing concern is not only a
matter of increasing technical and financial resources for aging, but
also involves moral and political concerns about what is an adequate
life in today's China. What is an acceptable system of eldercare? What
constitutes quality care? How should retirement and social welfare
supports be changed? And what does a good death mean? We can
feel the resonance with similar concerns in the United States and Europe, yet the Chinese context lends this globalized condition so distinctive a quality that the responses of Western societies seem more
limited and less appropriate. How China creates policy and program
responses will alter Chinese society and may have a global influence.

Similar to aging and eldercare challenges, mental health problems open a revealing window on Chinese society and offer a special
view of its problems and prospects. When I first visited China in 1978,
the minister of health, parroting a propagandist and utterly absurd
party line, informed me that there were no mentally ill patients in
China, because China was a communist culture without the capitalist sources of mental health problems. And in 1980, when I began
field research in Changsha at the old Yale-in-China Medical School,
less than 1 percent of patients carried a diagnosis of depression. The
research I conducted helped change this false picture by showing that

many patients with the anachronistic wastebasket diagnosis of neur-asthenia, which was a leading diagnosis at that time, could be re-diagnosed as suffering from depression and effectively treated with common psychological and chemical treatments. A 2001–2005 survey of four provinces documents that the rate of depression and other common mental health problems is of the same magnitude as in the United States. There is widespread concern with autism in children, eating disorders and substance abuse among adolescents, depression among patients with diabetes and cancer, and dementia among the aged. Again, this is not a dissimilar picture to the United States or Europe. And Chinese psychiatry has modernized so that the treat-ments heretofore regarded as "Western" are now global and increas-ingly available to Chinese sufferers.

While the stigma associated with psychoses (schizophrenia and bipolar disorder), which leads to discrimination, abuse, and enormous family burdens, remains an important human rights issue, the situa-tion for depression and anxiety is changing rapidly with increasing public awareness (especially in large, predominantly middle-class cities), earlier use of available mental health services, and interest in psychotherapy and self-help. As a visit to a Chinese bookstore will attest, there is today growing sophistication among readers in intel-lectual engagement with psychology and psychological treatments, and in the emotional, moral, and social implications of China's transition to a middle-class society.

As I have outlined elsewhere, individual Chinese are engaging in a variety of quests for meaning, including inner searches for hap-piness, justice, gender equality, sexual identity, religious and spiri-tual values, and new forms of subjectivity. In each of these domains, we are witnessing both the revivification of traditional pathways and the opening up of more globalized ways of living as an individual in the twenty-first century. As scholars have shown, this story of progressive individualization, in a culture and polity long defined by collectivist orientations, represents a highly significant generational change, one that is expressed in major societal movements from consumerism and materialism to cultural and technological innovations in the arts and social media.

The broader implications of these personal quests for meaning are substantial and potentially revolutionary. We need to begin thinking of the Chinese self as not just more individuated, but, especially among youth and young adults, a different, more globally connected personhood. This self is less caught up on contradictions between tradition and modernity, and much more fluid in negotiating different cultural imperatives and social relationships. It is still highly pragmatic, but it is more layered than divided, or, put differently, made less anguished by and more facile in handling divisions between desire and obligation, hierarchical relations of authority, and horizontal relations of love and friendship, choice and responsibility, past and future orientation, and so forth. So there is an agile shifting between these alternatives, and the anxiety has been taken out of the alternatives. It is the shifting itself that is the new reality.

This Chinese self in the future will be the dominant self-orientation of the middle class. It will come to be the normal self of future leaders in business and the professions and circles of political power. While some social theorists advance the attractive, though superficial, idea that such widespread changes in personhood respond to the requirements and opportunities of a neoliberal political economy, this global studies perspective needs to be balanced by a deeper appreciation of how the changing Chinese moral and emotional context is creating a distinctive kind of subjectivity, one in which the lineaments of tradition are not so much being superseded or replaced but mixed with these new orientations. The upshot is the kind of contradiction and irony that Chinese novelists and filmmakers become preoccupied with today. But it is also well represented by the widespread use of techniques of "layering" by contemporary artists. The latter represent both the tensions and possibilities of the collective cultural expressions of multiple, non-unified orientations existing side by side. The very nature of this multiplicity is greater sophistication, more tolerance of difference and ambiguity, a practical critical stance that makes misplaced loyalty, if not less likely, then less likely to be consequential, and an openness to new realities with fewer requirements for defensive nativism. One can see this selfhood at work among young Chinese students who are comfortable being both globalized and local. I also believe we see it at work in the more useful channeling of the widespread societal distrust into practical demands for higher-quality services.

Of course, whether the political system will build on this subjectivity or seek to control and discipline it remains an open question. But I believe that this new moral and emotional orientation of the ever-enlarging middle class is much more promising for the future. Even political liberalization (with a Chinese face, of course) is made more feasible, in spite of what the current repressive political climate and slowing economic growth would portend. After almost a half-century of studying Chinese society up close, I have come to recognize not just the emerging crises of aging and mental health; I now also see how those perspectives enrich our view of what the Chinese are becoming, what they must face in ordinary life, and, most important of all, how the moral and emotional sides of the subjectivity of ordinary Chinese are refashioning culture, social relationships, and everyday life.

Take what is happening in health-care policy, for example. The government has moved to provide insurance coverage for catastrophic health events and treatment systems for serious chronic illness, so as to reduce the large financial burden on families, which, in rural areas, often leads to bankruptcy and even suicide. For the same reason, health policies and programs are now organized around an emerging primary care option in which each person has his or her own provider. This is an entirely new model of professional caregiving. Even the barefoot doctors of the 1960s and 1970s were not true primary care physicians but, despite their importance, very low level public health and emergency workers. This new medical model is an excellent fit with the demands of patients for higher quality care and a highly appropriate, if difficult to realize, response to the patient-doctor distrust crisis. It means that, rather than contending with long lines of patients waiting to see hospital-based experts for a few minutes, patients will, in principle, be able to be screened, referred, and given integrated, comprehensive care—a middle-class approach if ever there were one. There is already evidence of a similar, middle-class responsiveness of government policies in the areas of food and drug regulation, smoking cessation, environmental health standards, and best-practices requirements for doctors and nurses. All are examples at the level of political governance of the impact of the processes I have described above. And all—even in an early stage—are promising.

Of course, the picture for China as a whole is mixed. I have emphasized the positive changes because there is a tendency for American and European commentators to approach Chinese society with an overly critical, ideologically negative viewpoint, and, in contrast, the health field provides, over the long term, a more nuanced and generally more positive perspective. The unprecedented reduction in poverty and creation of wealth are associated over the decades with great gains in longevity, improved health status, and the building of modernized health care and public health systems.

Now, as China faces the need for improved eldercare, a number of forces are at play that will determine how patients with dementia

and their families fare. Businesspeople are at work building retirement, assisted living, and nursing home facilities. It is yet to be seen
whether these will be serious contributions to the public's health or
new ways of extracting wealth, as the country transforms itself from
a manufacturing to a service-industry economy. Indeed, the aging
and health fields offer an unparalleled vision of how this new service
economy will look in the actual lived experience of Chinese people
and the real practices of China's businessmen, bureaucrats, and professionals who will cater to their needs and desires. Professionals are
using technology and equipment to scale up higher-level intervention programs for elderly adults with complex, co-morbid medical
conditions. Scientists are drawing upon stem cell technology to develop new ways of replacing failed organs and aging body parts. IVF
is flourishing. So entrepreneurial have bioscience researchers become
that medical tourism to China by wealthy Asians, Middle Easterners,
Europeans, and Americans is booming. Meanwhile, for the very first
time, the Chinese government is treating mental health problems as
a major public health concern: increasing awareness, popularizing
screening, raising professional standards, and sharing information
once treated as state secrets with leading international organizations.
The outcome of these and many other related developments is not
certain, but it is clear that these issues have become just as important
in China as they are in the United States.

And yet—the Chinese policy, regulatory, institutional, and
popular approaches are a mixture of things culturally Chinese and
global. And that is why historians, anthropologists, and language specialists, knowledgeable of what is local and traditional, are as relevant today as global health and bioscience experts, as well as global
studies professionals in fields as various as global trade, global environment, and international relations. This is the new world that we
need to study, and it is here to stay.

24 | HOW IMPORTANT IS RELIGION IN CHINA?

James Robson

IF AN ESSAY assessing the importance of religion in China had been written sixty years ago, the author might have been forgiven for concluding that religion was insignificant. During the 1920s, Hu Shih, a leading Chinese public intellectual, had famously proclaimed that "China is a country without religion and the Chinese are a people who are not bound by religious superstitions." That Western observers would largely follow Hu's and other Chinese elites' assessment about the fate of Chinese religion was due in part to the way his narrative corresponded with the problematic Western theory of how modernization would lead to secularization.

Hu's stark claims might best be understood, however, as the wishful thinking of a modern intellectual attempting to orchestrate China's transition into modernity by focusing on science and education rather than on China's traditional religious past. Hu's comments came as the Chinese state had embarked on a series of traumatic, anti-superstition campaigns that raged from the 1920s into the 1930s. By then, the Chinese state had already begun to implement the Western categories of "religion" and "superstition." Beliefs and practices fitting into the newly instituted category of religion, whose contours were largely modeled on the supposedly shared characteristics of "world religions" (including sacred founders and texts, hierarchical institutional structures, and clearly designated centers for the practice of religion), were to be tolerated. But diffused practices that did not fit neatly into the category of orthodox religion, including most traditional Chinese religious practices, were all marked as heterodox superstitions that needed to be eradicated.

The anti-superstition campaigns followed closely on the heels of an earlier "build schools with temple property" campaign that began in the waning days of the Qing dynasty, which ended in 1911, and continued into the new Republican era that followed. Between the Communist Revolution in 1949 and the end of the Cultural Revolution in 1976, the vast majority of China's religious institutions, including temples, churches, local shrines, and spirit writing altars, had their resources seized and were dramatically reduced in size, destroyed, or repurposed.

The state attitude toward religion in the late nineteenth century caused a radical reshaping of the Chinese religious landscape. Prior to the inauguration of reforms in 1898, Chinese local society was suffused with ascriptive religious affiliations that provided organization and meaning for individuals, families, and communities. The Chinese landscape and calendar were filled with sacred places for pilgrimage and sacred times for communal rituals and festivals. All of that changed in the most dramatic ways during the late nineteenth and early twentieth centuries. It is not possible to understand the importance of contemporary Chinese religion without taking into account the radical reformulation of religion that occurred at that time.

After the establishment of the People's Republic in 1949, it looked as if China's government were entering into a period of relative religious freedom, since it guaranteed the individual right to religious belief. This "religious freedom" was, however, a tightly controlled semblance of freedom, since the only acceptable versions had to be in accord with the state's new definitions, while religious practices had to remain within the law and not threaten social order. In the face of these new conditions, some religions, especially those that shared the characteristics of modern world religions, such as Buddhism, attempted to define themselves as being in accord with the state's definition of orthodox religion and also began to establish, or in some cases revive, official national associations. The Chinese Buddhist Association was founded in 1953, the Three-Self Patriotic Movement (representing the Protestant Church in China) was established in 1954, the Islamic Association of China was established in 1954, and the Daoist Association was instituted in 1957—the same year that Catholics, in defiance of the Pope, set up the Chinese Catholic Patriotic Association. Such national organizations provided official legitimacy for those traditions while also fostering state oversight of them. Indeed, the state established a Bureau of Religious Affairs in 1954 to implement its policies and ensure that its directives would be transmitted to members through the national associations. The situation was, however, very different for the diffused, local religious traditions. Since they did not have such organizations, they came to be classified as superstitions subject to critique and censure.

As the 1950s came to a close, no one was prepared for the sheer scale and severity of the religious destruction that was to follow. During the Anti-Rightist Campaign and the Great Leap Forward, both in the late 1950s, religious groups were subjected to ruthless attacks and had their property confiscated or destroyed. A brief respite came in 1962, when the Chinese Communist Party (CCP) critiqued the excesses of the traumatic Great Leap Forward, and restrictions on religion were loosened. That freedom did not last long. When the Cultural Revolution began in 1966, religion again came under fierce attack. The period from 1966 to 1976 was a traumatic time for all religious institutions and clerics, as temples were destroyed by marauding gangs of young Red Guards, and clerics were subject to ridicule, persecution, and physical violence.

Was religion now dead and gone in China, as some scholars and commentators in the 1970s concluded? While some even today would answer that question in the affirmative—and many in the media still register disbelief when results of new surveys are released—recent developments would suggest otherwise. Perhaps the only thing more shocking for some observers than the widespread destruction of religion through the mid-1970s was the sudden and dramatic revival and reconstitution of religion that began in the 1980s. The paroxysms of destruction unleashed by the Cultural Revolution had subsided by 1976. Previously antagonistic policies were repudiated, and, under national leader Deng Xiaoping, religion began to enjoy a revival. New government policies begun in this period created the context for the increased importance of religion for both the state and individuals in contemporary China.

Like the earlier policies, the Chinese Constitution of 1982 guarantees the people's right to believe in legitimate religion, as well as the right not to believe. Yet much hinges on the interpretation of what constitutes a "legitimate religion." In general, the state has maintained prohibitions against religions that disrupt public order, impair health, obstruct education, or are dominated by foreign interests. During the 1980s, China began to enjoy freedom of religion once again, but that freedom has also been hemmed in by constraints due to the CCP's ongoing fears about the potential threat to social order. That said, the CCP has also gradually recognized some of the economic and social benefits that orthodox religions could offer the state. It understood that religion could help foster social order and build what the previous administration called a "harmonious society." The state also attempted to harness the organizational capacities of the major religions, such as Buddhism, since they had witnessed how these could assist with charities and social services, such as the building of hospitals, schools, and convalescent homes.

Official acceptance and recognition has come rather easily for the major orthodox religions, but it has been much more difficult for small-scale, diffused local religious traditions. I still vividly recall a late-1980s trip into the countryside of Hunan Province; during a short break in the drive, I wandered out into a field to view a small local shrine. A few weeks later, on my return to the regional capital of Changsha, I asked to stop at the shrine, only to discover that it had been smashed and dismantled. This is just one small example of how a policy inimical to local religions was carried out across China until recently.

The Chinese government's attitude to local religious practice has shifted slowly as it has realized their importance. Indeed, an irony of the current situation is that local religious movements that had long suffered due to being categorized as heterodox superstitions have become sanctioned parts of China's "Intangible Cultural Heritage," "traditional culture," or "local customs." Those new affiliations have served to legitimatize and protect them from destruction. Further changes in the state's policies have included a rethinking of the status of "popular faith," further aiding local religious movements to exist and function in local society. This phenomenon has been a clever way for local traditions to align themselves with official policy and avoid being labeled a superstitious cult. This new experiment of trying to incorporate local religious movements into the sphere of orthodox religious practice is still being carried out and indicates that the state has begun to realize the profound importance of popular religion for local society. It is hoped that, one day, policy makers will realize that many problematic religious issues in contemporary China stem not from the actions of those groups, but from their attempt to apply Western categories of religion and superstition onto the Chinese religious landscape and enforce those artificial boundaries.

Even the most casual visitor today will witness the vibrant and active culture of the five major religions. China now has the largest number of Buddhists in the world. Daoism has undergone a rapid rise in recent years, and there is steady growth among Muslim, Catholic, and Protestant religious communities, even if some remain under the state's watchful eye. It is now common to hear, for example, that more Chinese attend church on Sundays than do all Europeans combined. In addition, and perhaps on a much larger scale, there are an immense number of vibrant local (mostly rural) religious traditions, ritual performances, and festivals. One can also encounter a revived Confucianism, diverse self-cultivation movements, redemptive societies (syncretic movements, which practice qigong-type practices and philanthropy, that flourished in the Republican Period and have persisted into the present), spirit writing groups, lay Buddhist groups proselytizing in vegetarian restaurants, yoga groups, and the presence of new religious groups such as the Bahá'í Faith, Mormonism, and the imported Japanese religion Soka Gakkai that is based on chanting the title of the *Lotus Sūtra*.

There is no question that the revival and growth of religion in China in the twentieth and twenty-first centuries have been dramatic. But such a revival represents more than merely the return of old-time religion; rather, it has involved the rise of something entirely new, embedded in new historical contexts, that provides a fertile field for the growth of religion. The repudiation of Marxist ideology and China's rapid economic transformation have inspired people to search for new meanings and orientations, leading to a dramatic social restructuring. In the so-called spiritual vacuum created by China's rapid modernization, urbanization, and internationalization, religion has become increasingly meaningful for individuals, especially those living in urban centers. They are no longer compelled to follow the traditional beliefs of their home villages, but can voluntarily choose, or experiment with, religions that interest them.

Contemporary scholars have noted a correlation between the modern shift to a market economy and the creation of a spiritual marketplace, just as the central planning in earlier years led to centralization of the five official religions. Nonetheless, if one were to travel from cities into rural China, the old-time communal religions that, for centuries, have structured and held together local societies are still of great importance. Chinese policies have reconfigured the contemporary religious landscape in profound ways that continue to have significant effects on what we witness today. As China draws on its past traditions and mixes them with new elements drawn from a variety of religious sources, it does so under constraints imposed in the late nineteenth and early twentieth centuries. But this new configuration of religion remains important and meaningful, albeit in different ways, for individuals, families, local communities, and the state.

Leonard W. J. van der Kuijp

THE INSTITUTION OF the Dalai Lama, arguably the most important and best known of the major reincarnation series that populate the Tibetan cultural area, can be traced to the late fifteenth century. But the very idea of a reincarnated *lama,* which means "teacher," goes back much earlier, and the reincarnated lama's presence is a special feature wherever Tibetan Buddhism is practiced: northern India; the northern regions of Nepal; the Tibetan Autonomous Region; northwestern Yunnan Province and large portions of Sichuan, Qinghai, and Gansu Provinces; Inner Mongolia; and, in Russia, the Republics of Kalmykia and Buryatia.

Based on certain interpretations of Buddhist thought, the earliest evidence of the idea of a reincarnated Tibetan lama dates to the twelfth century. The Tibetan term for such a reincarnation is *tulku,* which means something akin to "a wondrously manifest presence of enlightenment." During the Ming dynasty, this idea was translated into Chinese as "living Buddha," which was based on the mistaken idea that the *tulku* is an actual manifestation of the enlightened experience of Buddha, that is, *buddha* proper. An individual designated as a *tulku* is in fact considered to be almost a Buddha, and such an individual is known as a bodhisattva. While the bodhisattva's enlightened state is not as fully formed as *buddha,* it irrevocably progresses to the ultimate spiritual goal of Buddhist practice, to be *buddha.*

The title Dalai Lama originally refers to Sonam Gyatso (1543–1588), who was the third in a line of reincarnated teachers residing in the large Tibetan monastery of Draypung. The Mongol chieftain Altan Khan gave Sonam Gyatso the Mongol title *dalai lama*, meaning "oceanic teacher," after he accepted the Khan's invitation to meet with him in 1578 in Qinghai Province. He was thus the first of the reincarnated lamas who came to be called Dalai Lama.

The institution of the Dalai Lama is sectarian and belongs to the Gelugpa school of Tibetan Buddhism, now seated in the city of Lhasa. At some early point in Buddhist history, the Dalai Lama incarnation series was calculated backwards to the bodhisattva Avalokiteśvara, who had been a spiritual presence since a "beginningless beginning" atop Mount Potala in southern India. Avalokiteśvara represents the enlightened, compassionate aspect of *buddha* and is associated with the famous *Oṃ Maṇi Padma Hūṃ* mantra, among various other practices. For the devout, some sacred mountains are believed to be mobile rather than stationary objects, and the mountain on which the fifth Dalai Lama (1617–1682) built his residence was called Potala.

The Dalai Lamas are not considered the sole reincarnations of Avalokiteśvara. The Karmapa, or Black-hat hierarchs of the Karma Kagyüpa school of Tibetan Buddhism, as well as many significant lamas of other Tibetan Buddhist schools and sects, were considered to be reincarnations of this bodhisattva. The motif of a lama being considered a reincarnation of Avalokiteśvara is closely associated with the fact that, by the middle of the eleventh century, some Tibetans posited that Avalokiteśvara was the patron bodhisattva of the Tibetan area, whereas the other major bodhisattva, Mañjuśrī, was the patron bodhisattva of China. In fact, any Tibetan lama regarded as a particularly significant spiritual presence by various schools or sects could be designated a reincarnation of Avalokiteśvara.

Sonam Gyatso never returned to his home monastery in central Tibet. Instead, he traveled around northwestern China and Kham (eastern Tibet) at the invitation of several monasteries as well as Tibetan and Mongol notables. Upon his passing, the need arose to find his successor. Although we lack a clear account of how this was accomplished, we do know that the person in charge of identifying and finding Sonam Gyatso's successor was the steward of his estate, who visited the family controlling the Drigung monastery (the center of the Drigung sect of the Kagyüpa school) after the monastery's abbot let it be known that Sonam Gyatso's wife had just given birth to a son.

Except for the Gelugpa school, the major schools of Tibetan Buddhism do not require abbots to be celibate. The same holds for reincarnated lamas, although some chose to be celibate nevertheless. (The Gelugpa school's reincarnated lamas, as a rule, are celibate monks.) Sonam Gyatso's steward was not convinced of the Drigung family's candidacy—indeed, he probably wished to keep Draypung monastery's reincarnation line strictly within the Gelugpa school—and when he heard that Altan Khan's grandson had become the father of a newborn boy, he visited the Khan's encampment and recognized the baby as Sonam Gyatso's successor. He became the ineffectual Yonten Gyatso (1589–1617), the first reincarnation of a Tibetan lama who was not ethnically Tibetan.

But with the advent of the fifth Dalai Lama, the institution became a political powerhouse and the wealthiest of all such reincarnate institutions. He founded the Ganden Podrang government as a theocracy, and it was this government which, with ups and downs, the Dalai Lamas led. For some three centuries, the Ganden Podrang controlled or exerted a powerful influence over a large portion of the Tibetan cultural area, until it fell in 1959.

The economy of the Tibetan cultural area before 1959 was one in which monasteries and the landed aristocracy possessed most of the wealth, consisting mainly of land and cattle. (Families of the landed aristocracy were, in addition, often owners of monasteries and their estates.) Beyond farm profits, wealth accrued to the reincarnated lamas and monasteries through gifts offered in exchange for teaching or initiation into an esoteric practice. Buddhist notions of gifts and generosity were imported from the Indian subcontinent and China, when Buddhism began migrating to the Tibetan area from these regions in the eighth century. Ultimately, Tibetan Buddhism became thoroughly Indic, although some traces of Chinese Buddhism are still detectable.

Roughly, the concept of the gift in Buddhism concerns the expected offering rendered in return for a requested teaching or practice. The wealthier the person requesting instruction or initiation, the greater the expectation that a gift will be offered—and, often, the greater the size of the gift expected. Gifts could be monetary, but more often involved property such as land and cattle. All such gifts were minutely recorded, registered, and archived; management teams were needed to oversee and administer gifts as they accumulated over time. This gave rise to the notion of the *labrang*, a bureaucracy preeminently associated with the reincarnation series to which a given incarnated lama belongs. Some large monasteries may have a number of *labrangs*, depending on how many incarnated lamas reside there.

The Tibetan record indicates that in the thirteenth century, the Mongol ruler Kublai Khan offered his teacher, Lama Phagpa, the territory of central Tibet in return for initiation into esoteric Buddhist practices, and in addition rewarded him with the titles and offices of National Preceptor and Imperial Preceptor. Much later, when the fifth Dalai Lama traveled to Beijing in 1652 and 1653 to visit the young Shunzhi emperor at the Qing court, he traveled through the vast nomadic areas of northwest China that had large Tibetan and Mongol populations. His autobiography states that, capitalizing on the idea that he was a reincarnation of Avalokiteśvara, he accumulated enormous wealth by giving teachings and instructions in the practice of evoking Avalokiteśvara. This means that he was able to forge strong bonds of loyalty from them focused on himself. Thus he consolidated personal power, in addition to the power and wealth of the institution of the Dalai Lama, by means of what virtually amounts to a personality cult, one that continues to this day. Had it not been for him, the institution of the Dalai Lama would merely be one of a number of similar institutions and reincarnation series found in various Tibetan Buddhist communities and schools.

Ever since the fourteenth Dalai Lama and some 100,000 ethnic Tibetans fled to India, Nepal, and Bhutan in 1959, leaving several million Tibetans behind, the fourteenth Dalai Lama has been the subject of many conversations in China and elsewhere about the legal status of Tibet, the question of human rights in post-1959 Tibet, and other topics. Some of these have been substantial and informative; the vast majority, however, are propagandistic in tone, either pro-Dharamsala (the Indian home of the Tibetan government in exile) or pro-Beijing. Occasionally, other conversations have had a surrealistic air, having little to do with the realities of pre-1959 Tibetan society or the roles played by the Dalai Lamas and their governments. Questions about Tibet's historical status—whether it is independent of China and, if so, when it achieved independence—in addition to what area properly should be called Tibet, and what marks the extent of the territory controlled by the Dalai Lama's Ganden Podrang government, have been raised since 1959. These questions are extremely complex and have no easy answers.

Starting several decades ago, the current Dalai Lama has often said that he may be the last one. There have been other instances of reincarnation lines disappearing over time. The reasons are manifold: a lack of a charismatic leadership, inter- and intra-scholastic competition that led to civil unrest and the destruction of monasteries and temples, a lack of interest in finding a successor, and so forth. Sometimes reincarnate lines were ordered to disappear, as happened to the Red-hat reincarnation series of the Karma Kagyüpa school, whose involvement with the Gurkha War of 1792 led the Dalai Lama's government to forbid the line's continuation after the presiding reincarnation was killed or committed suicide. This ban lasted until 1963, when it was lifted by the Tibetan government in exile; the reincarnation line was then revived by Karmapa XVI (1924–1981), who had recognized his nephew, Mipam chokey lodrö (1952–2014), as the Red-hat reincarnation.

In the seventh century, the great Indian Buddhist philosopher Dharmakīrti argued that the principal cause for the willed and goal-oriented reincarnation of a bodhisattva is the profound level of compassion that drives such a person to return to the ocean of suffering, of everyday life in *samsara*, or to aid other people in a quest to become free from suffering. Achieved over countless lifetimes, so it is argued, the level of the bodhisattva's (and the Buddha's) compassion is so intense that he cannot do otherwise. For that reason, it is difficult to understand how the present Dalai Lama could proclaim that he will be the last Dalai Lama, unless, of course, this decision is based on motivations to which he alone is privy. To be sure, he may well be the last person to hold the office of Dalai Lama, but there is no question that, in the context of the Buddhist worldview, he, like all of us, will be reborn in some way.

26 | DOES LAW MATTER
IN CHINA?

William P. Alford

For this author, as a US national, the question, "Does law matter in China?" calls initially for a recognition of how charged inquiries by foreigners into the adequacy of Chinese law have long been. Assertions by Westerners about the brutal and inferior nature of pre-twentieth-century Chinese law were, after all, a precipitating factor of the Opium War of 1839–1842 (even as foreign merchants sold that drug into China knowing it was illegal). So, too, such claims led to the imposition, for close to a century thereafter, of a system of extraterritoriality, under which foreigners alleged to have committed crimes against Chinese nationals in China were immune from Chinese law and instead were to be tried by representatives of their own government using their home nation's law, if their cases weren't first dismissed. That this was initiated by Western powers in the name of promoting respect for human dignity and preserving sovereign equality only exacerbated what Chinese of many political persuasions have termed "the century of humiliation." While PRC authorities may at times invoke this history for tactical advantage in negotiations, anyone unaware of it who seeks to engage China is surely in for a big surprise.

Those of us examining law in China from a foreign vantage point would also do well to be mindful of our own assumptions regarding legal order more generally. Even in as law-centric a society as the

United States—the first nation, through its Constitution, formed around a written legal document—issues of class, race, gender, and disability, among other considerations, stand as sharp reminders that, however worthy we think the law's underlying ideals to be, "law on the books" is not necessarily the "law in action," at least in terms of equal protection for all. We should not spare China a comparably tough-minded scrutiny or suggest a cultural relativism that would elide the responsibility to foster values we believe to be universal. Yet, there is benefit to entertaining the possibility that China (among other societies) could advance human well-being in a manner that might rely less than we do on law, or utilize institutions that differ from our own.

Since the Cultural Revolution concluded in the late 1970s, the PRC has undertaken what elsewhere I have termed the most substantial state-led effort in world history to lay in place the foundations of a formal legal system—albeit not one intended to operate according to the principles of liberal legality. To this end, it has devoted vast sums, a goodly amount of energy, and some measure of its own credibility. Consider, by way of illustration, how over the past thirty-five years China has gone from having the most skeletal of legal frameworks to one of the most intricate, at least on paper, of legal orders (with tens of thousands of legal measures, covering everything from trading in derivatives to requirements to visit one's parents to prohibitions on the use of certain social media). Or, to take another example, think of how the Chinese legal profession during this period has grown well over a hundredfold, now numbering some 300,000 members (and this exclusive of judges, the procuracy, and basic level legal workers, essentially, quasi-professionals who provide legal services at the rice-roots level). Or consider the explosive growth in legal education, from roughly a dozen institutions granting degrees in law at the outset of the reform era to more than 630 now.

And yet, if our goal is to understand these developments (as a prerequisite to assessing whether and how they "matter"), we need to guard against the still all-too-frequent tendency of foreign observers to assume that these steps were intended to, or will perforce, operate as building blocks in an inevitable convergence toward a rule of law of the type toward which liberal democratic societies aspire. The Chinese Communist Party itself has been quite clear in declaring its goals for its work in legal development, as it stated unequivocally in devoting the October 2014 Decision of the Fourth Plenum of its 18th Party Congress to a blueprint for "ruling the country according to law." After commencing by proclaiming the importance to this undertaking of following "Marxism-Leninism, Mao Zedong Thought, Deng Xiaoping Theory . . . the Three Represents [of Jiang Zemin] and . . . the spirit . . . of important speeches by General Secretary Xi Jinping," the Decision announced, that

> The leadership of the Party is the most essential trait of Socialism with Chinese characteristics, and is the most fundamental guarantee for Socialist rule of law. Letting Party leadership penetrate into the entire process and all aspects of ruling the country according to the law is a basic experience of the construction of our country's Socialist rule of law. Our country's Constitution has established the leading position of the Chinese Communist Party. Persisting in Party leadership is a basic need for Socialist rule of law, it is where the foundations and the life-line of the Party and the State lie, the interests and happiness of the people of all ethnicities in the entire country are tied to it, and it is a proper element of moving ruling the country according to the law forward. Party leadership and Socialist rule of law are identical, Socialist

rule of law must persist in Party leadership, Party leadership must rely on Socialist rule of law.

And lest there be any doubt about what this means, the Decision repeatedly stresses the indispensable role of the Party as an entity (as distinct from individual members) and of its official ideology, in the conception and operation of legislation, state administration, the judiciary, the legal profession, legal education, and all other aspects of the legal system.

To acknowledge this is not to suggest that Chinese legal development has been intended as little more than window dressing (although there certainly has been more than a little of that). Rather, it is to underscore—as is indicated in what, after all, is a Party document about the purpose of the state's legal system—that the law ultimately is to be an instrument for the Party as it exercises its leadership in the name of the people. Order, which, of course, is a central dimension of any legal system, is in China paramount and defined by the Party to preserve the Party.

We can see the harsh results that this produces in the brutal treatment of the late Nobel Laureate Liu Xiaobo, left to die in prison of cancer. We can also see it in the approach taken toward *weiquan* (rights protection) lawyers, hundreds of whom have been arrested or otherwise detained in the last two years—even though it would seem that their willingness to seek peaceful resolution of politically contentious issues through the state's legal system should be welcomed by the Party-state. But it is also worth noting that the emphasis on order does not preclude and may, in some respects, advance legal regularity that in and of itself is not necessarily repressive. Note, for example, the Fourth Plenum's admonition against Party members who would "use their power . . . to bend the law for friends or relatives under any excuse."

Or consider that there are those, even among relatively senior Party members, who appreciate how crucial it is for the Party-state's legitimacy and China's future that legal institutions be seen by the populace as credible outlets for the resolution of legitimate grievances and that professionalism be fostered, albeit within the bounds set by the Party. Arguably, the Supreme People's Court's current President and Party Secretary Zhou Qiang has been exemplifying that—at least more so than did the previous head of the judicial system, Wang Shengjun (a former public security official unencumbered by any formal legal education). Witness the easing of the Wang administration's requirement that a majority of cases be settled by judicial mediation whether their facts warranted it or not (so that more cases are now to be decided in a procedurally rigorous manner); the increased promotion of "guiding cases" or instructive (as opposed to binding) precedents; and the recent expansion of the number and range of judicial decisions posted by the court system on the Internet. That noted, Zhou's January 2017 warning to the judiciary of the perils of "Western" style judicial independence, separation of powers, and constitutionalism underscores that legal development ultimately is intended to remain in service of the Party.

Of course, whatever the authorities may think or hope regarding the question of whether and how law matters, this does not necessarily speak definitively as to either the law's impact on China's populace or the ways in which citizens have assimilated it and aspire to use it. Both are extremely difficult to ascertain. This is due, in part, to such obvious factors as China's immense size and variety; the notorious unreliability (even for Chinese officials) of statistics; and the conundrum of what counts as credible public opinion in a one-party state with respect to such concerns as satisfaction with the judiciary or any other part of the official apparatus.

There are also, however, more subtle issues that add further complications in determining how law does (or doesn't) matter. At a practical level, for example, to what extent has China's spectacular economic growth, through which more than a half billion people have lifted themselves out of poverty in less than two generations, occurred because, despite, or wholly independently of the legal system's development (given that some observers, even in the West, believe the government's ability to act in a relatively unimpeded manner and the general fluidity of rules have been advantageous economically)? Assuming that the law has contributed to economic gains (per capita annual income has reportedly risen to roughly $8,000), how are we to balance these successes against growing inequality, an increasingly despoiled environment, and other problems for which law has provided little remedy? For instance, what are we to make of the complex and potentially conflicting ways in which law may apply to the highly contentious question of land expropriation, which allows some in the development business to lay stronger claim to what they may have gained (via vesting their holdings with the mantle of property rights) than would otherwise be the case, while leaving others (especially peasants dwelling on rural land reclassified as urban for development purposes) exasperated at the law's inability to provide them with meaningful redress? Nor is this a passing concern, as evidenced by the estimate of the eminent economist Wu Jinglian, that Chinese peasants through 2013 had failed to realize more than $700 billion in appreciated value of land to which they once had been entitled.

Other questions raise normative or conceptual challenges. For instance, how should one weigh the material improvements in Chinese life that may arguably be attributable in part to law against the use of law to curtail self-expression and limit access to ideas, be they of other Chinese or foreigners, that has been increasing in recent years? How should we respond to the likelihood that there may well be sharp differences of opinion about these issues among citizens of the PRC, and between Chinese and foreigners? And, at an even more basic level, as Chinese citizens interact with their government, to what extent are they distinguishing law from other expressions of state authority? After all, as concerns rural China, scholars such as former Beijing University law dean Zhu Suli, Kevin O'Brien, and Li Lianjiang report that peasants may treat law, policy pronouncements, and even speeches by leaders as somewhat interchangeable as they engage local authorities. And at the other end of the spectrum, to what extent is corporate governance in state-owned enterprises driven by legal considerations, as distinct from those of economic and political power?

Lying behind these questions are other fundamental ones to be mindful of as we seek to understand and evaluate law in China (or elsewhere). What are we counting as law and why? What are the trade-offs endemic to law anywhere in the world between, for example, order and freedom, or predictability and flexibility? What are the principal values we see law as intended to promote? To what extent are and should those values be the same in China and elsewhere? Who gets to decide this and on what basis? What are the different institutional forms through which such values may effectively be promoted? How, in assessing the institutional choices made in China, should we balance the importance (for both practical and normative reasons) of their adaptation to Chinese circumstances against instrumental invocations by some in power of China's uniqueness as an excuse to avoid global scrutiny?

To pose such questions is not a counsel of despair but, rather, crucial if we are to do justice in reviewing the possibilities that law may or may not hold for attaining justice in China.

27 | WHY DO SO MANY CHINESE STUDENTS COME TO THE UNITED STATES?

William C. Kirby

AT THE BEGINNING of the twenty-first century, Chinese students constituted approximately 10 percent of all international students enrolled in US institutions of higher education. Today, this share of Chinese students has increased to more than 31 percent. India is a distant second with about 17 percent. Accordingly, Chinese students contribute nearly one-third of the total international student payments to American universities. According to the Institute of International Education, during the 2015–2016 academic year, 328,547 Chinese students were enrolled in American colleges and universities, accounting for 31.5 percent of the total number of international students in the United States. At Harvard, the percentage of international students has grown from 16 percent in 2000 to 22 percent in 2015, and China has surpassed Canada as the home country of the largest number of the university's international students. Harvard is not an exception; many US universities have experienced similar trends.

Why is this happening? Is it because China lacks a sufficient number of university places for graduates of its high schools? No.

In 1978, after a decade when universities were closed during the Cultural Revolution, Chinese universities enrolled approximately

860,000 students. This number increased gradually until 1990, when about two million were enrolled in Chinese universities. By the year 2000, this number had increased to as many as six million students. Since then, the overall official numbers, including all types of tertiary institutions, have risen dramatically. There are at present more than thirty-six million students in Chinese institutions of higher learning. In 2000, China had approximately half the number of university students as the United States; now it has more than twice that number. Today, China graduates more university students than the United States and India combined. In short, there is no shortage of university spots in China.

Is it because China lacks good universities? No.

Modern Chinese higher education was among the most dynamic (if small) sectors in the world during the first half of the twentieth century, with outstanding universities, public and private, Chinese and foreign. After suffering during three decades of Maoist rule and Soviet influence, Chinese universities again emerged as a global presence. Two Chinese universities (Peking University and Tsinghua University) now regularly rank in the top thirty to forty of all global universities on various international league tables. By contrast, although German universities were the international gold standard in the nineteenth and early twentieth centuries, today, by almost any ranking, only one German university is listed among the top fifty in the world.

To be sure, American universities now dominate in the rankings of elite universities, but the best and brightest of Britain, France, Germany, and Japan do not enroll in large numbers in American universities, particularly for undergraduate study. They go to the elite universities in their home countries. Here, China appears to be different: a growing number of China's very best students—undergraduates now equal in number to graduate students—seek an American university education.

Chinese students come to the United States for a number of reasons, some of which are rooted in history. Before the 1949 communist takeover of China, the United States was the leading destination of Chinese who studied abroad. In the nineteenth century, the first educational mission sent abroad by the Qing dynasty court went to Hartford, Connecticut. Although Japan was a principal venue for foreign study in the early 1900s—and Germany and Britain were important destinations in specific disciplines—American universities were the destination of choice for the largest contingent of Chinese students who studied abroad.

Indeed, preparing young men to enter American universities was the founding mission of Tsinghua, one of China's greatest universities. Established by the Qing court as Tsinghua Academy, Tsinghua began as a preparatory school for students selected to study in the United States. At the urging of the president of the University of Illinois, Edmund J. James, the US government remitted a portion of the Boxer Indemnity Funds for the education of Chinese in the United States and for the establishment of Tsinghua in 1911. As James told President Theodore Roosevelt: "The nation which succeeds in educating the young Chinese of the present generation . . . will reap the largest possible returns in moral, intellectual, and commercial influence." During its first decade, Tsinghua built an American-style campus—its Jeffersonian grand auditorium inspired by the auditorium at Urbana-Champaign—to prepare its students for study in America. Tsinghua would go on to become a great, comprehensive university, and, in its first decades, the connection with the United States remained strong.

The first five individuals of Chinese background (from mainland China, Hong Kong, or Taiwan) who earned Nobel Prizes in the sciences had all either studied or taught at American universities. Returned students from the United States also included leading political figures in the Nationalist government that governed China from 1927 until 1949: T. V. Soong (Harvard); H. H. Kung (Oberlin); Hu Shi (Cornell); and Madame Chiang Kai-shek (Wellesley). In business, transformative figures of modern China's textile industry from the 1910s to the present, such as Cai Shengbai of Meiya Silk Manufacturing Company, Y. L. Yang of apparel powerhouse TAL, and Marjorie Yang of textile manufacturing giant Esquel—three generations of the same family—received engineering education at Lehigh, Lowell Tech, and MIT, respectively; and the next generation in this distinguished textile lineage, Dee Poon of fashion brand PYE, is a Harvard College graduate.

Chinese who studied in the United States have left their mark in notable ways. On the Harvard campus today there is a marble slab, or stele, presented to the university at its 300th anniversary in 1936 by its nearly one thousand Chinese alumni. Its inscription, believed to be in the calligraphy of Hu Shi, who received an honorary degree from Harvard that year, reads: "It is by virtue of its culture that a nation arises, but truly it is due to learning that a culture flourishes . . . That this is indeed the case is amply confirmed by the example of Harvard University in the United States of America . . . Our nation symbolizes an ancient culture of the East, but time irrevocably moves forward and the world evolves, constantly undergoing renewal and change. Those committed to learning once again have studied overseas to deepen their knowledge and self-understanding."

With the fall of the Chinese mainland to the communists in 1949, the flow of new students to the United States ended for thirty years. Some, like Ji Chaozhu, Harvard Class of 1952, returned to China before graduating; Ji would later become a senior diplomat and personal translator to Mao Zedong and Zhou Enlai. At the same time, the United States benefited in 1949, as it would again after the Tiananmen crisis in 1989, by an inflow of intellectual refugees from China who enriched American universities in the sciences, social sciences, and humanities for decades.

The flow of Chinese students to the United States today is built on these past experiences, but now it is on a much grander scale than ever before. This is in part because of the expansion, quality, and breadth of education in contemporary China. Its leading public high schools now rank among the best in the world, and their graduates qualify for admission to the world's most competitive colleges. Chinese university graduates are competitive to enter the world's leading doctoral programs—and the high percentage of Chinese in US Ph.D. programs, which admit students almost exclusively on the basis of academic merit, is proof of their quality. In 2016, Chinese doctoral candidates accounted for 34 percent of all first-year international doctoral students in the United States. And because no one can graduate from a Chinese university without having passed an English language examination, Chinese graduate students are linguistically capable of handling the challenge of study in the United States.

The growth in international and, especially, Chinese enrollments is due also to the expansion, diversity, and financial needs of American systems of higher education in recent decades, from community colleges, to liberal arts colleges, to public and private comprehensive universities. There is no single port of entry into American higher education. There are thousands. And if Chinese doctoral students come to study primarily on US-funded scholarships (Harvard, for instance, spends approximately $20 million annually to support Chinese doctoral students), most Chinese undergraduates come with no financial aid and pay top dollar (full tuition at private colleges; out-of-state tuition at public institutions) to American institutions that are still reeling from the financial meltdown of 2008. According to the US Commerce Department, Chinese students at American colleges and universities contributed more than $11 billion to the US economy in 2015. This is one reason why prospective Chinese undergraduates are recruited so aggressively by many American colleges. As a measure of this market, there is a robust new industry of education consultants in China helping young Chinese prepare their US college applications.

Beyond the openness and accessibility of American universities, there is the widespread perception on the part of Chinese parents that a US education is simply better than a Chinese education. Just as many American educators believe (not incorrectly) that young Chinese students are better educated in math and science than their American counterparts, many Chinese educators believe that it is the West, and particularly the Americans, who are "innovative" and "creative thinkers," whereas the Chinese (despite all their ancient inventions and modern revolutions) remain "traditional," "rule bound," and "rote learners" (despite recent research arguing that K–12 Chinese students outperform their "innovative" American counterparts in critical thinking skills). For what is assumed to be China's lag in innovation, some blame the tortured path to Chinese university admission through the National Higher Education Entrance Examination (NCEE, commonly known as *Gaokao*), with its modernized version of what one scholar has called "China's examination hell." How can students who are so completely focused on test scores in order to enter university possibly become innovators?

The much-feared and grueling NCEE is an important reason why Chinese students prefer to study abroad. Although 9.4 million sat for the exam in June 2016, this was 20,000 students fewer than in previous years. In Beijing, Liaoning, and Jiangsu, the number of students taking the NCEE in 2016 hit new lows. Part of this can be attributed to the fact that many elite high schools now offer two study tracks: one for students preparing to take the NCEE and another for students intending to study abroad. The latter curriculum trains students to take the TOEFL (Test of English as a Foreign Language) and the SAT, the standardized tests required for admittance to American universities. In 2015, a total of more than a half a million high school students pursued their higher education outside of China.

For undergraduate education, Chinese parents and educators apparently believe American colleges and universities when they pride themselves on their liberal arts–oriented or general education programs, which, they contend, produce "leaders" who are broadly educated to take on the world. The concept is at the heart of much undergraduate education in the United States: the need to educate students to be lifelong and critical learners, rather than simply to train them for their first job. Indeed, it is difficult to find an American college that does not produce "leaders." No college seems content to pursue the presumably larger market of followers. Presidents of Chinese universities have taken their American counterparts at their word and have devoted enormous efforts to crafting curricula for general and liberal education in a Chinese context. When Harvard College replaced its Core Program with a new General Education Program in 2006, its many curricular reports and recommendations were read as carefully in Beijing as they were in Cambridge, Massachusetts. As nearly every leading Chinese university is experimenting with forms of general education, emulation of American general education programs in China has raised the concept's prestige and has led parents to think: Why not go for the original product and study in America?

The strengths of China's education system are more appreciated abroad than at home. Although nowhere has higher education grown more rapidly in recent years, in both quality and quantity, than China, within China there is much criticism. Chinese rankings of global research universities are much tougher on Chinese institutions than British or American league tables, placing Peking and Tsinghua

Universities only in the top 50–100 group. And there is much that Chinese parents, students, and faculty disparage. Required classes are large. Good teaching is seldom rewarded. Good jobs do not necessarily await graduates of such a suddenly expanded system. And the open and unfettered exchange of ideas that is at the heart, at least in principle, of an American undergraduate education, is limited. The leading Chinese universities are all state-run, and the Chinese Communist Party (CCP) secretary normally outranks the university president (who in any event is subject to the Party). The enduring—indeed growing—role of the Party in higher education is surely the greatest challenge to the pursuit of "world class" status by Chinese universities.

The challenge for China's competitiveness in higher education comes down to a simple question: Can "world class" universities—however they are defined—exist in a politically illiberal system? Maybe, but only with a significant degree of autonomy. German universities in the nineteenth century faced many political pressures, but they were the envy of the world, in part because they also had traditions of institutional freedom that fostered and at times protected creative thinkers. China's universities today boast superb scholars and among the world's best students. But these students are also forced to sit through required courses on CCP ideology and politics, and they learn a comic-book version of the history of their own country. Despite new general education programs, in the realm of politics and history the distance between what Chinese university students have to learn in order to graduate and what they know to be true grows greater every year. In an era of increased political control under President Xi Jinping, in which empty political sloganeering takes up hours every week for students (not to mention for faculty and administrators), Chinese universities run the risk of graduating two kinds of "leaders": cynics and opportunists.

Perhaps by default, then, American universities still enjoy their hour in the sun as innovative places to educate leaders. After all, real Chinese leaders are sending their children to American universities, and in increasing numbers. One learns a lot about parents from where they send their children to study. In the 1920s and 1930s, China's paramount leader, Chiang Kai-shek, sent his sons to study in two of the leading powers of his day: to the Soviet Union (Chiang Ching-kuo, who attended Moscow's Sun Yat-Sen University, a school for revolutionaries) and to Germany (Chiang Wei-kuo, who was trained at the Kriegschule München, a military academy). Today, the sons and daughters of China's most powerful political figures—including President Xi and his archrival, former Chongqing Party Secretary Bo Xilai—have studied at the foremost American colleges and universities. Currently, even Peking University and Tsinghua University—the most prestigious and connected of institutions in China—lose students to top universities in America and elsewhere.

How long will this situation last? American universities may have been the envy of the world in the twentieth century, but that was not true in the nineteenth century, and there are no guarantees for the twenty-first century. Chinese universities can become the best and most attractive in the world, and truly extraordinary efforts (the Schwarzman Scholars Program at Tsinghua and Yenching Academy at Peking University) are being made to attract global talent to China. Yet, despite the aspirations of the US-sponsored "100,000 Strong" movement to have that number of American students studying in China—still only one-third of the number of Chinese students in the United States—the actual total of American students in China (21,975 in 2015, down from 24,203 in 2014) is modest and likely to remain so.

For now, the influx of Chinese students to the United States—and also to Britain, Australia, and Japan, in significant if lesser numbers—continues to grow. In time, most of these students are likely to return to China, where they will make important contributions. Meanwhile, however, the massive educational migration to the United States may be due less to confidence in American universities than to a sense of doubt and uncertainty about China's own institutions, especially in its current repressive and insecure political climate. In addition to sending their children—their most valuable human capital—abroad, Chinese parents today are also sending real assets overseas, getting their children and money out of the country at the same time. All this may not automatically redound to American benefit, at least as conceived by President James of the University of Illinois more than a century ago, but it is hardly a vote of confidence in China's immediate future.

VI | HISTORY AND CULTURE

28 | WHO IS CONFUCIUS IN TODAY'S CHINA?

Michael Puett

FOR MUCH of the twentieth century, Confucius was seen as the embodiment of what China had to reject in order to enter the modern world. Confucius was portrayed as the supporter of a traditional social order, in which humans had to be socialized through rituals to accept their given roles and duties. If people would then live out these roles and duties properly, society would become harmonious. Fathers would be proper fathers, sons would be filial sons, wives would be loyal wives. Along with these social roles, the rituals would also inculcate a proper belief in all humans that the cosmos was itself a harmonious system. If humans would follow their social roles properly, then not only would society be harmonious, but it would also be in accord with the larger harmony of the cosmos. The goal for humans was thus simply to accept society and the world as tradition had prescribed. As the purported philosopher behind such ideas, Confucius was the ultimate symbol of a traditional way of thinking.

In opposition to Confucius was a self-perceived modernist vision. According to this view, humans needed to destroy the traditional world altogether and create the world anew. For the first half of the twentieth century, the debate in China, as elsewhere, revolved around which modernist vision should be embraced: capitalism, socialism, or communism. In 1949, one of these modernist –isms, communism, won.

Mao Zedong called upon the population to rise up and forge a new, egalitarian society. And a key part of this was a full rejection of Confucius. The extreme point of such a rejection was reached during the Cultural Revolution, when texts and artifacts associated with Confucius were destroyed as part of a campaign to wipe out the past and create a new communist reality. Mao's claim was that, twenty years after the revolution, the officials of the Communist Party were becoming like a new scholarly class that would be in danger of reverting to traditional ways of thinking. Mao's call in the Cultural Revolution was for the people to rise up against the Party officials, just as they had (according to his reading of history) risen up against the Party officials of the last dynasty. Mao explicitly labeled his opponents—figures like Lin Biao—as Confucians who therefore needed to be destroyed.

But modernist rejections of a perceived traditional world are nothing new. In fact, during the Cultural Revolution, Mao explicitly compared himself to the First Emperor—the figure who, in 221 BCE, after unifying the competing states, tried to destroy the traditional world of the previous Three Dynasties. And the First Emperor also tried to destroy those intellectuals who wanted to model society on the past. The Confucians—then as well—were held in particular contempt. According to one source, the First Emperor had the Confucians buried alive. Mao argued that the only difference between himself and the First Emperor was that he, Mao, would be more ruthless, fully eradicating the ideas that the First Emperor correctly tried but ultimately failed to destroy.

If the First Emperor's modernist revolution failed, Mao's ultimately did as well. Mao's communist vision came to be discredited and was later replaced with a strong turn toward capitalism. Indeed, by the end of the twentieth century, China had become one of the most extreme laissez faire capitalist systems in the world. But the rhetoric of breaking from a traditional, Confucian society and entering the modern world continued—only now the modern world was defined as capitalism rather than communism.

The result of China's turn to an extreme form of neoliberal capitalism was an extraordinary period of economic growth. But the result was also a society increasingly polarized by radical income inequality. By the beginning of the twenty-first century, a self-conscious debate arose in China about whether China had lost its values, about whether it had become a world where everything was simply about wealth and power.

Out of this debate, Confucius returned.

The beginnings of the rethinking of Confucius began not in China itself but a couple of decades earlier, in another part of Asia. In the 1980s, Singapore began developing a form of state capitalism—one in which a market economy would be supported but also overseen by a bureaucracy of highly educated officials. The officials were not democratically elected but, rather, chosen through a form of meritocracy. Tellingly, the government explicitly claimed that such a meritocracy—in which the officials would be in charge of public infrastructure and the legal system, as well as moral governance of the populace—was based on Confucian values. Such a Confucian vision was also presented as being an antidote to the individualistic, amoral form of modernity being practiced in the West.

Instead of the tradition vs. modernity framework that had been so dominant for the previous decade, in which Confucius figured as the icon of the traditional world that had to be destroyed, Singapore was instead emphasizing a cultural divide between the West and East, and Confucius was now the icon of the East that needed to be extolled.

Increasingly, this became the framework embraced by the People's Republic of China as well. Over the past several years, China has been strengthening the meritocratic criteria for admission into the government and has been strongly emphasizing the importance of major state investment in public infrastructure, education, and green technology. Moreover, such an approach has increasingly been contrasted with the views dominant in the West. Unlike the form of neoliberalism that had become predominant for the past several decades, with a focus on limited government and privatization, China presents itself as a society with an extremely successful capitalist system, yet one which is re-developing forms of governance that it, following Singapore, associates with Confucius. Part of China's claim for world leadership thus increasingly rests on the argument that China, with its Confucian form of governance, will be able to tackle issues like economic inequality and climate change—issues that the United States, with its governance structures so controlled by lobbying interests, cannot address.

If Confucius was the figure Mao saw as most antagonistic to his dreams of a communist utopia, the new regime in China presents Confucius as precisely the figure offering an alternative to Western neoliberalism. Related to such claims has been an international outreach aimed at educating the world about what had once been disparaged as traditional Chinese culture. A series of government-sponsored, well-funded centers, called Confucius Institutes, are being built around the world to support the study of the Chinese language and Chinese culture. The traditions that were once being destroyed are now being presented as embodying a vision that offers a new possibility for twenty-first-century humanity. If Confucius previously represented the traditional worldview that held humans back, Confucius is now being presented as an alternative to the alienation, individualism, and anthropocentrism of Western modernity in general, and more specifically to the dysfunctional forms for governance seen in Western societies.

But where in the traditions are such readings of Confucius being found? The view of Confucius as a traditional thinker, forcing people to follow their roles submissively, was based upon a narrow reading of late imperial Chinese history. The new reading, on the contrary, takes much of its inspiration from the Han dynasty—the dynasty that came to power after the short-lived Qin dynasty of the First Emperor collapsed—as well as the later Tang dynasty. After the fall of the Qin dynasty of the First Emperor, the ensuing Han dynasty continued many of the First Emperor's innovations, but it also brought back the idea of building upon the traditions of the past. The Confucians, instead of being persecuted, were brought to court and eventually became a new class of officials staffing the imperial bureaucracy. They supported the creation of a meritocracy, in which the state would be run by an educated elite charged with building public infrastructure and running the legal system.

So is the current situation in China comparable to the early Han dynasty, with the regime building upon the innovations of Mao while creating a powerful state through the formation of a meritocracy? And will the next several centuries of Chinese history involve, as it did with the Han and later Tang, the emergence of China as one of the most successful states in the world?

These are among the major debates in China. Should the current moment be thought of in terms of tradition vs. modernity, East vs. West frameworks, some combination of these, or something else altogether? And is Confucius the salvation or the figure whose ideas must be destroyed?

This debate is playing out in many ways. Films about the Qin, Han, Tang, and late imperial periods have become common recently, as implicit ways to debate the current period and its relationship to earlier Chinese history. And films and books about Confucius have begun to proliferate as well—not the Confucius associated with the late imperial period, or even the Confucius associated with the Han and Tang periods, but the Confucius as portrayed in the *Analects,* the book of Confucius's teachings as recorded by his various disciples. Here, too, opposing visions have emerged—Confucius as a great sage who created a new moral vision (as in a highly popular book by Yu Dan), or Confucius as a human striving to be a good teacher (as in a competing book by Li Ling).

After a century of rejecting its traditions, we are witnessing an exciting moment in Chinese history, when the past is actively being debated, re-interpreted, and appropriated anew. How this will play out is impossible to say, but it is a debate that is worth following very closely. Which Confucius will emerge out of these debates, and how the current moment will be understood vis-à-vis earlier history, will have major ramifications for the type of society China will become and the way it will position itself in relation to the rest of the world.

29 | WHERE DID THE SILK ROAD COME FROM?

Rowan Flad

THE EXCHANGE OF technologies and ideas among individuals and communities has been a principal factor in the evolution of human culture, from the origins of our species, to the establishment of early states, and to the development of geographically massive empires. In the region now within the People's Republic of China, cultural development and identity similarly have long been affected by such intercultural transfers. Recent research on these transfers reflects a more interconnected and less geographically isolated origin to Chinese civilization than once assumed and, consequently, has not only transformed the way we understand its roots, but also provides a metaphor for the position of China in a globalized, twenty-first-century world. The recent emphasis specifically on the "One Belt, One Road" (OBOR) strategy for regional integration in Eurasia, led by China, is a particular manifestation of this and brings to the fore the idea of an interconnected, rather than isolated, economic and political world in both China's present and, presumably, the past.

In fact, the very origin of Chinese civilization owes a lot to interregional exchange. Some of the most important exchanges share geographical space with the Silk Road, a historical construct coined in the nineteenth century that is perhaps the most iconic example of long distance interregional exchange (and which, at least implicitly, is a construct drawn on in the OBOR strategy). But these formative exchanges both far predate the Silk Road proper (in that they did not involve silk) and involved a much more convoluted and locally diverse network of interactions and relationships. Nevertheless, just as the Silk Road helped connect far-flung cultures through commerce and exchange of ideas, these early interactions formed a "Proto–Silk Road" with a similarly profound impact on the societies and communities involved. The technologies they introduced into central parts of North China were fundamental to developing complex and politically expansive polities during the third and second millennia BCE—the period considered the beginning of Chinese civilization.

The historical Silk Road refers to the network of trade and transportation routes across Eurasia that was first solidified and fortified during the latter half of the first millennium BCE—developing into a well-travelled network particularly in the period from the Han (206 BCE–220 CE) through Tang (618–907 CE) dynasties. Historical accounts from Chinese sources emphasize attempts to control these routes by restricting the movement of people and through the establishment of military garrisons. Of course, the Silk Road was not only, or even primarily, a network involved in the transportation of silk, and branches of the trans-Eurasian Silk Road network leading toward Southeast Asia and across the Tibetan Plateau often refer to other important commodities, particularly tea and horses. Furthermore, it is not even clear that trade was a primary mode of interaction in all parts or periods, but we do see that these various routes, throughout history, brought into contact people with different languages, values, religions, ways of life, customs, and technologies.

Evidence for long-distance transfer of technologies across Eurasia is not limited to the historical period usually linked to the trade of silk and other commodities by merchants travelling over prescribed routes and monitored by imperial administrations or military outposts. In fact, recent research has started to detail technological transfers in the forms of new materials and practices, used in increasingly broad regions by communities that must have had some degree of connection with one another.

These practices and objects fit within a number of "technological domains," that is, assemblages of practices that involve the transformation of material resources and the related knowledge, beliefs, and social relationships. Some agricultural technologies illustrate long-distance contacts; for example, certain crops and animals first domesticated in Southwest Asia—including cattle, sheep, goat, barley, and wheat—have recently been shown to have been adopted by communities in East Asia sometime in the third to second millennium BCE. These newly domesticated animals and plants apparently were not part of a "package" associated with a single group of migrants, however. They were taken up by different communities, to different degrees, across the vast territory of central Asia and northwest China. In some cases, plants merely supplemented existing subsistence practices and were probably not important to the overall caloric intake of those who ate them. In some cases, they may have served as luxury goods, or as ingredients in the production of alcohol. In other cases, however, newly domesticated plants made new environmental zones possible for more extended occupation, opening up, for example, higher elevations in the Tibetan Plateau for farming.

Newly introduced domesticated animals, likewise, provided entirely new means of subsistence and focal points for ritual behavior. Cattle, for example, are known to have become an increasingly important focus of ritual activity during the latter half of the second millennium BCE, well after domesticated cattle were introduced from Southwest Asia through routes still not well understood. At the same time, however, wild cattle native to China were being used for the same purposes, suggesting that the status of animals as domesticates alone was not the only reason for their importance in ritual. However, once domesticated, access to cattle was certainly made easier, and possibly this played a role in the increasing focus on cattle as subjects of sacrifice and other ritual behavior.

One such ritual use of animals was the burning of animal bones, usually scapulae (shoulder blades) of mammals and plastrons of turtles, in a form of divination known as "pyro-osteomancy": the burning of bones to tell the future. Pyro-osteomancy became particularly important in the court of the Shang dynasty (ca. 1500–1050 BCE), the first dynasty in China for which we have primary historical attestation. Shang dynasty textual material is actually notations on objects traditionally called oracle bones that were burned for this sort of divination. While similar divination practices are not known from central Asia or points further west, we do see some of the earliest examples of it across the so-called "Northern Zone"—stretching from the traditional Silk Road in Gansu in northwest China through the northeast of China in Inner Mongolia and Liaoning Provinces. These early examples are often on scapulae of wild animals, such as deer, and other domesticates, such as pigs (an animal domesticated locally within China) and sheep (another domesticate introduced through the networks of the Proto–Silk Road).

Perhaps the most transformative animal technology transferred this way was the use of the domesticated horse and associated equipment, such as the chariot. Starting with the Shang dynasty, domesticated horses profoundly affected the nature of warfare and symbolism of status of the Chinese Central Plains. Not only is the process of domesticating horses somewhere in central Asia not well understood, neither is the precise timing and route of their introduction into East Asia, though some of the earliest evidence seems to be in northwest China. As with the aforementioned plant and animal introductions, horses were probably used in various ways at different times, and conditions that would have impacted their adoption would have varied widely depending on whether they could be accommodated in ways acceptable to the people concerned. In the absence of massive population movement, technological transfer must be understood as a process involving members of local communities wrestling with their own challenges and committed, to varying degrees, to their traditional ways of life.

Of course, the technological changes along the Proto–Silk Road are not limited to agriculture, nor limited primarily to a west-to-east trajectory. Bronze metallurgy, for example, reflects a particularly important pyrotechnology that seems to have been first practiced in the late third millennium BCE in northwest China, in ways related to earlier metallurgy in central Asia (especially the production of small tools and ornaments). By the middle of the second millennium BCE, bronze metallurgy in the Central Plains became one of the most significant economic activities of emerging centralized polities, such as the Shang. For the next thousand years, the manufacture of bronze weapons and ritual vessels commanded the attention and resources of the state beyond almost any other activity.

Among the evidence that reflects technological exchanges and influences with a primarily east-to-west trajectory are the traditions of pottery manufacture in northwest China. Ceramic production is important evidence for archaeological research into economic and technological practices and traditions because ceramics preserve well, and their production methods concern design similarities that may, some scholars think, relate to shared traditions and interactions. During the later part of the Neolithic period in northwest China (third millennium BCE), several traditions of painted pottery were manufactured and used across different parts of the region at different times. When the distributions of archaeological finds are mapped, they reveal an extension from the east to west over time and an expansion of the region of painted pottery used through this part of the Proto–Silk Road network.

Painted pottery actually plays a crucial role in one more aspect of how exchange of ideas and technologies in this region has affected our understanding of Chinese civilization. Early in the twentieth century, years of unequal economic relationships with Western governments and internal strife within the Qing dynasty court led to a profound sense of uncertainty among intellectuals in China. Some looked abroad for philosophical inspiration, and the new government that emerged in the second decade of the century explicitly looked abroad for assistance with all sorts of scientific and administrative tasks, importing experts to advise the new Republican government and bring "modern" ideas and technologies. One such expert was a geologist by the name of Johan Gunnar Andersson.

Andersson's story, and his somewhat contested role in the formation of Chinese archaeology, has been told many times. His geological interest in stratigraphy made him naturally suited to observe evidence of human activity that significantly predated the historical record of China's origins. Among his most significant contributions were the identification of the prehistoric site of Yangshao, in Mianchi (Henan Province), which we now associate with the Neolithic culture known as the Yangshao culture (ca. 5000–3000 BCE), and the identification of the Paleolithic cave site of Zhoukoudian, where the *Homo erectus* fossils, known as Peking Man, were discovered in large numbers. His documentation of a "prehistory" in China—a period predating the historical texts so vital to the notion of Chinese civilization—represented a sea change in the understanding of the origins of Chinese civilization.

Andersson proposed that the painted pottery of the prehistoric Yangshao culture must be connected to other painted pottery, for instance, the specimens found in excavations in Turkmenistan. Suggesting that Neolithic China owed its origins to western or central Asian prehistoric cultures seemed to imply that Chinese civilization as a whole may have been derivative of traditions, cultures, and practices that originated elsewhere. This does not seem to have been Andersson's intent, but he was interested in discovering evidence of these connections. Thus, he spent time in northwest China examining both the region's geology and unearthing yet more examples of painted pottery cultures at various sites.

These archaeological cultures represent traditions of various prehistoric communities that make up part of the Proto–Silk Road world. Had Andersson not engaged in his preliminary archaeological work or later attempts to trace connections to central Asia through evidence of painted pottery, an understanding of the deep origins of China would not have developed as it did. Furthermore, he also set the stage for current research that is revealing how the Proto–Silk Road contributed to the origins and development of Chinese civilization. Far from being a single route cutting across Asia, like a premodern superhighway, this Proto–Silk Road was a complex network of interactions and practices, and we are just beginning to understand it through active archaeological research across northwest China. Understanding it is vital, however, if we are to fully grasp the processes by which social hierarchy, and eventually expansive states, developed in the heartland of China. The origins of the Silk Road matter because they demonstrate how complex and diverse Chinese civilization is and has always been, and how exchange of ideas and technologies in multiple directions provides essential evidence of cultural and political development.

30 | WHY DO INTELLECTUALS MATTER TO CHINESE POLITICS?

Peter K. Bol

FROM ANCIENT TIMES, and certainly since the days of Confucius some 2,500 years ago, there has been a distinction between doing the work of government and articulating the justifications for having a government. Doing the work required administrators who could oversee the government's role in military affairs, judicial administration, and taxation. The institution of a centralized government in the third century BCE transformed the administrators from men of noble status, who often possessed independent power, into bureaucrats who advanced their professional careers by serving the system's interests. At first, articulating the justifications was a matter of practice. Governing required men conversant with the rites and ceremonies that tied together a lord and his vassals and allowed the ruler to fulfill his role as the intermediary between the living and the ancestors, and between human society and the cosmos in which it was embedded. But not only the rites.

But not only the rites. In the first millennium BCE, a different kind of vehicle of political justification and legitimacy appeared: writing. Rituals do things. They are a form of effective action. Writing may describe and call for effective action, but it is a step removed. How much more I would have preferred, said Confucius, to be doing things, but all I have are empty words. He was not quite right, for the claims made in writing often have consequences for action and politics. The poets who much earlier told of how "God in his sovereign might / . . . Gazed down upon the four quarters / . . . And hated the laxity of their rule / So he turned his gaze toward the west / And here he made his dwelling place" were not merely justifying the overthrow of the Shang dynasty by the Zhou in the eleventh century BCE, they were introducing the idea that sustaining political power—holding onto "Heaven's Mandate"—was contingent on the quality of rule. They were proposing a new standard by which the Zhou rulers could be held to account and denying that the Mandate was given in perpetuity. This challenges Max Weber's view that, historically, China relied on the "traditional" source of regime legitimacy, in which people obey the state's dictates simply because it is customary to do so, discussed by Elizabeth Perry in this volume.

Writing was thus also a means of exercising power, but it did so much more than the performance of the rite. It made a record of the past possible, and it would underlie the very idea of a civil rather than a military order, and of governance that could be effected through communication from a distance, whether by civil or military means. The writers proclaimed the legitimacy of dynastic power, but they also created the documents that portrayed the most ancient rulers as men selected on the basis of talent rather than hereditary privilege, and they collected poetry that spoke for the governed against the governors.

We can call those who provided the justifications for government "intellectuals," rather than bureaucrats, without necessarily implying that they stood apart from political power. Indeed, it is fair to say that for much of Chinese history most of those who gained fame as writers and thinkers outside of religious orders were likely to have spent some of their lives in government service and to have carried some kind of official status.

But the relationship between bureaucrats and intellectuals—between those who held political power and ran the government, and those who thought and wrote about what government should do—was hardly constant. Nor was it limited to politics. It was precisely during periods of political and social rupture that intellectuals went beyond their normal role as intermediaries. They became thinkers. They spoke to rulers about how rulers should act and about ideal political orders, and they spoke to individuals about how a person could be moral. They were the ones who held that there was an authority above the ruler and that they had the ability to speak of and for it.

In China's history, there has never been only one answer to the question of where that authority was to be found, or of how government and society needed to be transformed in order to accord with it. Some Zhou poets had one answer: look to the model of the sagely dynastic founder: "The doings of high Heaven / Have no sound, no smell. / Make King Wen your pattern, / And all the states will trust in you." This has been echoed at various times on behalf of the founders of the Tang and Ming dynasties, for example, and more recently by admirers of Mao Zedong. But there were other possibilities. The cosmic theory of universal empire proposed a necessary resonance between the quality of rule and the state of nature, so that any aberration—an earthquake, or an unpredicted eclipse—in the supposedly stable and predictable course of the natural world could be interpreted as a sign of misrule. Faced with the likelihood of such an interpretation, bureaucrats had to choose how to respond. By and large, government responded as best it could, but its opponents could, and did, find in natural disasters grounds for accusation of misrule, leading bureaucrats to downplay and even suppress bad news. Both reactions have been evident in China's most recent history.

There have been, and continue to be, other sources of authority to which intellectuals have appealed. The writing and rewriting of history has been taking place since Sima Qian's great interpretation of the history of civilization at the end of the second century BCE. Among other achievements, he showed how the problems of his day developed over time and could only be reversed based on an understanding of how they came to be. In addition, he pointed out the ways his ruler had adopted the ill-fated policies of past tyrants. A millennium later, Sima Guang, an historian and leader of the opposition, wrote a history of the preceding 1,500 years to show that for a dynasty to survive, it had ultimately to recognize the necessary limits on the government's power to transform society to fit its ideal model—in this case, an ideal that had been advanced by other intellectuals who found their authority in the Confucian Classics. A millennium after him, the historian Qian Mu found in middle period China (the age of Sima Guang) signs of the beginning of modern society in the potential of the civil service examination system to enable the common man to become a prime minister. The interpretation of history has always been about the present or, stated with greater nuance, about the past's significance for the present. Was it something to be continued or resisted? Remnants to be destroyed, or a past whose glories should be recovered? Who were the villains? The worthy figures? The writing of history has almost always been caught up in ideological debates.

Until recent times, the Confucian Classics have been the greatest vehicle for ideological debate in China, and with good reason: they are an account of the beginning of civilization. (Although, beginning three centuries ago, scholars began to conclude that some texts, thought to be the most ancient, were not, and, as Rowan Flad points out in this volume's chapter on the Silk Road, modern archaeology has given us a very different picture of the origins of civilization in China.) They were a foundation for political and moral thought as well as literature. Some saw these diverse books as giving a coherent account of an ideal integrated social order that had only existed in antiquity—something later ages had, in vain, attempted to recover. Befitting texts of such importance, intellectuals found that one of the best ways to make their arguments about what government should do, and how people should learn and think, was to offer a reinterpretation of the Classics. The Classics were repeatedly reinterpreted, sometimes in opposition to the orthodoxy of the moment, and sometimes with the aim of unifying conflicting interpretations. But what was originally a statement of disagreement could, if it gained a following, become a new orthodoxy. Every major commentator thought that he, at last, had gotten it right.

In the Tang dynasty of the early seventh century, the idea that the court was the center of political power became the source of a new interpretation of the Classics, one that sought to synthesize interpretations from the northern and southern scholars after three centuries of division. But the most consequential and long-lasting reinterpretation of the Classics came not from the court but from opposition intellectuals. This was the great Neo-Confucian interpretation of Zhu Xi in the twelfth century, who sought to combat the expansion of state power and its efforts to transform society through government intervention. It was consequential because Zhu's commentaries became part of the examination system and, thus, part of the schooling of everyone with a higher education into the early twentieth century. The path to political power went through education—an education that was the work of intellectuals. Passing an examination did not mean that educated people were convinced by what they read, but it did provide a common vocabulary and a set of templates for understanding and responding to events. The

Neo-Confucian interpretation did more than that, however; it shifted the focus from making the political system work to producing a morally and socially responsible individual. It accomplished this not only with a philosophical claim that all people possessed a moral nature that could be realized through individual effort, but also by giving what it called the "Four Books"—the *Analects of Confucius*, the *Mencius*, the *Great Learning*, and the *Doctrine of the Mean*—primacy over the traditional Classics. The Four Books, according to the Neo-Confucian interpretation, were texts that focused not on the political system but on the ways the individual could become a morally responsible actor through learning.

The civil service examination system had ancient roots, but it was only in the late tenth century that it became the primary means of recruiting officials. It was a test of talent, with talent first defined as literary accomplishment and later as an interpretive understanding of the Four Books. It went together with an education system that placed a state school in every county and included many hundreds of private academies. Even the Yuan dynasty of the Mongols, who conquered China in the thirteenth century and sharply limited the role of examinations, increased funding for schools and academies. In the eyes of sixteenth-century European observers, the examination system came close to the Platonic ideal of having philosophers become kings. That is dubious, but it is quite extraordinary that such a large country could make education necessary preparation for bureaucratic service.

But perhaps China's largeness had something to do with it (along with the breakdown of the medieval aristocracy, the growth of commerce, and the increasing influence of the literati, the educated elite, in local society). At any moment, hundreds of thousands of literati had acquired an examination education without achieving bureaucratic office, ensuring that across the land local literati had a similar standard of literacy, a shared body of knowledge and, it was hoped, a shared set of values. An examination education was a vocational education only in a very weak sense, in that it required a knowledge of past texts and current interpretations and a mastery of sophisticated literary forms. It was closer to what Confucius, and Confucians after him, called "learning for oneself," rather than "learning for others." Concerned with reasoning and critical thinking, breadth of vision and historical depth, moral challenges and choices, an examination education was closer to an ideal liberal arts education without the sciences. At a fundamental level, modern education also hopes to inculcate values, not just hone a student's ability to pass tests.

The debate, then, is always over which values education should seek to inculcate in those who learn. Benevolence and righteousness? Should it be loyalty (to state) and filial piety (in the family)? Investigating things and acquiring knowledge? But there have also been tensions: between reviving the ancient and creating the new, serving the state and advancing the family, building institutions and cultivating the self, and so on.

In contemporary China, such debates are once again out in the open. At first, it was a division between liberals who argued that freedom of choice in a globalizing market economy ought to lead to freedom of choice in politics, and a New Left that argued that the growing inequality that resulted from globalization and a market economy could only be remedied by a return to the collectivist policies of the socialist period. Then came proponents of a "third way" that would be uniquely Chinese and, by implication, neither liberal nor socialist. The key to China's greatness was to be found in its history—a history that had once been derogated as feudal. For some, it is a matter of power: China can only recover its proper place in the world by exercising dominion over others. For others, greatness lies in restoring a civilization founded on Confucian values (although there is no consensus about whether those values are humanistic or authoritarian). What is clear is that intellectuals from different camps have, as intellectuals did before them, sought to gain government support for their respective positions and establish themselves as those who could guide China's future.

Today, the Party leadership has decided to support both Confucianism and socialism. President Xi Jinping visited Peking University for a photo-op with the late Confucian philosopher Tang Yijie, who held that the restoration of the Chinese nation's greatness depended on the restoration of Confucianism, and Xi also lectured on the Confucian *Great Learning* as a foundation for socialist values. University institutes for "National Learning" have received ample funding from the government. It is a bad time for intellectuals whose criticism of the regime is grounded in the experience of other civilization and histories. But for those who are schooled in the Chinese humanities, it is an opportunity to establish themselves as the authoritative interpreters of the values that will make China truly Chinese and that, in turn, positions them to be both supporters and critics of the regime.

Since antiquity, China's history has shown an enduring commitment to tying the work of government, which requires bureaucrats and politicians, to the efforts of intellectuals. At times, those in power have wrested from intellectuals control over education and debates over values. But during the last millennium, the more common pattern has been a combination of, on the one hand, the government's recognition of the values of the dominant intellectual movement of the time, and, on the other hand, its attempt to co-opt intellectuals into being supporters rather than critics. When individual education is seen as essential to successful politics, however, this tension between political power and intellectual authority will be hard to avoid. Perhaps we should say it is in the nature of civilization as it is found in China.

31 | WHY DO CLASSIC CHINESE NOVELS MATTER?

Wai-yee Li

CLASSIC CHINESE NOVELS from the Ming (1358–1644) and Qing (1644–1911) dynasties have a vibrant presence in the contemporary Chinese-speaking world. Picture an amalgam of Shakespeare's plays and Disney movies, or imagine using Othello, Mr. Darcy, Uriah Heep, and Jane Eyre as points of reference in casual conversation with a random person: the usual distinctions in linguistic and cultural registers do not seem to apply when it comes to these works. Characters, plot details, and specific lines from them become part of everyday discourse and popular psychology. To a degree unmatched by the great literary works in the European tradition, these novels permeate every level of society. Among the most famous are the "four masterworks of Ming fiction": *Three Kingdoms*, *Water Margin* (also called *The Marshes of Mount Liang*), *Journey to the West* (also called *Monkey*), and *The Plum in the Golden Vase*. Perhaps even more prominent is *The Dream of the Red Chamber* (also called *The Story of the Stone*), recognized by many as the greatest Chinese novel. Another eighteenth-century work, *The Scholars*, is also widely admired but is less visible in modern popular culture.

It is important to regard these novels not merely as pages between two covers but rather as gateways into Chinese civilization and cultural history. Their prehistories and afterlives span centuries, granting insights into crucial cultural trends and transformations. For example, the earliest extant editions of *Three Kingdoms, Water Margin,* and *Journey to the West* date from the fifteenth and sixteenth centuries, but they represent culminations of centuries of historical and pseudo-historical accounts, myths, popular storytelling, anecdotal literature, and theatrical performance. In addition, all major Ming-Qing novels enjoy afterlives as sequels, rebuttals, and reinventions with new settings, sometimes in different genres. In the last three centuries of imperial rule ending in 1911, these Ming-Qing works also claimed a significant place in visual culture as operatic spectacle, book illustrations, card games, new year paintings (a type of folk art), and images on porcelain. (They almost never appeared in elite paintings, which often eschewed narrative and dramatic elements and rarely took up themes and figures from vernacular literature.) Their multimedia presence in contemporary culture is ubiquitous.

Accessible to students in middle school or high school, these texts are not difficult and are available in cheap editions (or can be downloaded for free), yet it is hard to gauge the size of the actual readership. What seems certain is that even those who have not read these books know versions of the stories in children's literature, animation, graphic novels, opera, movies, serialized drama on television, blog debates, or video games. From theme parks to decorative arts and even recipes (some restaurants feature "dishes from *The Dream of the Red Chamber*"), we find reminders of their power as markers of cultural literacy and indices to popular mentality.

I started out by calling these "classic Chinese novels," yet this very term may be a misnomer. These works became "classic" only in the twentieth century. Unlike traditional high literature, which was written in classical Chinese, they were written in premodern vernacular or, in the case of *Three Kingdoms,* simple classical Chinese. (Classical Chinese is very different from the spoken language, although many expressions and turns of phrase in classical Chinese inform modern written Chinese.) Ming-Qing readers voicing their admiration sometimes sounded defensive, averring the continuity of ethical or metaphysical concerns between classical and vernacular literature.

The situation changed drastically in the twentieth century. During the New Culture Movement of the late 1910s and early 1920s, a new written language that purported to be more popular, immediate, and closer to the spoken language came into being. It drew from, and sought its own lineage in, traditional vernacular fiction. The modern Chinese language thus owes much to traditional vernacular fiction, which was canonized as the "counter-tradition" by scholars and writers of the literary revolution. As a result, its ties to the spoken language, performance, popular culture, and folk memory, and its potential to subvert socio-political order (a more problematic proposition), have often been emphasized in modern criticism. In other words, precisely because so many intellectuals were raising questions about the role of Confucian precepts, social conventions, and political morality in defining the relationship between self and society, or the individual and the state, Ming-Qing vernacular fiction came to be prized for its "spirit of opposition." Such works became "classic" because of their previous exclusion from "the Great Tradition."

Whether they should be called "novels" is also open to debate; it may be merely a term of convenience. Aside from a general interest in narrative and their formidable length (comparable to, say, novels by Tolstoy, Dickens, or Eliot), these sprawling works bear little resemblance to European novels that often emphasize social and psychological realism. Ming-Qing vernacular fiction is a hybrid genre. Lyric poetry, songs, descriptive verses, poetic exposition, parallel prose, dramatic arias, doggerels, quotations from and summaries of historical texts and other fictional works, and the rhetoric of oral performance are often woven into the fabric of narrative. There seems to be no formal unity. Yet the more attentive reader will notice patterns and meanings emerging from contrast and complementarity within each chapter, between chapters and narrative units that comprise clusters of chapters, figural and structural repetitions, the gathering and dispersal of characters, and significant midpoints or middle sections. There also are framing sections that function as extended prologues and epilogues. Traditional commentaries published along with these works are often helpful in delineating the aesthetics of fiction.

Some modern writers, including Nobel Laureate Mo Yan, claim to have been inspired by the ideas and aesthetics of Ming-Qing fiction. Mao Zedong (1893–1976) offered assiduous commentary on three canonical works—*Water Margin, Journey to the West,* and *The Dream of the Red Chamber*—because of their spirit of opposition.

The historical kernel of *Water Margin* is based on the early twelfth-century exploits of the Song dynasty bandit-rebel Song Jiang and his followers. Surviving 100-chapter editions from the sixteenth century recount the adventures of 108 bandit-heroes, their paths to outlawry, their eventual congregation in the Marshes of Liangshan, their military victories over government troops, their reconciliation with the government and subsequent military expeditions against the foes of the Song dynasty, leading to their dispersal and death as a result of those campaigns and a final betrayal by the government. In the mid-seventeenth century, scholar Jin Shengtan truncated the text and produced a seventy-chapter version, which concludes with the congregation at Liangshan, followed by one character's dream in which all 108 rebels are summarily executed. This became the most widely read version.

Although *Water Margin* apparently endorses a counter-government or counter-culture based on secret-society morality and defiance of socio-political order, its common title in Ming–Qing editions is *The Loyal and Righteous Water Margin*, implying that banditry expresses political frustration and yearning for an uncorrupt order. Modern criticism tends to eulogize *Water Margin* as an anti-authoritarian saga protesting against repressive forces in Chinese civilization. The truth is, *Water Margin* fits as uneasily with late-imperial assertions of its "loyalty and righteousness" as with modern interpretations of "peasant uprising" or anti-authoritarian utopia. This is no pastoral Robin Hood–like community. The glorification and justification of vengeance, indiscriminate violence, bloodlust, misogyny, and ruthless power struggles pose special problems for interpretation. Is it possible that what is distasteful to the modern reader might have served as effective propaganda for organizing gangs and galvanizing anti-Jurchen, anti-Mongol, or simply anti-government popular movements? (The Jurchens ruled north China from 1115 to 1234; the Mongol, or Yuan, dynasty lasted from 1271 to 1368.) Did naïve authors fail to note the discrepancy between heroic rhetoric and violent reality? Is this a realistic portrayal of different sides of human nature in situations of persecution, violent appropriation of power, and alternative socio-political organization?

Mao Zedong was characteristically untroubled by these dark undertones. From the 1920s on, he referred to *Water Margin* numerous times as a source of inspiration for organizing insurrection and strategic planning. In 1975, however, he dubbed it worthwhile only as a "negative example" that "let the people see through advocates of surrender." He complained about Jin Shengtan's ambiguous ending: does he make surrender more or less distasteful? After all, the bandits "only opposed corrupt officials, not the emperor." Some believe that the targets of these critiques by Mao of a "flawed rebellion" were Zhou Enlai and Deng Xiaoping. The furor over *Water Margin* as a political movement in the 1970s is now a distant memory. Recent discussions of its appropriateness for inclusion in middle school textbooks demonstrate, however, how it still channels rancor. Those disdainful of critiques of violence in *Water Margin* maintain that the injustices of contemporary Chinese society cry out for such outbursts of anger.

Journey to the West also has its share of anger and violence, but any sense of danger is ameliorated by playfulness, fantastic invention, and magical transformations. Historical and fictional accounts of the great monk-scholar and translator Xuanzang, chronicling and elaborating his seventh-century journey to India to obtain Buddhist scriptures, inspired this 100-chapter work. It begins with Monkey's birth from a stone impregnated by the essences of heaven and earth, his ascension as ruler of the monkey kingdom, his acquisition of magical powers and attempt to overcome mortality and mutability, the great havoc he wreaks in heaven and his successive confrontations with the celestial hierarchy, and his final subjugation by Buddha. After five hundred years of imprisonment, Monkey is released by the monk Tripitaka (Xuanzang) and joins him, along with three other disciples (including Monkey's comic foil, Zhu Bajie, or Pig Eight-Abstinences), on the westward journey to obtain scriptures. After enduring eighty-one ordeals, which often involve successive captures by monsters, demons, and renegade celestial beings, they successfully complete their mission.

This saga about coming into being, attaining self-awareness, confronting mortality, rebelling against authority, and reaching enlightenment and salvation through an arduous journey has always invited allegorical interpretations. For three centuries, Buddhist, Daoist, and Confucian readings have mined the text for lessons in accumulating merit, attaining transcendence, controlling the vital flow of energy in the body, or pursuing moral self-examination. Some twentieth-century scholars emphasize its buoyant good spirits and dismiss allegorical readings as overly subtle and ultimately irrelevant. The introduction to the best-known abridged translation (entitled *Monkey*) describes it as "simply a book of good humor, profound nonsense, good-natured satire and delightful entertainment." More recently, there has been renewed emphasis on religious and allegorical readings.

Political readings interpret Monkey's confrontations, first with the celestial hierarchy and then with numerous monsters during the journey, as allegories of socio-political struggles. In 1941, the pioneer animation artist Wan Laiming made *Princess Iron Fan* in Shanghai (then under Japanese occupation), turning the pilgrims' crossing of the Flaming Mountain by borrowing the Iron Fan from the Princess into a story of struggle for national survival. Monkey's initial rebellion is celebrated as triumphant revolution in Wan's *Havoc in Heaven* (made in the early 1960s), hence it ends not with Monkey's subjugation by Buddha but his defiant return to his monkey kingdom. Yet there was enough unease about this anti-establishment stance—there were suspicions of covert analogy between Mao Zedong and Monkey's foe, the Jade Emperor—to cause a delayed release of this animation classic. Political applications of *Journey to the West* are infinitely malleable. In 1945, Mao Zedong compared communist guerrilla warfare against the Kuomintang (Nationalist Party) to Monkey's wreaking havoc in heaven. In 1963, Mao used the same "havoc" to describe the break with the Soviet Union: "Remember: don't take heavenly rules too seriously. We have to forge our own revolutionary way." Ultimately, political readings, like all allegorical readings, exist in tension with the "profound nonsense" of comedy.

Just as laughter can explode allegorical structures in *Journey to the West*, the sensuous details of *The Dream of the Red Chamber* may distract from its purported moral and religious meanings. It begins with a myth about flaws and disequilibrium. In order to repair a hole in heaven, the goddess Nüwa refines 36,501 stones, one more than she needs. The superfluous stone, refined into consciousness and spirituality and yet deemed unfit to repair heaven, is discarded at the foot of a mountain whose name is roughly homophonous with "roots of desire." The stone laments its destiny and is taken to the human world by a Buddhist monk and a Daoist priest, to be reborn as the protagonist Jia Baoyu (fictive Precious Jade), scion of a rich, powerful but declining family. Baoyu is born with a piece of jade—the transformed stone—in his mouth.

Aside from the intermittent intrusion of supernatural elements, most of the novel is taken up with details of daily existence in the Jia household—the endless feasts, birthday celebrations, family gatherings, and dramatic performances. In the midst of these, intrigues unfold, affections deepen, jealousies and misunderstandings develop, and, eventually, disaster strikes. A garden, built in the space between the two branches of the family, becomes an idyllic space for Baoyu and the girls (cousins, half-sisters, and maids) he admires and loves. Narrative focus shifts between the irrevocable decline of the Jia family, explained in part by extravagance, greed, corruption, mismanagement, and abuse of power, and Baoyu's emotional and spiritual world, his relationship to the girls surrounding him (especially two cousins) and to his family, his perceptions, love, disappointments, moments of enlightenment and final renunciation of worldly attachment to become a monk. The author Cao Xueqin, who drew upon personal and family history in writing the book, did not live to finish it. The eighty chapters he wrote circulated as hand-copied manuscripts for about three decades before the novel's publication in a 120-chapter version in 1791. Another author wrote the last forty chapters.

Mao Zedong often asserted that one should read *The Dream of the Red Chamber* "at least five times." He claimed to have read it as history—he saw (predictably enough) evidence of "class struggles" and the inevitable collapse of "feudal society." Mao's 1954 campaign to criticize the autobiographical readings of the novel proposed by eminent scholars heralded strictly Marxist readings of all literature as the new orthodoxy. Mao's more astute comments are found not in his public pronouncements but in his marginalia parsing the language of love used by Baoyu and the objects of his longing. Like readers before and after him, being seduced by the novel's romantic aura sometimes takes precedence over ideology and philosophy.

Even as scholars debate the meanings of love, desire, transcendence, and fictionality in the book, grassroot enthusiasts argue about the interpretation of every detail in Internet forums, often pursuing clues to the "real story" supposedly embedded in seventeenth- and eighteenth-century Chinese history. At the same time, many readers of the book or consumers of it in other media are content to enjoy its beautiful sights and sounds or complex human relationships. In some ways, the nostalgia for and the idealization of a lost world in *The Dream of the Red Chamber* capture the modern Chinese reader's feelings about the entire Chinese culture. At the same time, the inevitable collapse of that world implies irony, critical distance, and a questioning or even oppositional stance.

Why do classic Chinese novels matter? One can make the argument based on relevance: one needs to know them to gain cultural literacy, understand their role in modern politics, or be attuned to their uses in popular culture. But perhaps the pleasure of reading ultimately carries more weight. These texts open up worlds where one can roam and get lost; the moral, religious, or political messages can always wait.

HOW HAVE CHINESE WRITERS
IMAGINED CHINA'S FUTURE?

David Der-wei Wang

MODERN CHINESE LITERATURE was born with a call for utopia. In 1902, toward the end of the beleaguered Qing dynasty, Liang Qichao published *The Future of New China* in the newly founded magazine, *New Fiction*. The novel opens with an overview of a prosperous China in 2062, sixty years after the novel's fictive publication date of 2002. As citizens of the Republic of Great China celebrate the fiftieth anniversary of their nation's founding, a revered scholar, Kong Hongdao, the seventy-second-generation descendant of Confucius, is invited to give a lecture at the Shanghai World Exposition on how Chinese democracy has been implemented. His lecture draws a huge enthusiastic audience, including hundreds of thousands from overseas.

If the grand opening of *The Future of New China* feels uncanny, perhaps it is because the "future" of new China seems to have become reality in the current millennium. At a time when China is ascending to a role as a leading political and economic power worldwide, having hosted not only a World Exposition but also the Olympics, and more impressively, founded hundreds of Confucius Institutes in places as far from China as Pakistan and Rwanda, Liang Qichao's futuristic utopia may prove to have already been realized by socialist China. Indeed, as if taking up where Liang left off more than a century earlier, President Xi Jinping gave a speech on the

"Chinese Dream" in 2013, projecting the future of new China as one thriving on "the way of socialism," "the spirit of nationalism," and "the force of ethnic solidarity."

Although "utopia" has always been a suspect term in the lexicon of socialist China, the "Chinese Dream" partakes of a strong utopian dimension insofar as it invokes an ideal political and cultural vision. As a matter of fact, the "Chinese Dream" may represent the summation of a string of recent discourses about futuristic China. From "the great nation is rising" to "all under the heaven," from "repoliticizing" China to "unification of three orthodoxies"—Confucianism, Maoism, Dengism—we are witnessing a cornucopia of treatises and declarations that again aspire to forge a powerful Chinese polity through their visions. While these treatises are ordinarily not treated in literary terms, they nevertheless point to the rhetorical gesture and imaginary aptitude that inform the "structure of feeling" of a time. They share the fantastic mode of a "grand narrative," and it is this mode that brings us to rethink utopia and its literary manifestation in contemporary China.

Utopia entered the Chinese lexicon as a neologism in Yan Fu's late-1890s translation of Thomas Huxley's *Evolution and Ethics*. In his annotation, Yan Fu contemplates the relationship between sovereign rule and national governance, concluding that education and enlightenment are keys to national prosperity. In his treatment, Yan Fu downplays the fact that utopia is a fictitious construct. Rather, he considers utopia a goal to be achieved by any nation committed to the dictum of the survival of the fittest. In other words, he equates utopia to a teleological project predicated on the Darwinian ethics he yearned for.

The way Yan Fu broached the idea of utopia leads to a larger question regarding the instrumentality of literature at his time. That is, the "fictitiousness" of literature is regarded as intelligible only when it proves to be a manifestation of historical experience or expectation. As such, fiction is said to serve as both the end and the means of transforming China. Echoing the advocacy of Yan Fu and like-minded intellectuals for reforming China by re-forming Chinese fiction, Liang Qichao made the famous statement in 1902, "To renovate the nation, one has to first renovate fiction . . . Fiction has the incalculable power of transforming the Chinese mind." At some mysterious point of time, as Liang would have it, fiction and nation, or for our concern, utopia and history, become exchangeable notions.

Utopia constitutes one of the most important themes in modern Chinese literature at its budding stage. Besides Liang's *The Future of New China*, Wu Jianren's *The New Story of Stone* and Biheguan Zhuren's *New Era* imagine either a futuristic time in which China regains its superpower standing or a fantastic context in which China has transformed into an ideal state. By the act of writing the incredible and the impractical, late-Qing dynasty writers set the terms of China's modernization project, both as a new political agenda and as a new national myth.

This utopian impulse, however, dissipated in the 1920s May Fourth era. Writers appeared to be so occupied by the canon of realism that they could not even entertain any fantastic thought. In the few non-realistic works produced during this time, it is dystopia, not utopia, that became the norm, as evinced by Shen Congwen's *Alice in China*, Zhang Tianyi's *Diary of a Ghostly Land*, and Lao She's *City of Cats*.

But utopia had found a new venue—communist discourse—in which to demonstrate its power. Chinese communist revolutionary theory is predicated on the vision that a socialist "promised land" is accessible through a radical shakeup of the status quo. To that end, literature is only part of a grand narrative projecting what China should become. One could even argue that the utopian trope has always occupied a space in mainstream Chinese literature from 1942 to 1976, be it called socialist realism, revolutionary realism, or revolutionary romanticism. Whatever happens to the past and present, the Party-state is supposed to lead Chinese people to "the best of all best possible worlds."

In conjunction with utopia is science fantasy, a genre that features technological marvels and novelties in service of a utopian (or dystopian) agenda. Scholar Rudolf Wagner has indicated that the genre enjoyed a short-lived boom, from the mid-1950s to the end of 1960s, as part of the campaign of "marching toward science." The genre then staged a brief comeback in the late 1970s, following the fall of the Gang of Four. It assumes, as Wagner argues, a new role as "lobby literature," "presenting scientists' group aspirations in the form of the fantasy, and portraying how scientists would operate in the larger framework of society if their demands were met."

Utopia and science fantasy underwent an ambiguous transformation toward the end of the twentieth century. Despite the ongoing murk of politics, writers were able to create more personal visions and, to that effect, they remind us of their late-Qing predecessors. For instance, Bao Mi's *Yellow Peril* (1991) casts an eschatological look at China engulfed by civil wars and nuclear holocaust, which result in an exodus and a new "Yellow Peril" worldwide. Liang Xiaosheng's *Floating City* (1993) describes a southeastern Chinese metropolis mysteriously disconnected from the mainland. By envisioning China on the verge either of a miraculous rejuvenation or an eternal destruction—or by prophesying China either as a post-nuclear wasteland or an instigator of a new "Yellow Peril"—these writers create different temporal and spatial zones through which to ponder the fate of their nation.

The new century witnesses the resurgence of writing and reading utopia with a vigor reminiscent of the late-Qing era. Ironically, one

finds few works that can be described as utopian in its traditional definition. It is dystopia that better characterizes these works. In Han
Song's *2066: Red Star over America,* 2066 marks a turning point in
Chinese-American relationships. America is imagined to have suffered from a series of economic and political disasters while China has
become a "gardenlike" superpower. As such, Han Song seems to relate a revanchist fantasy that has obsessed many writers since the late
Qing. But Han has more to tell us. China is said to have achieved its
superpower status by succumbing to "Amando," an artificial intelligence that preprograms everyone's life and oversees its happiness in
every possible way. Even then, Amando proves to have collapsed
when the mysterious "Martians" descend on earth, turning China
into the Land of Promise, or *fudi* (a Chinese expression that, not co-
incidentally, is also a euphemism for "cemetery," a land for the dead).

Liu Cixin's *The Three-Body Problem* trilogy (2007–2010) assumes
an epic scope that spans millions of years. Mixing the Cultural Revolution and *Star Wars,* historical pathos and outer space marvels, Liu's
saga ought to be regarded as one of the most ambitious works of contemporary Chinese fiction, one that is not only a fantastic spectacle
but also an inquiry into the ethics of spectacle. *The Three-Body Problem*
relates a woman scientist's revenge of her father's purge and death in
the Cultural Revolution by inviting the extraterrestrial creatures
known as Three Body to invade earth. A group of Chinese citizens
are drafted to help prevent the impending global holocaust. These
heroes travel through the tunnel of time, using ingenious tactics to
fight cosmic battles. Even then, all civilizations on earth are doomed
to be ruined in the long run.

But it is in a novel such as *The Fat Years* (2009), by the Beijing-
based author Chan Koonchung, that one finds the most polemic dialogue between utopia and dystopia. The novel starts with a global
economic crash in 2011 that paralyzes all leading countries except

China. Thanks to shrewd national leadership, China is able to take advantage of the crisis and further its economic development and sociopolitical solidarity. As a result, China can boast, as early as 2013, the arrival of *shengshi*, a historical epoch of prosperity. While a majority of Chinese citizens welcome the golden time, there are signs, such as a prevailing mood of jubilation called "high lite lite" and massive amnesia, that arouse suspicion among a few nonconformists. In order to find out the truth, they kidnap a national leader, only to learn something that they never could have imagined.

Published during the sixtieth anniversary of the People's Republic of China, *The Fat Years* reminds one of *The Future of New China*, though a reader familiar with Liang's novel would be surprised by the paradoxes permeating *The Fat Years*. Sixty years after the Chinese Communist Revolution, China has accomplished what Liang Qichao could only have dreamed of at the turn of the twentieth century. Meanwhile, Chinese citizens appear to have succumbed to the benevolent hegemony of the Party-state. That Chan marks 2013 as the year when the Chinese leader came to declare Chinese supremacy over the world uncannily anticipates Xi Jinping's announcement of the "Chinese Dream."

In contrast with dystopian fiction in the vein of *Brave New World* or *1984*, *The Fat Years* is less concerned with exposing the evil scheme of a seemingly benign rule than in telling the other side of the story, thus making the captive national leader its unlikely hero. Suave, cool, and a little jaded, the national leader surprises everyone with a night-long, tell-all confession. According to him, the primary goal of the government is to make people happy; to that end, necessary means— from "marketization with socialist characteristics" to thought control— should be adopted so as to "maintain social order."

We are also told that the Chinese people are served with MDMA, the "ecstasy" drug, in their drinking water, which helps them forget anything that hampers a healthy revolutionary memory. This bio-political episode is a predictable device of science fiction. What Chan really underscores is that he has told a story in which the "national leader" turns out to be not only a Machiavellian administrator but also the most mesmerizing storyteller. His tale about the "golden time" to come turns out to be a more potent prescription for national ecstasy.

Chinese utopia thus comes full circle. A sublime conclusion has been reached, though more in the sense of the "phantom sublime" than the "Maoist sublime." Still, Chan Koonchung arranges for his dissident characters to turn their backs on the golden time at the novel's end, a conclusion that brings to mind the words of Lu Xun, the founding father of modern Chinese literature, in his essay "Farewell of a Shadow": "There is something I dislike in heaven; I do not want to go there. There is something I dislike in hell; I do not want to go there. There is something I dislike in your future golden world; I do not want to go there."

33 | HAS CHINESE PROPAGANDA WON HEARTS AND MINDS?

Jie Li

The East is red, the sun has risen
Mao Zedong has appeared in China.
He is devoted to the people's welfare,
Hu-er-hai-yo,
He is the people's great savior.

There is no song more familiar to the ears and lips of Chinese over the age of forty than "The East is Red." From the 1950s to the 1970s, the song was blasted at dawn and dusk over tens of millions of loudspeakers nationwide. In 1964, "The East is Red" became a multimedia "song-and-dance epic" extravaganza that turned China's revolutionary history into a foundation myth. Carried by tens of thousands of mobile movie projection units, the musical's film version illuminated the dark nights of even China's most remote countryside.

This epitome of Mao's personality cult, however, has humble origins in a folk love-song from the area near Yanan that served as the communist base in the 1930s and 1940s, one that later became the Mecca of the Chinese Revolution. The original lyrics read:

Sesame oil, cabbage hearts,
Wanna eat string beans, break off the tips

Get really lovesick if I don't see you for 3 days
Hu-er-hai-yo
Oh dear, Third Brother mine.

In 1938, as China waged a war of resistance against Japanese invasion, a poet gave new lyrics to the old tune to mobilize the people to fight:

Riding a white horse, carrying a rifle
Third brother is with the Eighth Route Army
Wanna go home to see my girl
Hu-er-hai-yo,
But fighting the Japs I don't have the time.

A few years later, with Mao's rise to the top of the Communist Party's power hierarchy, a schoolteacher reworked the song into "The East is Red" as we know it today. For all its reincarnations from an earthy ditty to a celestial paean, the song has remained a love song, except that personal desire is rechanneled, first into military valor, then into quasi-religious ardor. While denouncing "feudal culture," communist cultural workers had systematically turned traditional folk culture into revolutionary propaganda. As Mao prescribed in a seminal 1942 speech on literature and art, "these old forms, remolded and infused with new content, also become something revolutionary in the service of the people."

Besides giving new words to old tunes, communist artists produced propaganda posters by appropriating the medium and auspicious symbolism of traditional New Year prints, which farmers used for home decoration. People's Liberation Army soldiers replaced Door Gods as the new guardians of homes; Mao and other communist leaders replaced the Kitchen God and ancestors at the altar. Even today, New Year prints of Mao and his successors preside over many rural homes. It is worth keeping in mind, however, that among the common people, fearful gods and vindictive ghosts have had as much symbolic currency as merciful and benevolent bodhisattvas. In this sense, the worship of Mao also can be understood as the worship of power.

Power, as Mao famously proclaimed, grows out of the barrel of a gun. Yet more than a military strategist, Mao himself was a master propagandist, and propaganda made great contributions to the communists' rise to power. In a 1927 report on the peasant movement in Hunan, Mao wrote of how "political slogans have grown wings" and "found their way to the young, the middle-aged and the old, to the women and children in countless villages." Revolutionary songs and slogans had "penetrated into their minds and are on their lips." Although initially backward in their access to mass media technologies, the communists thus turned the bodies and voices of the masses into propaganda carriers.

We may consider such tactics the cultural counterpart of Mao's influential 1937 treatise *On Guerrilla Warfare*, which prescribed that every guerrilla company had to have its own mobile propaganda troupe. Unlike industrialized modern warfare, guerrilla warfare does not rely so much on machinery as on human beings to conduct mobile battles in enemy territory, often using weapons seized from the enemy. The revolutionary transformation of folk songs and New Year prints are both examples of cultural guerrilla warfare.

Prior to taking over Mainland China, communist propaganda in the form of posters, songs, slogans, plays, and stories had only a limited local circulation. After 1949, however, the CCP inherited and extended the existing mass-media infrastructure to bring propaganda to the most remote corners of the land. Alongside the growth of urban cinemas, an itinerant film projection network grew from 100 to 100,000 teams by the late 1970s, whereas a hundred million wired loudspeakers (one for just about every household) reconfigured the nationwide soundscape. Indeed, the utopian dreams and violent upheavals of Maoist China could not have reached their massive scale without the mass media that mobilized a largely illiterate populace over a vast geography. In this sense, the Chinese Revolution was not only a political, economic, and social revolution, but also a media revolution.

Movie teams traveled by foot, horses, tractors, boat, or self-tinkered automobiles, setting up cinemas on threshing fields and pastures, forests and deserts, construction projects and battlefields. Projectionists not only showed films but also used a storyteller's bamboo clapper to summarize a film's plot and tell the good characters from the bad. They live-dubbed for audiences who did not understand Mandarin and produced lantern slides about local histories. Films served to authenticate "socialist miracles" and help audiences envision a communist paradise. As the only legitimate form of "nightlife" people had, movies attracted the biggest crowds, so that village cadres often summoned movie teams when they needed to congregate the masses for a meeting.

Projectionists reported that Chairman Mao remained the biggest movie star for country folk, who often asked them to "slow down, let Chairman Mao stay a bit longer!" For an audience exposed to film for the first time, newsreels of national leaders helped establish a quasi-direct rapport between the rulers and the ruled. In 1966, newsreels of Mao's eight meetings with the "revolutionary masses" on Tiananmen Square—each beginning with the song "The East is Red"—were screened free of charge to hundreds of millions of people. This served to launch the Cultural Revolution and bring Mao's personality cult to unprecedented heights.

With the intensification of class struggle, cinema also took on qualities of political shamanism. Like Chinese traditional ritual theater that staged hell at temple festivals, screenings about the evil pre-Liberation "Old Society" supposedly made audiences weep with rage; with some local militias moved to the point of shooting the onscreen villains. Following the lead of propaganda, audiences denounced local landlords or "spoke bitterness" in public, so audiovisual media became spirit mediums that conjured up the ghosts of the feudal past and exorcised them to ensure the purity of the revolutionary community.

But public responses to propaganda were not always genuine. The 1963 film *Serfs*, for instance, depicted the harrowing life of a Tibetan "serf" eventually emancipated by the communists. Although the film presented a travesty of Tibetan history and religion, Tibetan scholar Tsering Shakya recalls that audiences in Lhasa were required not only to attend the screening, but also to shed tears. Otherwise, one "risked being accused of harboring sympathy with the feudal landlords." So his mother and her friends put tiger-balm under their eyes to make them water.

Still, propaganda films had enormous aesthetic power over their audiences, especially in their use of songs. Even if they weren't full-fledged musicals like *The East is Red*, most works of Maoist cinema featured a few theme songs repeated throughout the film, as if the film's very purpose was to teach audiences how to sing. The songs stayed in their ears and on their lips even as they had forgotten the film's plot and characters. More importantly, the same songs were broadcast again and again from local loudspeakers, first installed at every school, factory, and farm, and then in every residential courtyard.

Like church bells and tribal drums, omnipresent loudspeakers came to collectivize and structure people's everyday lives, calling on them to work or rest, to congregate or fight. Every morning, students, workers, and employees of state-owned work units gathered on drill grounds to perform mass calisthenics to marching music.

During the Cultural Revolution, many factional battles culminated with one group's seizure of the broadcast station as the throne, even if they continued propagating the same slogans and songs.

Also in the Cultural Revolution, every mass rally began with "The East is Red" and ended with "The Internationale." Between singing "he is the people's great savior" and "no savior from on high delivers," many people began to think through the revolution's many contradictions. Those with access to short-wave transistor radios began listening to Voice of America, Radio Moscow, and Taiwan's Voice of Free China. Between the blasting of government propaganda and the whispers of "enemy propaganda," listeners harbored alternative undercurrents of thought beneath their performances of public slogans and collective rituals.

After Mao's death and the end of the Cultural Revolution, songs like "The East is Red" stopped playing. Although people still listened to "Big Deng" (referring to the PRC's preeminent leader, Deng Xiaoping) over the loudspeakers during the day, they tuned into "Little Deng" (Taiwan singer Teresa Teng) at night. Crooning softly over transistor radios and cassette recorders, her syrupy love songs—considered "yellow" or pornographic music by the Communist Party—melted the hearts of a nation hardened by a decade of "red songs" with the beat of military marches. Listening to Teresa Teng also inaugurated a new era of mass-media consumption in China that marked a shift from the collective to the individual, from the public to the private, from centralized control to rampant piracy. Loudspeakers and films, once the primary mediators of party propaganda, were increasingly displaced by home entertainment in the form of stereo and karaoke, television and video.

As television became more widespread in the 1990s, most rural movie projectionists lost their jobs and, hence, any form of social security. In recent years, tens of thousands of them organized and

demonstrated at provincial broadcasting bureaus to petition for retirement pensions. Since the new millennium, the Chinese Ministry
of Culture has revived mobile cinema, aiming to show "one movie
per month per village," serving in part as the government's spiritual
competition with flourishing Christian churches.

In the spiritual vacuum of the post-Mao years, "red songs," with
all their nostalgic associations, have made a powerful comeback with
disco beats. Today, you can still hear "The East is Red" chiming from
the old Customs House on the Bund in Shanghai: incrementally, one
bar each quarter-hour, culminating in the entire song at the top of
the hour. Modeled after London's Big Ben and built by the British in
1927, the Customs House played the "Westminster Quarters" until
the Cultural Revolution, when the tune was changed to "The East
is Red." This changed back to the Westminster Quarters in the 1980s,
only to change once again to "The East is Red" in 2003. Like the
red flags atop every colonial building on the Bund, the song signi-
fies Chinese nationalism. But what do elderly Chinese tourists feel
when they recognize the song? Nostalgia or repulsion? Pride or irony?

In spring 2016, upon the fiftieth anniversary of the Cultural Revolution, a new music video of "The East is Red," with revised lyrics,
bounced around Chinese social media, only to be censored shortly
afterward:

> The East is red again, the sun rises again.
> Xi Jinping inherits Mao Zedong.
> He strives for the nation's revival
> Hu-er-hai-yo,
> He is the people's great lucky star.

With a visual montage overlaying footage of both Mao and Xi against
the backdrop of a rising sun, "The East is Red Again" is one of sev-

eral viral music videos (including such songs as "Big Daddy Xi Loves Mama Peng") that commentators considered a part of Xi's growing personality cult as well as an indication of his increased ideological control over mass media. After all, Xi openly proclaimed that "the Party- and government-run media are a propaganda front and must be surnamed 'Party.'"

Rather than the Department of Propaganda, however, the music videos came anonymously from the grassroots. It remains unclear if the creators are sycophants fawning over the Great Leader or cultural guerrillas mocking and undermining Xi by associating him with the Cultural Revolution. Netizens, however, responded with mostly negative comments, and after the song was scrubbed from the Chinese Internet, it reappeared on YouTube with a quip: "Dictatorship will collapse from the people's laughter." Indeed, if Chinese propaganda is no longer winning hearts and minds—or forcing out tears—it surely is winning some laughs.

34 | WHY IS IT STILL SO HARD TO TALK ABOUT THE CULTURAL REVOLUTION?

Xiaofei Tian

I WAS BORN in the second half of the Great Proletarian Cultural Revolution, a political movement launched by Chairman Mao Zedong in 1966 and, later on, always referred to as the "great calamity lasting ten years" that caused much physical and psychological devastation across China. The bits and pieces I remember of it are flashes in white and black or, more accurately, in the non-colors of dream imagery, except for the ubiquitous rosy picture of Chairman Mao hanging on the wall. One such fragment involves small crumpled notepapers with classical-styled poems scribbled on them, copied and brought back from Tiananmen Square by my father in the spring of 1976. I was not yet quite five years old and had just begun to read; I had little idea of what the verses were. What branded them into my memory was the air of utter secrecy surrounding them when my father showed them to my mother, their hushed voices, and their anxious warning to me and my brother to say nothing about them to anyone.

Only years later did I learn what the poems were: they were mourning poems, protesting poems. They were composed, posted, recited aloud, and copied by hundreds of thousands of people who gathered in Tiananmen Square from March to early April 1976; the people were there to take part in the popular demonstration mourning the recent death of Premier Zhou Enlai and protesting against the government, especially against Mao's wife, Jiang Qing, and her allies, who subsequently became known as the Gang of Four after their downfall. On April 5, thousands of demonstrators were driven from the square by police, People's Liberation Army (PLA) soldiers, and militia with clubs and batons. Arrests were made then and there and in the months following the incident, which was denounced as "counter-revolutionary" by the government. Mao died and the Gang of Four met their end later that year, and many poems from the demonstration were eventually collected in a volume entitled *Selected Poetry of Tiananmen* and published in 1978. As I was reading those poems in that volume, the words looked distant and unfamiliar on printed pages, but they evoked the memory of jotted lines on crinkled note-papers and of whispers behind closed doors. Words and danger are closely intertwined. I also learned to appreciate the intriguing fact that the majority of the poems were written in classical style, some of which were *ci*—song lyrics in centuries-old meter.

Though a medievalist, I have been teaching a course called "Art and Violence in the Cultural Revolution" since 2001. There is a double play of continuity and rupture in the periodization project of twentieth-century China. China's imperial past is made to serve as the origin giving coherence to modern China's national identity, and as the background against which modern China emerged in revolt. What has always fascinated me about the Cultural Revolution, however, are the twin paradoxes at its heart: (1) the paradox of the movement's pledge to demolish the past and create a new society, even though the movement was itself deeply embedded in the past; and (2) the violence attendant on such a cataclysmic historical event and the movement's continuous interlocking with literature and arts. With regard to the first paradox, despite the sworn aim to rid China of the "Four Olds" ("Old Customs, Old Culture, Old Habits, and Old Ideas"), many old cultural forms of expression persisted, albeit in distorted or disguised configurations. With regard to the second paradox, the full-scale launching of the movement had been augured by a propaganda war waged by the state against a historical drama featuring an official from the Ming dynasty (1368–1644), written by a historian of the Ming. We also should note that the "Eight Revolutionary Peking Opera Model Plays" produced during this period became woven into the daily lives of millions of Chinese and remain very much part of contemporary popular culture.

Indeed, the Cultural Revolution began as a bad hermeneutic exercise in the form of a virulent attack, undertaken by one of the Gang of Four and backed by Mao, on the "Three-Family Village"—a group of three writers who contributed essays to a magazine managed by the Beijing Communist Party Committee. The attack led one of the writers to commit suicide and sparked a nationwide paranoia about hidden meanings lurking between the lines. People learned that what they said or wrote could condemn them, and that a friend or neighbor could perform an ingenious interpretation and one's own spouse or child could turn into an informant. The so-called "prison of words" harks back to the first such case in Chinese history. It happened in the eleventh century when the poet, writer, and statesman Su Shi was thrown into prison for his poems, and a legal case was built around a close analysis of the poems. But in the twentieth century, the interpretation craze spread from famous members of the scholar elite to common citizens.

The power of words to destroy was manifested in "big-character posters"—wall-mounted posters written by hand in large Chinese characters. These posters would denounce the alleged counterrevolutionaries, and they could be anyone: the purged chairman of the People's Republic (i.e., Liu Shaoqi), the manager of a factory, a colleague, an associate, or a neighbor living two houses down the street. In my course on the Cultural Revolution, I always show students a photograph from the 1960s of people climbing a ladder to put up posters and asked them if they notice anything strange. It usually takes the students a while to realize that nobody could read much of the posters, because they were hanging from the third floor of a building and the size of the characters was not large enough for anyone to read. But the content hardly mattered. The posters were there to create an atmosphere of oppressive visual weight and violence. One was surrounded by ferociously brutal words; there was nowhere to flee and to escape. My maternal grandfather was an "old revolutionary" who ran away from his well-to-do family—parents, young wife, and two children—to join the communists and fight in the Sino-Japanese War. His actions led to his entire family's death at the hands of the local militia, and his father's concubine and my mother were the massacre's only survivors. During the Cultural Revolution, he was censured at one of the so-called struggle sessions and, unable to withstand the verbal onslaughts, died of a stroke at age forty-nine.

Rather than focusing on the Cultural Revolution as a purely political movement, as Mao's maneuvers to maintain personal power, or as a manifestation of the ideological struggles among communist leaders, I wanted to teach a course exploring the Cultural Revolution's *cultural* implications. What did it mean to begin a mass movement with literary criticism? How could art turn violent, and how could violence be turned into an exquisite art? The Cultural Revolution promised, as a popular slogan had it, to be "a revolution touching the soul." It did. How it did that, through what means, and what the effects were of having one's soul "touched"—these are questions that must be asked. The means through which the movement was carried out tell us much about the culture and society that it purported to change.

Many people living through the Cultural Revolution chose to write memoirs as a way of coming to terms with, and making sense of, their traumatic experiences. Both personally written memoirs and oral accounts compiled by interviewers and researchers are invaluable sources to help understand the movement, but they also have a way of raising yet more questions about the relationship between memory, especially traumatic memory, and history. Memory is subject to interference. The past is not fixed but constantly shifting, always being determined by the present of the person who has already integrated the past into his or her being and recalls the past under drastically different circumstances. Thus, the attempt to understand the past cannot be separated from the attempt to understand the person remembering the past in its aftermath. Memory is also mediated by writing, which is governed by its own rhetorical tradition, strategies, and devices. Literary tradition intervenes in the way in which memory is articulated; language is not a transparent medium in the writing of history and must itself be an object of critical inquiry.

To take a bottom-up approach to the Cultural Revolution—examining it from the perspectives of individuals—enables one to see the movement "up close and personal" and, in many ways, as it really was, for the Cultural Revolution was a mass movement in which numerous Chinese people—workers, peasants, the city-street cleaning crew, not just high-level communist leaders or members of the intelligentsia who are the modern-day avatars of the scholar elite from imperial China—all participated to various degrees. Much attention has been paid to the political ideology motivating the movement, or to the writers, artists, and intellectuals who became embroiled in it. That attention is certainly justified, but it is not enough.

The Cultural Revolution may be described as a movement fractured and fragmented by regions and individuals. There was no single "Cultural Revolution" because every Chinese, in every city and village across the country, was involved in a unique, individual way. The movement was nonetheless woven into the textures of ordinary people's daily lives in shared multimedia venues: through the voices of news anchors broadcasted from radios and loudspeakers; through Mao's portraits and bright-colored wall posters; through newspapers and magazines; through the Revolutionary Peking Opera arias played over and over again; through songs and slogans; and through the Little Red Books and memorized passages of Chairman Mao's teachings.

A student from my class, while doing archival research, accidentally discovered a photo of long-lost family friends in the uncatalogued, unmarked boxes, acquired by a librarian in the 1980s, of Cultural Revolution material in the Harvard-Yenching Library. Many of the Chinese students taking my class told me that their parents or grandparents had been deeply affected by the Cultural Revolution but were reluctant to talk about it because they feared their children or grandchildren, growing up in vastly different contexts and speaking a different language both linguistically and culturally, would not understand. Working on projects that involved interviewing family members, those students felt that taking a class on the Cultural Revolution helped them know their family history better and connect more deeply with their parents and grandparents. For their non-Chinese classmates, it was an inspiring experience because they observed how the memories of the Cultural Revolution lived on in real people's lives—something one cannot get from simply reading about it in books and articles. Those individual memories, taken together, form a memory mosaic that brings more parts of a massive historical event into light.

It was an unforgettable decade for people of all ages, for different reasons. Beginning with personal reminiscence about classical-styled Chinese verses written on scraps of paper, I want to end the essay with an English quatrain by the Iowa poet Paul Engle, husband to the famous Chinese American writer Nieh Hualing, and co-founder with her of the International Writing Program in Iowa City. This and many other poems were, as Nieh said, "created in scraps of time" during Engle's trip to mainland China in 1980.

My hand picked up a stone,
I heard a voice inside
Crying: Leave me alone,
I came down here to hide.

The poem's title is "Cultural Revolution." It reminds us of the impenetrable, and the ever-present, nature of the "past." We must learn where to bend down and listen—to entities and objects that seem to contain no inner life at all—and we must also learn there are many different ways, approaches, and methods by which we can get inside.

35 | WHAT IS THE FUTURE OF CHINA'S PAST?

Stephen Owen

SOME WORDS merit reflection. We use such words too easily. We presume to know what the past means; but, in fact, the very concept of "the past" has some profound divisions, which themselves belong to history. There is a great difference between the past as something ongoing behind us, and the past as everything before a certain date or period, after which we enter some older version of a "present," which is itself acquiring a history even as the past is beyond change. Such a radical closure of the past was a part of the modernist project; the closure of the past is now institutionalized and has even been given its own word: "premodern."

There is considerable debate exactly when modernity happened; its proposed beginnings range from German thinkers of the late eighteenth century to the Industrial Revolution of the nineteenth century to the 1920s. With a peculiar combination of conviction and irony, Virginia Woolf famously observed: "On or about December 1910, human character changed" ("Mr. Bennett and Mrs. Brown," 1924). The heart of the matter is the problematic claim that after a certain point, everything was different.

China inherited the idea of modernity as a breach in history and institutionalized it with characteristic precision, allowing for a long transitional period. The "recent past" begins with the Opium War, and modernity begins (delineated with even greater precision than

Virginia Woolf offered) on May Fourth, 1919. This breach in history created the ahistorical construct of "traditional China" and the peculiar conviction that China before the Opium War had all been pretty much the same. It is an easy and banal exercise to show the deep differences between eighteenth-century China and modern China. It is, however, just as easy to demonstrate that, in very basic ways, eighteenth-century Chinese society was far closer to modern Chinese society than it was to Chinese society in the fourth century CE. The former claim is a matter of faith; the latter claim invites surprise and skepticism.

The Chinese word most commonly used to refer to the closed cultural past as it survives in the present is *yichan*, "heritage." This is an old word, "inheritance," extended to make the recipients not just family heirs, but the entire Han Chinese population. Every legacy implies an exclusion; in this extended sense of *yichan*, those excluded from the inheritance are non-Han peoples. This is particularly interesting in regard to other East Asian ethnicities whose elite had once believed that this received culture was also theirs—indeed, more theirs than it was the possession of Han Chinese commoners. This modern redistribution of cultural wealth was obviously a part of the project of forming national identity through the medium of the new Republican and, later, PRC school system. What had earlier been the possession that distinguished one small group within the population from other Han folk was distributed to the general population, irrespective of class, gender, or region. It is now a matter of faith that any Han Chinese who knows a dozen Tang poems understands them better than any foreign scholar possibly could—precisely because they are the inherited possession of Han Chinese. The profound differences consequent to more than a millennium of phonological, semantic, and cultural change are immaterial; the poems are a recited heirloom that confers identity.

A heritage implies death and closure, the second idea of the past mentioned above. It is indeed an heirloom, not capital, and can only be preserved unchanged. It is treated as something already known and not open to serious reinterpretation—unless something is dug out of the ground (or purchased on the black market in the hope that it was dug out of the ground). Under this regime of "the heirloom," scholarship becomes largely a re-performance of a familiar score or a nuanced exploration of some darker corner of the cultural archive. The task of scholarship becomes to secure the heirloom's place with greater detail in the history of the people, and not to ask questions about it.

If Western apocalyptic modernity ("On or about December 1910, human character changed") was one factor in the modern / contemporary construction of the Chinese premodern, a second factor came from premodern China itself—more specifically, from China's last dynasty, the Qing. This is the assumption that the earlier past was essentially the same as the later past. Any claim that basic changes occurred over the course of Chinese history always invites the response that whatever was supposed to have changed already existed earlier.

A changing medium within which a small part of the Chinese population lived has become a clearly defined product, "traditional Chinese culture," packaged in various forms for domestic consumption and an export market through lavishly state-supported "Confucius Institutes."

There are very smart graduate students and younger scholars in China excited by new ideas coming in. They form study groups. But when they teach, they are required to teach the standard literary histories, which all say the same thing and in which they have lost faith. When they are in public venues, they are often silent about the new ideas they discuss in private. They do not cite—or perhaps dare not cite—what they clearly have been reading.

I do not mean to paint too grim a situation, or to claim that this situation is unique to China. Similar phenomena are common in state school systems teaching national culture everywhere. American state universities sometimes have to struggle with legislatures to maintain academic freedom. The state is footing the considerable bill, and the state knows what it wants taught.

What then is the future of China's past? I see it in those study groups of graduate students and young faculty, on the margins of academic culture, and in the aficionados on the outside. They complicate contemporary China's cultural mix of a vibrant avant-garde, a no less vibrant popular web culture, and the conservatism of academic culture (remarkably senior and male). Simply by publishing, scholars from outside China have a role in this. Their books will sometimes end up in a foreign enclave in Chinese bookstores—marked as overseas scholarship—but they seem to attract a much greater concentration of shoppers than the vast shelves of academic Chinese scholarship. When we talk to those graduate students, young faculty, and the aficionados, there is a real dialogue, which does not happen in formal academic venues.

A venerable principle in Chinese thought is *bian er tong*: by changing, something gets through, succeeds, and continues. The antonym of *tong* is *se*: blocked, stagnating. This is where the understanding of the Chinese cultural past is now. Serious critical reflection on the Chinese cultural past—allowing our understanding to change—is what we can hope for from these marginal communities around the academy and the aficionados. It is a smart and exciting tradition if one but looks carefully and with new eyes. Its texts and artifacts can be rescued from the vast reservoir of stereotypes. These are not heirlooms.

European and American thought in the 1960s and 1970s was exciting and left a deep (if not always acknowledged) legacy on how contemporary intellectuals understand the world. Those thinkers are more often read in second-hand summary than in primary works. Few appreciate that much of their best work came explicitly out of rereading the thinkers of the past: Plato, Rousseau, Hegel, Balzac. This is a past not ossified and worshipped, but something that returns to the present as food for serious thought. That is what the past can be: *bian er tong.*

This is what we can hope for. I have no idea what younger Chinese scholars will find under such a critical gaze, but it would be neither the stereotypes of an ossified and essentialized "traditional China" nor Western thought, including postcolonial thought wearing Chinese clothes. I do not believe the contemporary academic commonplace that when we read the past, we find only ourselves. We are ourselves in change; we learn and change.

36 | HOW HAS THE STUDY OF CHINA CHANGED IN THE LAST SIXTY YEARS?

Paul A. Cohen

THERE ARE MANY FACTORS that can be brought into play in responding to this question. Three of the most important are technology, politics, and sociocultural change. Parts of my discussion necessarily will go beyond the question how the study of China in particular has changed, since, in certain respects, the Chinese case reflects a broader process of transformation that has taken place in much of the world.

TECHNOLOGICAL FACTORS

When the typewriter was replaced by the personal computer, not only did erasing become a thing of the past, but the word-processing capacity of the computer enabled you to copy and paste, move whole chunks of text from one place to another, and perform many other tricks. Word processing, in comparison with typing, proved a godsend. The typewriter was now reclassified as an antique.

But personal computers served not only to facilitate the creation of written text. They also, in combination with the Internet, provided the physical means by which you could do all sorts of things that were previously impossible. Libraries now traded in their low-tech card catalogues for online ones that enabled scholars the world over to determine, in an instant, whether a particular library had a particular book. You didn't have to go there to find out. The Internet also enabled scholars to make keyword searches; to pore over digitized archives, newspapers, and journals without ever having to leave their office or home study; to connect via the web with thousands of sites globally; to probe vast databases that revolutionized the process of carrying on research; and, with their computers, to engage in instantaneous email correspondence and exchange of documentation with colleagues around the world.

Here is a simple example from my own research. In preparing the final chapter of my book *Speaking to History: The Story of King Goujian in Twentieth-Century China* (2009), I made extensive use of *China Academic Journals*, a Chinese database, that enabled full-text searches of more than 7,200 journals, magazines, newsletters, and other sources, representing a vast range of specialized interests and covering the years from 1994 to 2007 (the year in which my research was concluded). To give some idea of the power of such a database, as of January 2007, a search for "Goujian" (a ruler of the state of Yue during the Eastern Zhou dynasty) resulted in hits in 5,549 articles, and a search for "*woxin changdan*" (a famous proverb associated with the Goujian story), yielded hits in 7,292 articles. Clearly, without such a search engine and the process of digitization that lay at its heart, the research on which much of the chapter was based would simply not have been possible. Digitization can convert virtually anything—text, sound, graphic images, parts of the human body—into digital form, making immense quantities of data readily accessible to researchers everywhere. It is now a basic tool for students of Chinese history in China, America, and elsewhere around the world.

POLITICAL FACTORS

Politics determines who can go to China and do research there; what kinds of archives are accessible (and to what degree); what sorts of contact, if you are a foreigner, you can have with Chinese scholars with whom you might wish to exchange information and ideas, or even perhaps collaborate; whether, as a foreigner, you are invited to take part in scholarly conferences; and so on. When I got my doctorate in 1961, it was impossible for Americans to visit China at all, although you could, of course, do research in Taiwan as well as other places that possessed archival materials pertaining to China (such as missionary papers at Harvard's Houghton Library or Yale's Divinity School Library), or the Toyo Bunko (Oriental Library) in Tokyo, or government and church archives in Paris, London, Rome, and elsewhere. Of course, at that point in time, long before computers and digitization, you had to make a physical trip to the archive to read the original materials, which was inconvenient, expensive, and time-consuming.

China's closed-door policy, at least for American scholars, began to change toward the end of the 1970s. Joseph Esherick, for example, for his path-breaking 1987 work *The Origins of the Boxer Uprising*, was able to spend a year in China beginning in the fall of 1979 and carry on extensive research in the oral history surveys of former Boxers done by students and faculty of the Shandong University History Department in the 1960s. I went to China for the first time in 1977, but my intellectual contact with Chinese scholars only really began in August 1981, when I attended a conference on "Chinese Society during the Late Qing and Early Republican Periods," hosted by Fudan University in Shanghai. Although it was a sizable gathering, few foreigners were invited, and Albert Feuerwerker and I were the only American participants. The conference was pretty freewheeling, with Chinese participants able to criticize or praise one another publicly, on substantive grounds, and also do the same with Feuer-werker and me. The conference papers were later published in Chinese, and in my case at least, there was no effort to reshape what I wrote to make it more politically acceptable. I came away from the conference feeling, perhaps a trifle prematurely, that real progress was being made in freedom of communication in China.

My first experience doing actual research in China came in 1987, when I spent a fruitful period at Shandong University, reading oral history documentation relating to the Boxers, and at Nankai University in Tianjin, where I was able to make copies of a sizable quantity of unpublished oral history material dealing with the Boxers in Tianjin and elsewhere in Hebei Province, which had been collected mainly by the Class of 1956 of the Nankai University History Department. During my Shandong visit, I spent almost an entire day talking with Lu Yao, one of China's foremost Boxer historians and the prime mover behind the Shandong oral history surveys. During our conversation, Professor Lu talked with complete openness about the limitations on the interviewing process as carried on years earlier by the Shandong History Department students.

By this point in time, it was possible to maintain regular communication with Chinese scholars, a few of whom had begun to spend time abroad pursuing their individual research interests. Also, non-Chinese scholars, in addition to having access to the collections of the First Historical Archives in Beijing and the Second Historical Archives in Nanjing, could now conduct important research in provincial and county archives in various parts of China. The Chinese, moreover, had begun to publish substantial collections of documents from their archival holdings, which made them readily available to people outside China.

Chinese government authorities, for political reasons, have occasionally denied visas to foreigners, and to people of Chinese extraction living abroad, in response to publications or publicly aired criticism that gave Beijing offense—and continue to do so. They also have periodically limited access to specific archives, and it remains relatively difficult to do research on politically sensitive topics in China. However, on the whole, access both to people and to documentation has improved dramatically over the past sixty years. The same is true in regard to the conducting of interviews with individuals who have taken important parts in China's recent history, or who could shed light on what life was like at various levels of Chinese society at specific points during the years of Mao Zedong's rule. Here again, although plenty of obstacles remain, the situation is far better than it was sixty years ago.

Another context that is politically related, and where dramatic change has taken place over the past sixty years, is China's emergence as a major force in the global economy of the early twenty-first century, something unimaginable from the perspective of my graduate school days. This has transformed the questions historians now ask. It has also resulted in an astonishing increase in the numbers of Chinese studying abroad: over 328,000 in 2015–2016 in the United States alone (according to the Institute of International Education). This figure constitutes 31.5 percent of all international students in the United States during the same period. Most of the Chinese students will return home after completion of their studies, bringing with them new perspectives on their lives in China and, hopefully, a greater interest in histories of China written by non-Chinese specialists.

SOCIOCULTURAL FACTORS

When I refer to "sociocultural factors," what I have in mind mainly are new developments that have taken place in the interests of historians globally over the past half-century and that have affected the kinds of questions we ask about China. Some of these developments represent elaborations of tendencies already under way in the 1970s and 1980s. A notable example is the study of popular culture, including how it both differed from and interacted with elite culture. There has been a veritable explosion of writing within this subfield, beginning with the publication in 1985 of *Popular Culture in Late Imperial China*, a pioneering volume edited by David Johnson, Andrew J. Nathan, and Evelyn S. Rawski. Subsequent high points have included, in the realm of labor history, work on groups as diverse as Shanghai prostitutes, Beijing rickshaw pullers, and factory workers in Shanghai and Tianjin; and, in the area of popular communication, studies of almanacs, folk literature, operatic performance, and wartime propaganda.

Another development that has increased enormously in importance has been the impact of the anthropological field on historical writing on China (mirroring a trend in the historical profession generally in the United States and elsewhere). Again, gender and women's studies, which were just beginning to attract attention when my first book was published (1963), have expanded significantly since that time. As the editors of the landmark work, *Engendering China: Women, Culture, and the State* (1994), put it: "China viewed through the lens of gender is not just more inclusive; it is different." Other new areas of research in recent years have included the history of medicine and disease, the roles of non-Han groups in Chinese history, Chinese migration abroad, and environmental history.

There was a time (certainly in the nineteenth century) when it was not uncommon for Westerners to see China as sui generis, something fundamentally different from their own countries. China was a static, unchanging civilization. It was a strange place, hard to understand. And it existed in a state of isolation, hermetically sealed from the rest of the world. Then, as Western scholars came to understand China better, especially over the past half-century or so, these myths were upended, one by one. Most importantly, change was seen to be as much a staple of Chinese history as of the histories of other major civilizations, and it became clear that, through trade, religion, and other forms of contact, the Chinese had been closely engaged with the rest of the world for a very long time.

The principal new context in which China has come increasingly to be seen in recent decades has been that of Eurasia as a whole. By enlarging our field of vision from the easternmost end of this landmass to the continent's entirety, we have come to see Qing dynasty China as only one Eurasian empire among several, including the Hapsburgs, the Ottomans, the Muscovites, the Mughals, and, in time, the British. As we began to compare China with these empires—and to shed some of our earlier preconceptions—our understanding of the Qing and its place in the world evolved. Scholars began, among other things, to see the Qing Empire not just as a victim of imperialism but as a colonial power itself, like other Eurasian empires expansionist and ruling over a sizable multiethnic realm. We also began to see the transformation of the Chinese polity from empire to nation, beginning in the latter decades of the nineteenth century, as in some respects a late iteration of a process that had already taken place in other parts of the Eurasian landmass. The point, here as elsewhere, is not that, as we got to understand China better, it became more and more like us. Rather, it is that as we came to see China in less fanciful terms, we began to see with increasing clarity that China has had to address problems over time that are often surprisingly similar to the problems other civilizations, including our own, have also had to deal with.

FURTHER READING

We don't pretend this book is the last word on China and recognize some readers may want greater detail about the topics covered here as well as other issues. For them, we include suggested further readings of general interest here. However, with so much new and interesting material being published, we recognize that offering only a static list is of limited use. For as long as this book remains in print, we will also maintain and update a dynamic list of further reading on the Fairbank Center website: http://fairbank.fas.harvard.edu/china-questions/, which also lists more specialized sources used by this volume's authors.

POLITICS

Cheek, Timothy. *A Critical Introduction to Mao.* Cambridge: Cambridge University Press, 2010.

Elliott, Mark. "The Case of the Missing Indigene: Debate over the 'Second-Generation' Ethnic Policy." *The China Journal* 73 (January 2015): 1–28.

Fukuyama, Francis. "Reflections on Chinese Governance." *Journal of Chinese Governance* 1, no. 3 (September 2016): 379–391.

———. *The End of History and the Last Man.* New York: Simon and Schuster, 2006.

Leibold, James. *Ethnic Policy in China: Is Reform Inevitable?* Honolulu: East West Center, 2013.

———. *Reconfiguring Chinese Nationalism: How the Qing Frontier and Its Indigenes Became Chinese.* New York: Palgrave Macmillan, 2007.

Li, Cheng. *Chinese Politics in the Xi Jinping Era: Reassessing Collective Leadership.* Washington, DC: Brookings Institution Press, 2016.

Lü, Xiaobo. *Cadres and Corruption: The Organizational Involution of the Chinese Communist Party.* Stanford, CA: Stanford University Press, 2000.

MacFarquhar, Roderick, and Michael Schoenhals. *Mao's Last Revolution.* Cambridge, MA: Harvard University Press, 2008.

Nathan, Andrew. "Authoritarian Resilience." *Journal of Democracy* 14, no. 1 (2003): 6–17.

Pantsov, Alexander V., and Steven I. Levine. *Mao: The Real Story.* New York: Simon and Schuster Paperback, 2012.

Pei, Minxin. *China's Crony Capitalism: The Dynamics of Regime Decay.* Cambridge, MA: Harvard University Press, 2016.

Perdue, Peter C. *China Marches West: The Qing Conquest of Central Eurasia.* Cambridge, MA: Harvard University Press, 2005.

Perry, Elizabeth J. *Challenging the Mandate of Heaven: Social Protest and State Power in China.* Armonk, NY: M. E. Sharpe, 2001.

———. "Reclaiming the Chinese Revolution." *Journal of Asian Studies* 67, no. 4 (November 2008): 1147–1164.

"The Politburo's Growing Number of Influential Leaders." *New York Times,* November 15, 2012. http://www.nytimes.com/interactive/2012/11/14/world/asia/the-politburos-growing-number-of-influential-leaders.html?_r=0.

Sautman, Barry. "Paved with Good Intentions: Proposals to Curb Minority Rights and Their Consequences for China." *Modern China* 38, no. 1 (2012): 10–39.

Tang, Wenfang. *Populist Authoritarianism: Chinese Political Culture and Regime Sustainability.* New York: Oxford University Press, 2016.

Tullock, Gordon. *Autocracy.* New York: Springer Science & Business Media, 2012.

Xiang, Lanxin. *China's Legitimacy Crisis.* Lanham, MD: Rowman & Littlefield, 2017.

Zang, Xiaowei, ed. *Handbook on Ethnic Minorities in China* (Handbooks of Research on Contemporary China). Cheltenham, UK: Edward Elgar Publishing, 2016.

INTERNATIONAL RELATIONS

Art, Robert J. "The United States, East Asia, and the Rise of China: Implications for the Long Haul." *Political Science Quarterly* 125, no. 3 (Fall 2010): 359–391.

Blasko, Dennis J. *The Chinese Army Today: Tradition and Transformation for the 21st Century.* 2nd ed. New York: Routledge, 2012.

Brook, Timothy. *Collaboration: Japanese Agents and Local Elites in Wartime China.* Cambridge, MA: Harvard University Press, 2005.

Bush, Richard C. *Uncharted Strait: The Future of China-Taiwan Relations.* Washington, DC: Brookings Institution Press, 2013.

Cheung, Tai Ming, ed. *Forging China's Military Might: A New Framework for Assessing Innovation.* Baltimore: Johns Hopkins University Press, 2014.

Christensen, Thomas J. *The China Challenge: Shaping the Choices of a Rising Power.* New York: W. W. Norton & Company, 2015.

Chung, Jae Ho, ed. *Assessing China's Power.* New York: Palgrave Macmillan, 2015.

Cliff, Roger. *China's Military Power: Assessing Current and Future Capabilities.* Cambridge: Cambridge University Press, 2015.

Erickson, Andrew S. *Chinese Anti-Ship Ballistic Missile (ASBM) Development: Drivers, Trajectories and Strategic Implications.* Washington, DC: Jamestown Foundation, 2013.

———, ed. *Chinese Naval Shipbuilding: An Ambitious and Uncertain Course.* Annapolis, MD: Naval Institute Press, 2016.

Goldstein, Steven M. *China and Taiwan.* Cambridge: Polity Press, 2015.

Hui, Victoria Tin-bor. *War and State Formation in Ancient China and Early Modern Europe*. Cambridge: Cambridge University Press, 2005.

Johnston, Alastair Iain. *Cultural Realism: Strategic Culture and Grand Strategy in Chinese History*. Princeton, NJ: Princeton University Press, 1995.

Lin, Hsiao-ting. *Accidental State: Chiang Kai-shek, the United States, and the Making of Taiwan*. Cambridge, MA: Harvard University Press, 2013.

McDevitt, Rear Admiral Michael, USN (ret.), ed. *Becoming a Great "Maritime Power": A Chinese Dream*. Arlington, VA: CNA Corporation, June 2016, https://www.cna.org/CNA_files/PDF/IRM-2016-U-013646.pdf.

McReynolds, Joe, ed. *China's Evolving Military Strategy*. Washington, DC: Jamestown Foundation, 2016.

Military and Security Developments Involving the People's Republic of China 2016, Annual Report to Congress. Arlington, VA: Office of the Secretary of Defense, May 13, 2016. http://www.defense.gov/Portals/1/Documents/pubs/2016%20China%20Military%20Power%20Report.pdf.

Mitter, Rana. *Forgotten Ally: China's World War II, 1937–1945*. New York: Houghton Mifflin, 2013.

Rigger, Shelley. *Why Taiwan Matters: Small Island, Global Powerhouse*. Lanham, MD: Rowman & Littlefield, 2013.

Ross, Robert. "The Revival of Geopolitics in East Asia: Why and How?" *Global Asia* 9, no. 3 (Fall 2014): 8–14.

———. "The Rise of the Chinese Navy: From Regional Naval Power to Global Naval Power?" In *A Changing China in a Changing World*, edited by Avery Goldstein and Jacques deLisle. Washington, DC: Brookings Institution, 2017.

Wachman, Alan M. *Why Taiwan? Geostrategic Rationales for China's Territorial Integrity*. Stanford, CA: Stanford University Press, 2007.

Westad, Odd Arne. *Restless Empire: China and the World since 1750*. New York: Basic Books, 2015.

ECONOMY

Chang, Leslie T. *Factory Girls: From Village to City in a Changing China*. New York: Spiegel & Grau, 2009.

Cho, Mun Young. *The Specter of the People: Urban Poverty in Northeast China*. Ithaca, NY: Cornell University Press, 2013.

Chow, Gregory C. *China's Economic Transformation*. Malden, MA: Blackwell, 2002.

Cunningham, Edward. *China's Most Generous: Understanding China's Philanthropic Landscape*. This can be accessed at https://chinaphilanthropy.ash.harvard.edu. This website is updated regularly.

Dillon, Nara. *Radical Inequalities: The Revolutionary Chinese Welfare State in Comparative Perspective*. Cambridge, MA: Harvard University Press, 2015.

Goodman, David S. G. *The New Rich in China: Future Rulers, Present Lives*. London: Routledge, 2008.

Hsing, You-tien. *The Great Urban Transformation*. Oxford: Oxford University Press, 2010.

Johnson, Paula D., and Tony Saich. *Values and Vision: Philanthropy in 21st Century China*. Ash Center for Democratic Governance and Innovation, 2017.

Lardy, Nicolas R. *Markets Over Mao*. Peterson Institute for International Economics, 2014.

Li, Shi, Hiroshi Sato, and Terry Sicular, eds. *Rising Inequality in China: Challenges to a Harmonious Society*. Cambridge: Cambridge University Press, 2013.

Looney, Kristen. "China's Campaign to Build a New Socialist Countryside: Village Modernization, Peasant Councils, and the Ganzhou Model of Rural Development." *China Quarterly* 224 (2015): 909–932.

Office of the United States Trade Representative, Washington, DC: 2016 Report to Congress on China's WTO Compliance. https://ustr.gov/sites/default/files/2016-China-Report-to-Congress.pdf.

Perkins, Dwight. *East Asian Development*. Cambridge, MA: Harvard University Press, 2013.

———. *The Economic Transformation of China*. Singapore: World Scientific Press, 2015.

Riedel, James, Jing Jin, and Jian Gao. *How China Grows*. Princeton, NJ: Princeton University Press, 2007.

Rithmire, Meg. *Land Bargains and Chinese Capitalism: The Politics of Property Rights under Reform*. Cambridge: Cambridge University Press, 2015.

Tsai, Lily L. *Accountability without Democracy: Solidary Groups and Public Goods Provision in Rural China*. Cambridge: Cambridge University Press, 2007.

Webster, Timothy. "Paper Compliance: How China Implements WTO Decisions." *Michigan Journal of International Law* 35 (2013): 525–578.

Whyte, Martin King. *The Myth of the Social Volcano: Perceptions of Inequality and Distributive Justice in Contemporary China*. Stanford, CA: Stanford University Press, 2010.

Wu, Mark. "The China, Inc. Challenge to Global Trade Governance." *Harvard International Law Journal* 57 (2016): 261–324.

ENVIRONMENT

Anderson, E. N. *Caring for Place: Ecology, Ideology, and Emotion in Traditional Landscape Management.* London: Routledge, 2014.

Duara, Prasenjit. *The Crisis of Global Modernity: Asian Traditions and a Sustainable Future.* Cambridge: Cambridge University Press, 2015.

Elvin, Mark. *The Retreat of the Elephants: An Environmental History of China.* New Haven, CT: Yale University Press, 2004.

Kahn, Matthew E., and Siqi Zheng. *Blue Skies over Beijing: Economic Growth and the Environment in China.* Princeton, NJ: Princeton University Press, 2016.

Mao, Yushi. "Evolution of Environmental Ethics: A Chinese Perspective." In *Ethics and Environmental Policy: Theory Meets Practice,* edited by Frederick Ferre and Peter Hartell, 42–57. Athens: University of Georgia Press, 1994.

McElroy, Michael. *Energy and Climate: Vision for the Future.* 1st ed. Oxford: Oxford University Press, 2016.

———. *Energy: Perspectives, Problems and Prospects.* Oxford: Oxford University Press, 2010.

Shapiro, Judith. *Mao's War against Nature: Politics and the Environment in Revolutionary China.* Cambridge: Cambridge University Press, 2001.

Smil, Vaclav. *China's Past, China's Future: Energy, Food, Environment.* London: Routledge, 2004.

Thornber, Karen Laura. *Ecoambiguity: Environmental Crises and East Asian Literatures.* Ann Arbor: University of Michigan Press, 2012.

SOCIETY

Ashiwa, Yoshiko, and David L. Wank, eds. *Making Religion, Making the State: The Politics of Religion in Contemporary China.* Stanford, CA: Stanford University Press, 2009.

Bol, Peter K. *Neo-Confucianism in History.* Cambridge, MA: Harvard University Asia Center, 2008.

Brauen, Martin, ed. *The Dalai Lamas: A Visual History.* Chicago: Serindia, 2005.

de Bary, Wm. Theodore, and Irene Bloom, comps. *Sources of Chinese Tradition.* New York: Columbia University Press, 2000.

Goossaert, Vincent, and David A. Palmer. *The Religious Question in Modern China.* Chicago: University of Chicago Press, 2011.

Greenhalgh, Susan. *Cultivating Global Citizens.* Cambridge, MA: Harvard University Press, 2010.

Katz, Paul R. *Religion in China and Its Modern Fate.* Waltham, MA: Brandeis University Press, 2014.

Kaufman, Joan, Arthur Kleinman, and Tony Saich. *AIDS and Social Policy in China.* Harvard East Asian Monographs. Asia Public Policy Series. Cambridge, MA: HIV/AIDS Public Policy Project, Kennedy School of Government, Harvard University, 2006.

Kleinman, Arthur, and James L. Watson. *SARS in China: Prelude to Pandemic?* Stanford, CA: Stanford University Press, 2006.

Kleinman, Arthur, Yunxiang Yan, Jing Jun, Sing Lee, Everett Zhang, Pan Tianshu, Wu Fei, and Guo Jinhua. *Deep China: The Moral Life of the Person: What Anthropology and Psychiatry Tell Us about China Today.* Berkeley: University of California Press, 2011.

Lei, Ya-Wen. *The Contentious Public Sphere: Law, Media and Authoritarian Rule in China.* Princeton, NJ: Princeton University Press, 2017.

Liu, Sida, and Terence Halliday. *Criminal Defense in China: The Politics of Lawyers at Work.* Cambridge: Cambridge University Press, 2016.

Overmyer, Daniel L., ed. *Religion in China Today.* Cambridge: Cambridge University Press, 2003.

Palmer, David A., Glenn Shive, and Philip Wickeri, eds. *Chinese Religious Life.* Oxford: Oxford University Press, 2011.

Schwieger, Peter. *The Dalai Lama and the Emperor of China.* New York: Columbia University Press, 2015.

Ya, Hanzhang. *The Biographies of the Dalai Lamas.* Translated by Wang Wenjiong. Beijing: Foreign Languages Press, 1991.

Zhang, Qinfan. *The Constitution of China: A Contextual Analysis.* Oxford: Hart Publishing, 2012.

Zhu, Suli. *Sending Law to the Countryside: Research on China's Basic-Level Judicial System.* New York: Springer, 2016.

HISTORY AND CULTURE

Cao Xueqin, and Gao E. *The Story of the Stone.* Translated by David Hawkes and John Minford. 5 vols. Harmondsworth, UK: Penguin, 1973–1986.

Chan, Koonchung. *The Fat Years.* Translated by Michael Duke. New York: Doubleday, 2011.

Cohen, Paul A. *Discovering History in China: American Historical Writing on the Recent Chinese Past.* New York: Columbia University Press, 2010.

Gilmartin, Christina K., Gail Hershatter, Lisa Rofel, and Tyrene White, eds. *Engendering China: Women, Culture, and the State.* Cambridge, MA: Harvard University Press, 1994.

Hansen, Valerie. *The Silk Road: A New History.* Oxford: Oxford University Press, 2012.

Hsia, C. T. *The Classic Chinese Novel: A Critical Introduction.* Hong Kong: Chinese University Press, 2015.

Johnson, David, Andrew J. Nathan, and Evelyn S. Rawski, eds. *Popular Culture in Late Imperial China.* Berkeley: University of California Press, 1985.

The Journey to the West. Attributed to Wu Cheng-en. Translated by Anthony C. Yu. 4 vols. Chicago: University of Chicago Press, 2012.

Lao She. *The Philosophy of Old Zhang: The City of Cats.* CNPeReading, 2012.

Li, Wai-yee. "Full-Length Vernacular Fiction." In *Columbia History of Chinese Literature,* edited by Victor Mair, 620–658. New York: Columbia University Press, 2001.

———. *Enchantment and Disenchantment: Love and Illusion in Chinese Literature.* Princeton, NJ: Princeton University Press, 1993.

Lieberman, Victor, ed. *Beyond Binary Histories: Re-imagining Eurasia to ca. 1830.* Ann Arbor: University of Michigan Press, 1999.

Liu, Cixin. *The Three-Body Problem.* Translated by Ken Liu. New York: Tor, 2016.

Makeham, John. *Lost Soul: "Confucianism" in Contemporary Chinese Academic Discourse.* Cambridge, MA: Harvard University Asia Center, 2008.

———. *New Confucianism: A Critical Examination.* New York: Palgrave Macmillan, 2003.

The Marshes of Mount Liang. Attributed to Shi Nai-an and Luo Guanzhong. Translated by John and Alex Dent-Young. 5 vols. Hong Kong: Chinese University Press, 2002.

Mittler, Barbara. *A Continuous Revolution: Making Sense of Cultural Revolution Culture.* Cambridge, MA: Harvard Asia Center, 2012.

Monkey. Attributed to Wu Cheng-en. Translated by Arthur Waley. New York: Grove Press, 1958.

The Monkey and the Monk: A Revised Abridgment of The Journey to the West. Translated by Anthony C. Yu. Chicago: University of Chicago Press, 2006.

Morning Sun. Hinton, Carma, Geremie Barme, and Richard Gordon. [Distributed by] Center for Asian America Media, 2003. Documentary film.

Morning Sun. http://www.morningsun.org/. Long Bow Group, Inc.

Outlaws of the Marsh. Attributed to Shi Nai-an and Luo Guanzhong. Translated by Sidney Shapiro. Bloomington: Indiana University Press, 1981.

Plaks, Andrew. *The Four Masterworks of the Ming Novel*. Princeton, NJ: Princeton University Press, 1987.

The Plum in the Golden Vase, or, Chin P'ing Mei. Translated by David Roy. 5 vols. Princeton, NJ: Princeton University Press, 1993–2013.

Three Kingdoms: A Historical Novel. Attributed to Luo Guanzhong. Translated by Moss Roberts. Berkeley: University of California Press, 1999.

The Water Margin: Outlaws of the Marsh. Attributed to Shi Nai-an. Translated by J. H. Jackson. Clarendon, VT: Tuttle, 2010.

Wu, Jingzi. *The Scholars*. Translated by Yang Hsien-yi and Gladys Yang. New York: Columbia University Press, 1992.

Yu, Anthony C. *Comparative Journeys: Essays on Literature and Religion East and West*. New York: Columbia University Press, 2009.

———. *Rereading the Stone: Desire and the Making of Fiction in "Dream of the Red Chamber."* Princeton, NJ: Princeton University Press, 1997.

ACKNOWLEDGMENTS

The editors would like to thank Mark Elliott, former director of the Fairbank Center, for his inspiration; Robert Keatley, journalist and former newspaper editor, for his invaluable editorial assistance in preparing the essays for a non-academic audience; Kathleen McDermott, our editor at Harvard University Press, for her critical support of this project; and the entire staff of the Fairbank Center for Chinese Studies, who implement the Center's many programs and initiatives.

CONTRIBUTORS

WILLIAM P. ALFORD is the Henry L. Stimson Professor of Law at Harvard Law School. He also serves as Vice Dean for the Graduate Program and International Legal Studies, Director of East Asian Legal Studies, and Chair of the Harvard Law School Project on Disability (which he co-founded in 2004).

PETER K. BOL is the Charles H. Carswell Professor of East Asian Languages and Civilizations and the Vice Provost for Advances in Learning at Harvard University. His research is centered on the intellectual history of China's cultural elites at the national and local levels from the seventh to the seventeenth century. He is the author of *"This Culture of Ours": Intellectual Transitions in T'ang and Sung China* (Stanford University Press, 1992)*; Neo-Confucianism in History* (Harvard University Press, 2008); coauthor of *Sung Dynasty Uses of the I-ching* (Princeton University Press, 1990); and co-editor of *Ways with Words* (University of California Press, 2000). He also directs two international digital scholarship projects: the China Historical Geographic Information System and the China Biographical Database.

PAUL A. COHEN is the Wasserman Professor of Asian Studies and History, Emeritus, Wellesley College, and a long-time Associate of the Fairbank Center for Chinese Studies, Harvard University. Among his books are *Discovering History in China: American Historical Writing on the Recent Chinese Past* (Columbia, 1984) and *History in Three Keys: The Boxers as Event, Experience, and Myth* (Columbia, 1997), with the latter named the winner of the American Historical Association's 1997 John K. Fairbank Prize in East

Asian History. Cohen's work has been translated into Chinese, Japanese, and Korean.

RICHARD N. COOPER is the Maurits C. Boas Professor of International Economics, Harvard University. He was formerly Vice Chairman of the Global Development Network, Chairman of the National Intelligence Council, Chairman of the Federal Reserve Bank of Boston, Undersecretary of State for Economic Affairs, and Professor and Provost of Yale University.

NARA DILLON is Lecturer in the Government & East Asian Languages and Civilizations Departments, Harvard University. The author of *Radical Inequalities: China's Revolutionary Welfare State in Comparative Perspective* (Harvard University Press, 2015), Dillon is a political scientist who specializes in Chinese politics and comparative politics. Her current research focuses on welfare in developing countries, especially food programs and subsidies.

MARK ELLIOTT is the Mark Schwartz Professor of Chinese and Inner Asian History in the Department of East Asian Languages and Civilizations and the Department of History at Harvard University and is a former director of the Fairbank Center for Chinese Studies; he is currently Harvard's Vice Provost for International Affairs. An authority on post-1600 China and the history of relations across the nomadic frontier, he is known as a pioneer of the "New Qing History," an approach emphasizing the imprint of Inner Asian traditions upon China's last imperial state.

ANDREW S. ERICKSON is Professor of Strategy in, and a core founding member of, the US Naval War College's China Maritime Studies Institute. He has been an Associate in Research at

Harvard's Fairbank Center for Chinese Studies since 2008. Erickson is also an expert contributor to the *Wall Street Journal*'s China Real Time Report. In 2013, while deployed in the Pacific as a Naval Postgraduate School Regional Security Education Program scholar aboard the flagship aircraft carrier USS *Nimitz,* he delivered twenty-five hours of lectures on Chinese and Asian security issues. Erickson received his Ph.D. from Princeton and runs the China research website www.andrewerickson.com.

JOSEPH FEWSMITH is Professor of International Relations and Political Science at Boston University's Pardee School of Global Studies. He is the author or editor of eight books, including, most recently, *The Logic and Limits of Political Reform in China* (Cambridge University Press, 2013). Other works include *China since Tiananmen* (Cambridge University Press, second edition, 2008) and editor of *China Today, China Tomorrow* (Rowman & Littlefield, 2010). From 2004–2015, he was one of the seven regular contributors to the *China Leadership Monitor,* a quarterly web publication analyzing current developments in China. He is an Associate of the Fairbank Center for Chinese Studies at Harvard University and travels to Asia frequently.

ROWAN FLAD is the John E. Hudson Professor of Archaeology in the Department of Anthropology at Harvard University and holds degrees from the University of Chicago and the University of California, Los Angeles. His research, primarily in Chongqing, Sichuan, and Gansu, is focused on the emergence and development of complex society during the late Neolithic period and the Bronze Age in China. This work incorporates interests in diachronic change in production processes and technology, the intersection between ritual activity and production, animals in early Chinese society, and the processes involved in social change in general.

ARUNABH GHOSH is Assistant Professor of Modern Chinese History at Harvard University. His interests span the social, economic, and environmental histories of twentieth-century China, the transnational histories of science and statecraft, and China–India history. He is currently completing a book manuscript on statistics during the first decade of the People's Republic of China. Future projects include a history of dam-building in twentieth-century China. His work has been published or is forthcoming in peer reviewed journals such as *BJHS—Themes, The PRC History Review,* and *The Journal of Asian Studies.* He received his Ph.D. in History from Columbia University.

STEVEN M. GOLDSTEIN is Director of the Taiwan Studies Workshop and an Associate of the Fairbank Center for Chinese Studies at Harvard University. He was a member of the Department of Government at Smith College from 1968 to 2016 and also has been a visiting faculty member at the Fletcher School of Law and Diplomacy, Columbia University, and the Naval War College. His writings have focused on issues of Chinese domestic and foreign policy as well as cross-strait relations. His most recent publication is *China and Taiwan* (Polity Press, 2015).

SUSAN GREENHALGH is Professor of Anthropology and the John King and Wilma Cannon Fairbank Professor of Chinese Society at Harvard University. Her books include *Cultivating Global Citizens: Population in the Rise of China* (Harvard University Press, 2010), *Just One Child: Science and Policy in Deng's China* (University of California, 2008), and, with political scientist Edwin A. Winckler, *Governing China's Population: From Leninist to Neoliberal Biopolitics* (Stanford University Press, 2005). More recently she has been working on the emergence of public health as a problem of twenty-first-century science and governance.

ALASTAIR IAIN JOHNSTON is the Governor James Albert Noe and Linda Noe Laine Professor of China in World Affairs at Harvard University. He is the author of *Cultural Realism: Strategic Culture and Grand Strategy in Chinese History* (Princeton University Press, 1995) and *Social States: China in International Institutions, 1980–2000* (Princeton University Press, 2008).

WILLIAM C. KIRBY is the T. M. Chang Professor of China Studies at Harvard University and Spangler Family Professor of Business Administration at Harvard Business School and a University Distinguished Service Professor. Professor Kirby serves as Chairman of the Harvard China Fund and Faculty Chair of the Harvard Center Shanghai. At Harvard he has served as Director of the Fairbank Center for Chinese Studies, Chairman of the History Department, and Dean of the Faculty of Arts and Sciences. His current projects include case studies of trend-setting Chinese businesses and a comparative study of higher education in China, Europe, and the United States.

ARTHUR KLEINMAN is the Esther and Sidney Rabb Professor of Anthropology in the Department of Anthropology in the Faculty of Arts and Sciences, Professor of Medical Anthropology in the Department of Global Health and Social Medicine and Professor of Psychiatry at Harvard Medical School. He was the Victor and William Fung Director of Harvard University's Asia Center from 2008–2016 and has conducted research in China since 1978.

YA-WEN LEI is Assistant Professor in the Department of Sociology at Harvard University. Trained in both law and sociology, she holds a J.S.D. from Yale Law School and a Ph.D. in Sociology from the University of Michigan. After graduating from Michigan in 2013, she was a Junior Fellow at the Society of Fellows at Harvard University between 2013 and 2016. She is the author of *The Contentious Public Sphere: Law, Media and Authoritarian Rule in China* (Princeton University Press, 2017).

JIE LI is Assistant Professor of East Asian Languages and Civilizations at Harvard, with research interests in modern Chinese literature, film, media, and cultural history. She is the author of *Shanghai Homes: Palimpsests of Private Life* (Columbia University Press, 2014) and co-editor of *Red Legacies in China: Cultural Afterlives of the Communist Revolution* (Harvard University Press, 2016). Her published articles include "A National Cinema for a Puppet State: The Manchurian Motion Picture Association," and "From Landlord Manor to Red Memorabilia: Reincarnations of a Chinese Museum Town." She is completing two books: *Utopian Ruins: A Memorial Museum of the Mao Era* and *The Reception of Cinema in Modern China*.

WAI-YEE LI is Professor of Chinese Literature at Harvard University. She works on Ming-Qing literature and early Chinese thought and historiography. Her recent publications include *Women and National Trauma in Late Imperial Chinese Literature* (Harvard University Press, 2014) and an annotated translation of the canonical classic *Zuozhuan / The Zuo Tradition* (University of Washington Press, 2016), done in collaboration with Stephen Durrant and David Schaberg.

RODERICK MACFARQUHAR is the Leroy B. Williams Research Professor of History and Political Science and former Director of the Fairbank Center for East Asian Research. His publications include *The Hundred Flowers Campaign and the Chinese Intellectuals* (Praeger, 1966); *China under Mao* (MIT Press, 1966); *Sino-American Relations, 1949–1971* (Praeger, 1972); *The Secret Speeches of Chairman*

Mao (Harvard University Press, 1989); *The Origins of the Cultural Revolution* (Columbia University Press, 1999); and the jointly-authored *Mao's Last Revolution* (Belknap Press of Harvard University Press, 2006). Founding editor of *The China Quarterly,* he has also been a fellow at Columbia University, the Woodrow Wilson International Center for Scholars, and the Royal Institute for International Affairs, as well as a journalist, TV commentator, and Member of Parliament.

MICHAEL B. MCELROY is the Gilbert Butler Professor of Environmental Studies at Harvard University. His research interests include changes in the composition of the atmosphere with an emphasis on the impact of human activity, chemistry of the atmosphere and oceans, evolution of planetary atmospheres, and the global carbon cycle. His research also addresses challenges for public policy posed by the rapid pace of industrialization in developing countries such as China and India while exploring alternative strategies for more sustainable development in mature economies such as the United States. He is the author of more than 250 technical papers and several books.

STEPHEN OWEN is the James Bryant Conant University Professor, and a member of the Department of East Asian Languages and Civilizations and of Comparative Literature at Harvard University. He has held a Fulbright and a Guggenheim Fellowship, and he is a member of both the American Academy of Arts and Sciences and of the American Philosophical Society. In 2005 he received the Mellon Distinguished Achievement Award. He is the author of a dozen books on Chinese literature, most recently a complete translation of Du Fu's poetry in six volumes. All the books, except for translations from Chinese, have been published in Chinese versions.

DWIGHT H. PERKINS is the Harold Hitchings Burbank Professor of Political Economy, Emeritus, of Harvard University. Previous positions at Harvard include Associate Director of the East Asian Research Center (now the Fairbank Center for Chinese Studies), Chairman of the Department of Economics, Director of the Harvard Institute for International Development, and Director of the Harvard Asia Center. He has authored, coauthored, or edited twenty-four books and over 100 articles on economic history and economic development of China and of other Asian and developing economies. His research and published writing about China began in the early 1960s and continues today.

ELIZABETH J. PERRY is the Henry Rosovsky Professor of Government at Harvard University and Director of the Harvard-Yenching Institute. A former president of the Association for Asian Studies and Director of Harvard's Fairbank Center for Chinese Studies, she is a fellow of both the American Academy of Arts and Sciences and the British Academy. Her work focuses on China's history of revolution and its implications for contemporary Chinese politics. Her latest books include *Anyuan: Mining China's Revolutionary Tradition* (University of California Press, 2012) and (in Chinese) *What is the Best Kind of History?* (Zhejiang University Press, 2015).

MICHAEL PUETT is the Walter C. Klein Professor of Chinese History in the Department of East Asian Languages and Civilizations and the Chair of the Committee on the Study of Religion at Harvard University. He is the author of *The Ambivalence of Creation: Debates Concerning Innovation and Artifice in Early China* (Stanford University Press, 2001) and *To Become a God: Cosmology, Sacrifice, and Self-Divination in Early China* (Harvard-Yenching Institute Monograph

Series, 2004), as well as the co-author, with Adam Seligman, Robert Weller, and Bennett Simon, of *Ritual and Its Consequences: An Essay on the Limits of Sincerity* (Oxford University Press, 2008).

MEG RITHMIRE is Associate Professor and Hellman Faculty Fellow at Harvard Business School. Her book on urbanization and property rights in China, *Land Bargains and Chinese Capitalism,* was published by Cambridge University Press in 2015.

JAMES ROBSON is the James C. Kralik and Yunli Lou Professor of East Asian Languages and Civilizations at Harvard University. He specializes in the history of Chinese Buddhism and Daoism. He is the author of the *Power of Place: The Religious Landscape of the Southern Sacred Peak in Medieval China* (Harvard University Asia Center, 2009), the editor of the *Norton Anthology of World Religions: Daoism* (W. W. Norton, 2015), and the author of the forthcoming *The Daodejing: A Biography* for the Princeton University Press, Lives of Great Religious Books Series.

ROBERT S. ROSS is Professor of Political Science at Boston College and an Associate of the Fairbank Center for Chinese Studies, Harvard University. Since 2009 he has been Adjunct Professor, Institute for Defence Studies, Norwegian Defence University College, and he has served as Senior Advisor of the Security Studies Program, Massachusetts Institute of Technology. He is a member of the Academic Advisory Group, US–China Working Group, United States Congress; the Council on Foreign Relations; and the National Committee for US–China Relations. His recent publications include *Chinese Security Policy: Structure, Power, and Politics* (Routledge, 2009) and *China in the Era of Xi Jinping: Domestic and Foreign Policy Challenges* (Georgetown University Press, 2016).

JENNIFER RUDOLPH is Associate Professor of Chinese History and International and Global Studies at Worcester Polytechnic Institute and an Associate of the Fairbank Center for Chinese Studies, Harvard University, as well as former executive director of the Fairbank Center and the Harvard China Fund. Her publications include *Negotiated Power in Late Imperial China: The Zongli Yamen and the Politics of Reform* (Cornell University East Asia Program, 2008). Her current research focuses on construction of political identity for Taiwan on both sides of the Taiwan Strait.

TONY SAICH is the Daewoo Professor of International Affairs and Director of the Ash Center for Democratic Governance and Innovation at Harvard University. He is the author of *Governance and Politics of China* (fourth edition, Palgrave, 2015) and, with Biliang Hu, *Chinese Village, Global Market* (Palgrave, 2012). Currently he is working on models of rural development in China and a new history of the origins of the Chinese Communist Party.

MICHAEL SZONYI is Professor of Chinese History and Director of the Fairbank Center for Chinese Studies at Harvard University. A historian of the Ming dynasty and the twentieth century, his books include *Practicing Kinship: Lineage and Descent in Late Imperial China* (Stanford University Press, 2002); *Cold War Island: Quemoy on the Front Line* (Cambridge University Press, 2008); and the forthcoming *The Art of Being Governed: Everyday Politics in Late Imperial China*. He recently edited *Companion to Chinese History* (Wiley Blackwell, 2017).

KAREN THORNBER is Professor of East Asian Languages and Civilizations and of Comparative Literature at Harvard University, where she is also Victor and William Fung Director of the Harvard University Asia Center and Director of the Harvard

Global Institute Environmental Humanities Initiative. An international prize-winning author and translator best known for *Empire of Texts in Motion: Chinese, Korean, and Taiwanese Transculturations of Japanese Literature* and *Ecoambiguity: Environmental Crises and East Asian Literatures* (Harvard University Press, 2009), Thornber publishes on East Asian (Chinese, Japanese, Korean, Taiwanese) literatures and cultural history, comparative and world literature, diaspora, gender, postcolonialism, translation, trauma, and the environmental and medical humanities.

XIAOFEI TIAN is Professor of Chinese Literature and Chair of Regional Studies East Asia at Harvard University. Her books include *Tao Yuanming and Manuscript Culture* (University of Washington Press, 2005, named a *Choice* Outstanding Academic Title in 2006); *Beacon Fire and Shooting Star: The Literary Culture of the Liang (502–557)* (Harvard University Press, 2007); *Visionary Journeys: Travel Writings from Early Medieval and Nineteenth-century China* (Harvard-Yenching Institute Monograph Series, 2011); and *The Halberd at Red Cliff: Jian'an and the Three Kingdoms* (Harvard-Yenching Institute Monograph Series, 2018). Her translation of a nineteenth-century memoir, *The World of a Tiny Insect: A Memoir of the Taiping Rebellion and Its Aftermath* (University of Washington Press, 2014), was awarded the inaugural Patrick D. Hanan Prize by the Association for Asian Studies in 2016.

LEONARD W. J. VAN DER KUIJP is Professor of Tibetan and Himalayan Studies at Harvard University. Born in the Netherlands, he holds a D.Phil. from Hamburg University, where he studied Indology and Tibetology, Sinology and Philosophy. He has taught at the Free University, Berlin, and the University of Washington, Seattle, and has been at Harvard University since 1995. He is

Chairman of the Inner Asian and Altaic Studies program. He published and co-published a number of books and articles on Indo-Tibetan intellectual and literary history, and on Tibetan-Mongol relations during the Yuan dynasty. For his work, he was awarded a MacArthur Fellowship and a Guggenheim Fellowship.

EZRA F. VOGEL is the Henry Ford II Professor of the Social Sciences, Emeritus, at Harvard University. He served as Deputy Director of the East Asia Research Center under John Fairbank before becoming the Center's second director. He served as National Intelligence Officer for East Asia at the National Intelligence Council, the Director of the Fairbank Center for Chinese Studies, and the founding director of the Asia Center. He is author of *Japan's New Middle Class* (University of California Press, 1971); *Japan as Number One* (Harvard University Press, 1979); *Canton Under Communism* (Harvard University Press, 1969); *Four Little Dragons* (Harvard University Press, 1991); *One Step Ahead in China* (Harvard University Press, 1989); and *Deng Xiaoping and the Transformation of China* (Belknap Press of Harvard University Press, 2011), and editor of *Living with China*. (W. W. Norton, 1997).

DAVID DER-WEI WANG is the Edward C. Henderson Professor in Chinese Literature and Comparative Literature at Harvard University. Wang's specialties are modern Chinese and Sinophone literature, late Qing fiction and drama, and comparative literary theory. His recent publications include *The Lyrical in Epic Time: Modern Chinese Intellectuals and Artists through the 1949 Crisis* (Columbia University Press, 2015) and the Harvard University Press edition of *A New Literary History of Modern China* (2017).

YUHUA WANG is Assistant Professor in the Department of Government at Harvard University. His research has focused on state institutions and state-business relations in China. He is the author of *Tying the Autocrat's Hands: The Rise of the Rule of Law in China* (Cambridge University Press, 2015). He received his B.A. and M.A. from Peking University and his Ph.D. in Political Science from the University of Michigan.

ODD ARNE WESTAD is the S. T. Lee Professor of US–Asia Relations at Harvard University. Among his books are *The Global Cold War* (Cambridge University Press, 2007), which won the Bancroft Prize, and *Decisive Encounters* (Stanford University Press, 2003), a history of the Chinese civil war. He also co-edited the three-volume *Cambridge History of the Cold War* (Cambridge University Press, 2010). His most recent books are *Restless Empire: China and the World since 1750* (Basic Books, 2012) and *The Cold War: A World History* (Basic Book, 2017).

MARK WU is Assistant Professor of Law at Harvard Law School. He is a faculty co-director of the Berkman Klein Center for Internet & Society and of the East Asian Legal Studies Program. He also serves as a member of the advisory board of the WTO Chairs Programme and of the World Economic Forum's Global Future Council on Trade and Investment. He formerly served as the Director for Intellectual Property in the Office of the US Trade Representative and as an economist and operations officer at the World Bank in China.

INDEX

The letter *t* following a page number denotes a table; the letter *f* following a page number denotes a figure.

Belt and Road Initiative. *See* One Belt, One Road (OBOR)
Bo Xilai, 19–21, 227
Bureau of Religious Affairs, 201
Bush, George W. and Bush administration, 82, 111

Cao Xueqin, 259
Carson, Rachel, 174
CCP Central Party History Research Office, 23
Censorship, 43–44, 47–49, 174, 217
Central Discipline Inspection Commission (CDIC), 18
Central Military Commission, Deng Xiaoping chairmanship, 52, 75
Chai Jing, 174
Chan Koonchung, 265, 267
Chen Jining, 174
China Daily, 169
China National Image Global Survey, 96
China Philanthropy Research Institute, 153
China Red Cross, 149
Chinese Buddhist Association, 201
Chinese Catholic Patriotic Association, 201
Chinese Coast Guard: Japanese sovereignty challenged, 88; Philippine sovereignty challenged, 88
Chinese Communist Party (CCP), 3–4; 19th People's Congress, 51; authoritarian resilience, 51; claimed Taiwan, 100; Confucius as alternative to

Western neoliberalism, 234; corruption and legitimacy, 18–19, 21, 23–24, 29–30; Discipline Inspection Commissions, 24; economic reforms announced at Third Plenum, 132; "eight immortals," 19; factional Boundaries, 56; historical legitimacy, 14–16; historical nihilism, 22–23; legal system goals at Fourth Plenum, 214–215; Mao and colleagues rule, 29; "New-Style Urbanization" plan, 138, 140; Party discipline, 19–21; popular support, 13; promises to ethnic minorities, 37–38; propaganda through mass-media infrastructure, 270–271; reform era, 29; regime change worry, 59; rule of law, 21–23; security priorities, 75; 17th Party Congress, 19; threat from elites in Party, 63–64; use of public opinion by, 47; war on nature, 178. *See also* Corruption; Philanthropy in China; Wealth management in China
Chinese cultural past: change or stagnate (*bian er tong*), 286–287; in study groups of graduate students, 286
Chinese international students, 219; leaders' children, 227; perception of quality of American education, 224–225; in the United States, 221, 223; to universities around the world, 227–228, 292
Chinese self, moral and emotional context, 195
Chinese self-image, 96–98